Supervision
THAT
Improves
Teaching AND Learning

THIRD EDITION

*I would like to dedicate this book to my daughters,
Mara, Alene, and Elena, for their supportive love and for providing
the opportunity to try out all my interpersonal skills as they grew to young adulthood.*

—Susan Sullivan

*I would like to dedicate this volume to my father; may peace be upon him,
because he taught me the value of education and urged me to achieve my potential.*

—Jeffrey Glanz

Supervision
THAT
Improves
Teaching AND Learning

Strategies and Techniques

THIRD EDITION

Susan Sullivan / Jeffrey Glanz   Foreword by
Karen Osterman

CORWIN
A SAGE Company

For information:

Corwin
A SAGE Company
2455 Teller Road
Thousand Oaks, California 91320
(800) 233-9936
Fax: (800) 417-2466
www.corwinpress.com

SAGE India Pvt. Ltd.
B 1/I 1 Mohan Cooperative Industrial Area
Mathura Road, New Delhi 110 044
India

SAGE Ltd.
1 Oliver's Yard
55 City Road
London EC1Y 1SP
United Kingdom

SAGE Asia-Pacific Pte. Ltd.
33 Pekin Street #02-01
Far East Square
Singapore 048763

Printed in the United States of America

Library of Congress Cataloging-in-Publication Data

Sullivan, Susan
Supervision that improves teaching and learning : Strategies and techniques/Susan Sullivan and Jeffrey Glanz ; foreword by Karen Osterman. — 3rd ed.
    p. cm.
Rev. ed. of: Supervision that improves teaching. 2nd ed. c2005.
Includes bibliographical references and index.
ISBN 978-1-4129-6713-6 (pbk.)

    1. School supervision—United States. 2. Teacher effectiveness—United States. 3. Effective teaching—United States. I. Glanz, Jeffrey. II. Sullivan, Susan, Supervision that improves teaching. III. Title.

LB2806.4.S85 2009
371.2′03—dc22   2009002812

This book is printed on acid-free paper.

    10   11   12   13   10   9   8   7   6   5   4   3

Acquisitions Editor:	Arnis Burvikovs
Associate Editors:	Megan Bedell and Desirée A. Bartlett
Production Editor:	Jane Haenel
Copy Editor:	Cheryl Rivard
Typesetter:	C&M Digitals (P) Ltd.
Proofreader:	Sue Irwin
Indexer:	Kirsten Kite
Cover and Graphic Designer:	Rose Storey

Contents

Foreword to the Third Edition

Sullivan and Glanz rightfully maintain that supervision is central to the renewal of classroom teaching and learning. This is particularly true if you believe that education, like other professions, requires continuous learning. Although needs and goals differ at different stages of career growth, everyone, whether teachers or administrators, should be engaged in a constant process of assessment and renewal. Ideally, schools should be places where professional educators, regardless of their specific roles, work as a team, sharing their expertise and contributing their efforts to continually improve student learning.

Since this book was first published in 1999, there are several things about schools that we have come to know with even greater certainty. The quality of teacher practice is most directly influenced by whether or not teachers experience schools as learning communities (Silins, Mulford, & Zarins, 2002). If the school supports collaborative work, sharing of information, and open communication among staff, it is more likely that teachers will utilize effective teaching strategies. Leaders play a direct role in determining how their schools function. Although the leadership role is complex, if leaders "encourage staff to reflect on what they are trying to achieve with students and how they are doing it" (Silins, Mulford, & Zarins, 2002, p. 621), and enable them to establish and pursue their own professional goals, it is more likely that teachers will perceive their school as a learning organization.

In this text, Sullivan and Glanz provide educators with the analytic and technical tools that they need to be able to create a climate for learning. Despite our knowledge about the effectiveness of learning organizations, schools rest in the shadow of a bureaucratic and hierarchical tradition that characterizes individuals as superior and subordinate, differentially distributes power and authority, and creates artificial and often antagonistic role-based divisions. In recognizing the strength of these mindscapes that so directly shape practice, Sullivan and Glanz encourage the readers to explore and challenge their own traditional beliefs about authority and control. They then present basic but very important communication skills that facilitate reflection and dialogue and contrast these with more traditional approaches that rely on judgment, direct control, and appeasement—disempowering strategies that reinforce hierarchical barriers, preclude collaborative problem solving, and constrain personal growth and initiative (Osterman & Kottkamp, 2004).

One of the most frequent complaints from teachers is that the supervisory process is seldom useful. They sit through the preobservation, observation, and feedback cycle, but it doesn't help them improve their teaching. There are two aspects of the process that limit supervisory effectiveness (Osterman, 1994). The first is a lack of descriptive data and/or the failure to share those descriptive data directly with the teacher. There will be no change in practice if teachers are unaware of the need for change. Because our perceptions are shaped by so many factors, most of us have only an incomplete understanding of our own behavior and the effects of our actions. The new teacher, for example, may perceive only her failures. A more senior teacher, shaped by years of experience, may unknowingly adopt very different patterns of interaction with different groups of students, limiting their effectiveness with some. Data-based feedback enables teachers to "see" their practice in a new light. For that reason, clear descriptive data about practice and its effects on student learning are critical if the goal is continuous improvement.

The second problem is the tendency to use the feedback conference to offer teachers suggestions for improvement. Teachers need to have information about their work, but, if the purpose of the supervisory process is to encourage learning, they also need the opportunity to assume responsibility for their own professional growth. From research and experience, we know that even when supervisors gather and share objective data with teachers, rather than encouraging dialogue about teaching and collaborative planning, they quickly shift attention to suggestions for improvement. Rather than empowering teachers to analyze and critically assess their own work, the supervisors fall into traditional patterns and provide the answers. Although well intentioned, this prescriptive approach limits teachers' potential to function as professionals.

To address these concerns, Sullivan and Glanz rightly direct the supervisor's attention to data collection and feedback. They provide a rich variety of tools to gather data about multiple dimensions of teacher practice and its connection to student learning. Equally important, they also illustrate how supervisors—whether administrators or fellow teachers—can provide feedback and engage in reflective dialogue, optimizing professional growth and avoiding the judgmental and prescriptive approaches that limit effectiveness. In this collaborative dialogue about teaching, the responsibility for problem analysis and problem resolution shifts. Although the supervisor can still share ideas, he or she no longer assumes the *sole* responsibility for solving the teacher's problems. Basically, this approach offers educators a practical way to challenge traditional top-down models of authority and control, respect teachers' professionalism, and create positive, supportive, and collaborative relationships between teachers and their supervisors.

Even more important, this approach to supervision is one that supports deep learning. It is relatively easy to achieve some types of change. For example, a district can require teachers to use a particular curriculum. Meaningful change, however, requires change in underlying beliefs about teaching. Thus, teachers who believe that didactic methods of instruction are appropriate are unlikely to adopt constructive approaches to teaching (Torff & Warburton, 2005). Good professional development, in whatever form, encourages teachers to explore and assess their beliefs in order to facilitate change. It respects their professionalism and is based on assumptions that teachers are not only willing but anxious to improve, and that they have the expertise (at whatever level) to take an active and direct role in shaping their own development.

The strategies that Sullivan and Glanz highlight in their text are techniques that ensure that supervision really will support professional learning. Even though the techniques they describe are not unique, the authors' presentation is. Not only do they provide information about various techniques that improve the quality of feedback, they also provide a learning framework based on principles of constructivism and reflective practice that facilitates not just understanding but application.

Reflective practice and constructivism share a common set of beliefs about learning (Osterman & Kottkamp, 2004). First is the belief that learning is an active process requiring student engagement. Learning is the ultimate responsibility of the learner, and the role of the instructor is to facilitate growth by focusing inquiry, engaging students, exploring and challenging ideas, and providing resources. The second belief is that ideas influence action. Through experience, people develop theories about how the world works, and these theories shape their behavior. Learners construct their own knowledge, building on prior experiences. Accordingly, students must have opportunities to articulate, represent, and assess as well as extend their knowledge. The third important belief is that learners construct knowledge through experience, particularly problematic experience. Pedagogically, then, it is necessary to build conceptual conflict by challenging current understanding and offering opportunities to develop and test new ways of thinking and acting.

The supervisory model Sullivan and Glanz describe is built on these pedagogical principles, and the text itself admirably incorporates these ideas. Each section poses problems to engage and challenge the learner. Realistic cases illustrate the relationship between beliefs and practice and describe the personal and organizational obstacles that perpetuate bureaucratic practices. Reflective activities in each section raise challenging questions, stimulate interest, and encourage the articulation and critical assessment of personal beliefs. The text also provides for development of skills through a series of progressively challenging activities. Initially, learners experiment with strategies in a supportive classroom environment. The second step involves testing the new strategies in the work setting. In the classroom and in the work setting, the learning process models the principles of supportive supervision. In the classroom, the students utilize a wide variety of observation strategies and practice descriptive feedback and collaborative problem solving with one another. In the work setting, they work closely with a colleague, testing the same strategies. Each of these activities develops skill, but more importantly, the actual experimentation establishes the validity of the specific technique and builds learner confidence in his or her ability to use these techniques effectively.

In constructivism and reflective practice, in contrast to more traditional educational models, the relationship between teacher and learners is that of a partnership based on common goals to improve practice rather than on hierarchical differences related to presumed differences in expertise. The structure of the text facilitates dialogue and creates a climate of openness. The language is accessible. The tone is personal, warm, respectful, and collegial. The authors share responsibility for learning with the readers, presuming that the readers are intelligent, informed, and capable. They invite learners to supplement the text with their own suggestions, and, in fact, use creative strategies suggested by their own students. These are empowering strategies that support the learning process and model the ideas about supervision that they espouse. In contrast with the "inspection" model that too often characterizes school supervision, the supervisory process envisioned by Sullivan and Glanz is collaborative rather than hierarchical, dialogic versus didactic, descriptive rather than judgmental, and supportive rather than punitive. This is a major shift. Although the idea is appealing and even convincing, bringing about change in the practice of supervision is no easy task. To do so, to align action more closely with theory, involves more than simply presenting a range of feasible and effective strategies. According to Argyris and Schon (1974), ideas like these will be integrated into practice only when existing theories and patterns of behavior are identified, explored, challenged, and modified. This theoretical premise has important implications for learning. If the learning process is to be effective, its learning goals must extend beyond the mere transference of knowledge to incorporate the appropriate and effective application of knowledge.

Normally, the challenge to facilitate the application of ideas rests on the shoulders of the instructor. The text provides the information and the instructor provides the pedagogical expertise. Here, Sullivan and Glanz have developed a text that provides information, but more importantly one that engages the readers in a reflective process of observation, analysis, and experimentation designed to facilitate behavioral change. By extending well beyond the normal scope of a text and exploring dimensions of belief and practice in the context of schools and leadership, the authors provide a valuable resource. The use of this text, its learning strategies and supervisory techniques, should support realization of the book's stated purpose: the development of educational leaders— whether administrators or teachers—who are able to engage in supervision designed to improve the quality of learning.

—Karen Osterman
Hofstra University

REFERENCES

Argyris, C., & Schon, D. A. (1974). *Theory in practice: Increasing professional effectiveness.* San Francisco: Jossey-Bass.

Osterman, K. F. (1994). Feedback in school settings: No news is bad news. *Journal of Management Science, 6*(4), 28–44.

Osterman, K. F., & Kottkamp, R. B. (2004). *Reflective practice for educators: Professional development to improve student learning.* Thousand Oaks, CA: Corwin.

Silins, H. C., Mulford, W. R., & Zarins, S. (2002). Organizational learning and school change. *Educational Administration Quarterly, 38*(2), 613–642.

Torff, B., & Warburton, E. (2005). Assessment of teachers' beliefs about classroom use of critical-thinking activities. *Educational and Psychological Measurement, 65,* 155–179.

Preface to the Third Edition

Supervision is and always will be the key to the high instructional standards of America's public schools.

—Spears, 1953, p. 462

As the first decade of the 21st century draws to a close, theory and practice of supervision have regained the attention of those who wish to improve schools. Educational reformers have come to understand that, unless attention is drawn to deep changes in instructional practice, change will remain ephemeral (e.g., Fullan, 2006). A renewed and potent focus on classroom instruction requires attention to important technological developments as well as to issues of diversity, both of which form the fabric of the educational landscape in the 21st century. Within this context, supervisory practices that appreciate diverse learning styles, of teachers and students alike, and the technologies necessary to promote quality teaching form the core of this third edition. Therefore, we have built this third edition around diversity within a technological environment. Our new scenarios describe teaching and learning dilemmas for English language learners. An additional case study also highlights English language learners within the context of "Critical Friends" groups. And new observation tools center on the diversity of our schools, emphasizing the need for differentiated instruction in order to reach all children and ongoing assessment of learning. Finally, suggestions abound for use of the book within a technological environment—from blogs and wikis to strategies for teaching a hybrid or completely online course.

Additionally, we have drawn clearer distinctions between evaluation and supervision in this third edition. We revised the timeline in Chapter 1 and made Chapter 3, "Observation Tools and Techniques," more reader- and user-friendly. However, our commitment to supervision through critical reflection remains unchanged. We hope you find this new edition practical and user-friendly. We welcome your input for additional changes in future editions. Contact us at Sullivan@mail.csi.cuny.edu and at glanz@yu.edu.

We believe that supervision, as a dynamic process that facilitates dialogue to promote instructional improvement, is central to the renewal of classroom teaching and learning in the 21st century. Rather than merely describing and explaining varied models of supervision, this book presents the reader with research-based and empirically tested strategies and techniques.

By offering an overview of approaches for instructional improvement and some specific supervisory strategies, this volume encourages the reader to develop her or his own supervisory platform or personal principles of practice. The main feature of this text is the hands-on development of essential supervisory skills.

This text is meant for use in undergraduate and graduate courses on instructional improvement and by individuals in leadership positions in schools and districts, including teams of teachers and teacher leaders. It contains unique features that set it apart from similar works. The text, designed to be user-friendly, provides examples of summary sheets and observation charts as well as "crib sheets" to enhance review and actual use in the classroom. Throughout each chapter are reflective microlabs and other activities designed to reinforce new material and concepts.

Why is a book of this nature important? In an era in which supervision as a field and practice is being attacked, sometimes vociferously, those individuals who argue that supervision is vital to instructional improvement must remain vigilant to preserve the best that supervision has to offer. With the continual emphasis on student outcomes and state and national standards, supervision is, more than ever, an indispensable link that inspires good teaching and promotes student learning. We believe that when teachers are encouraged to reflect on their teaching and when individuals with supervisory responsibilities engage teachers in conversations about classroom instruction, the stage for instructional improvement is set.

This book, along with other publications, such as the *Handbook of Research on School Supervision* (Firth & Pajak, 1998); *Educational Supervision: Perspectives, Issues, and Controversies* (Garman, 1997); *Handbook of Instructional Leadership: How Really Good Principals Promote Teaching and Learning* (Blase & Blase, 1986); *Mentoring and Supervision for Teacher Development* (Reiman & Thies-Sprinthall, 1998); *Differentiated Supervision* (Northern Valley Regional High School District, 1996); *SuperVision and Instructional Leadership: A Developmental Approach* (Glickman et al., 2004); *Interpersonal and Consultant Supervision Skills: A Clinical Model* (Champagne & Hogan, 2006); *Cognitive Coaching* (Costa & Garmston, 1997); *Instructional Supervision: Applying Tools and Concepts* (Zepeda, 2007); *Teacher Supervision and Evaluation: Theory Into Practice* (Nolan & Hoover, 2007); and *Approaches to Clinical Supervision* (Pajak, 2000), indicates the resurgence and attention given to supervision. We believe that such attention is not only warranted but necessary so that the integrity of instructional improvement within classrooms across America and around the world will be maintained. Although scholars may busy themselves with philosophical intricacies or theoretical nuances about the viability and definition of supervision, practitioners know too well how important effective supervision is for maintaining and encouraging instructional excellence.

A number of critical assumptions about supervision underlie this work. First and foremost, although supervision as a function and a process may not be fashionable or "pedagogically correct," we maintain that its primary aim is to assist teachers in improving instruction. As long as this purpose remains vitally important, we believe that supervision can remain a potent force toward promoting instructional excellence in schools. Moreover, the goal of supervision is to facilitate the process of teaching and learning through a multitude of approaches that can encompass curriculum and staff development, action research, and peer, self-, and student assessment.

This text follows a logical and orderly progression, all the while encouraging the reader to understand the changing context of supervision and to develop requisite knowledge, skills, and dispositions about supervision. It culminates in the development of a personal supervisory platform and offers suggestions for a collaborative plan for supervision.

Chapter 1 provides a historical and theoretical framework for supervision. This foundation, along with an initial belief inventory *that should be completed before reading the chapter* and again at the end of the course, permits the reader to begin laying the groundwork for a personal supervisory platform.

Chapter 2 introduces basic interpersonal tools for initiating and providing feedback on classroom observations. The reader is introduced to "crib sheets" to practice feedback dialogue between professionals and for use onsite. The theory and practice of reflection in action, a crucial tool for self-reflection and assessment, is also introduced. Chapter 3 reviews sample classroom observation tools and techniques in a way that allows readers to practice them in the college classroom or workshop and onsite and to develop this essential skill. In Chapter 4, the previously learned observation tools and techniques and feedback approaches are integrated into our reflective clinical supervision cycle framework. Opportunities for practice and simulations precede recommendations for site-based initiation.

Chapter 5 presents seven alternative approaches to supervision currently in practice. Authentic case studies introduce each approach, followed by a definition and suggested steps for implementation. Chapter 6, the final chapter and the culmination of the learning process, encourages readers to create their own personal supervisory platform, that is, a personal theory or principles of practice. In addition, this chapter includes a guide to facilitate the development of a collaborative site vision and plan for supervision.

In sum, this book reviews the supervisory strategies and techniques necessary for future educational leaders so that they can promote teaching and learning, the essence of what effective supervision is really all about.

Acknowledgments

We thank our graduate students at the College of Staten Island and at Yeshiva University for allowing us to develop various ideas of this book with them and for offering useful feedback.

Susan Sullivan would like to thank David Podell, the former Provost and Vice President for Academic Affairs at the College of Staten Island, for his ongoing support in all of her academic endeavors. She would also like to express appreciation to the faculty and administration of Ditmas Intermediate School, in Brooklyn, New York, and, in particular, Nancy Brogan, Lynne Pagano, Elke Savoy, Madeline Castaneda, and Nasreen Farooqui for their willingness and enthusiasm in developing a peer coaching model in the International Institute at their school. Eric Nadelstern and Carmen Farina and their staffs were models not only in the development of alternatives to traditional supervision but in their proactive open sharing of their successes and challenges. Karen Osterman of Hofstra University introduced the world of reflective practice to Susan and continues to reflect with her on teaching and intellectual endeavors.

Jeffrey Glanz would like to acknowledge his colleagues in the Council of Professors of Instructional Supervision (COPIS) for stimulating, over the years, many of the ideas in this volume. Special thanks to Bert Ammerman, Principal, and Jim McDonnell, Vice Principal, of Northern Valley Regional High School District for their innovative work, which formed the basis for some of the case studies in Chapter 5.

PUBLISHER'S ACKNOWLEDGMENTS

Corwin gratefully acknowledges the contributions of the following individuals:

Vincent A. Anfara, Jr., Associate Professor
College of Education, Health, and Human Sciences
The University of Tennessee
Knoxville, TN

Kenneth Arndt, Superintendent
Community Unit School District #300
Carpentersville, IL

Susan Bolte, Principal
Providence Elementary School
Aubrey, TX

Linda G. Brown, Principal
Parkview Arts/Science Magnet High School
Little Rock, AR

Judy Brunner, Author/Consultant
Instructional Solutions Group
Missouri State University
Springfield, MO

John Fitzpatrick, Superintendent in Residence
Pepperdine University, Graduate School of Education and Psychology
Westlake Village, CA

Christy M. Moroye, Assistant Professor
Curriculum and Supervision
University of Iowa, College of Education
Iowa City, IA

About the Authors

 **Susan Sullivan** received her BA from Elmira College, her MAT from The Johns Hopkins University, and her MEd and EdD from Teachers College, Columbia University. She served as an instructor in the Department of Romance Languages of The Johns Hopkins University for 10 years and as a teacher and administrator in Baltimore, Maryland; Rome, Italy; and the New York City area. She was Chair of the Department of Education of the College of Staten Island, the City University of New York, for six years and previously Coordinator of the Program in Educational Administration. She is currently Director of Collaborative Programs in the Department of Education and continues to teach graduate courses in supervision of instruction and educational leadership. In addition to their staff development book, *Supervision in Practice*, she and Jeffrey Glanz also published *Building Effective Learning Communities* for Corwin. You can reach her via Sullivan@mail.csi.cuny.edu.

 **Jeffrey Glanz** received his BA from the City University of New York and his MA and EdD from Teachers College, Columbia University. He currently holds the Raine and Stanley Silverstein Chair in Professional Ethics and Values in the Azrieli Graduate School of Jewish Education and Administration at Yeshiva University. He is a former chair, dean, schoolteacher, and school administrator. He is the author of twenty books including the new 2nd edition of *Teaching 101*, the *Assistant Principal's Handbook*, and the seven-volume set on School Leadership, all with Corwin. You can reach him via glanz@yu.edu and visit his Web page at www.yu.edu/faculty/glanz.

A Brief Note to Instructors

We are certain that this text can be used in many effective ways in your classroom or in your school. We would like to highlight some of the strategies that we have found most successful in developing supervisory and interpersonal skills. Detailed instructions for several of these strategies are provided in the text. We know that you will think of additional suggestions and hope that you will share your ideas with us.

1. *Journal writing.* Encourage students to reflect on their and others' class and site supervisory experiences in a personal journal. Reflections on supervisory practices that the students observe in their buildings and in other schools are invaluable in forming their own beliefs. The suggested *reflections* in the text also can be thought out in the journal. Students can choose to share journal entries online to solicit feedback on their ideas.

2. *Microlabs.* As explained in the Microlab Guidelines in Resource A, the microlab permits individualized collegial sharing, while at the same time developing reflective and nonjudgmental listening skills. Groups of three to five people address two to four questions suggested in the text or inspired by students or instructor. Small-group and whole-class debriefing ties thoughts together, promotes more ideas, and brings closure to the process. Again, microlabs are effective online on a Blackboard site or as wikis, and can also be set up interactively.

3. *The fishbowl.* This process can be used to discuss the ideas generated in small groups within a large-group setting. Representatives from each small group form a circle in the middle of the room and share the ideas generated in the small groups while the rest of the class listens and observes. We also use the fishbowl to allow volunteers to model feedback approaches for the rest of the class. The class learns the approach and at the same time serves as observers of the process. Directions for this approach are provided in Resource B.

4. *Videotaping or audiotaping.* We strongly encourage the use of videos and audiotapes of classroom and site practices, particularly of the planning and feedback conferences. The tapes can be used in two ways: They can

be part of the actual assignment and graded, or they can be used for the students' own learning; the knowledge that the tapes will not be shared with instructors or colleagues may increase their authenticity and acceptance. Many students tape themselves several times for scaffolded learning from their own practice.

5. *Intervisitation.* In all of our work with teachers, aspiring administrators, and practicing leaders, we have found that intervisitation within schools, between schools, and between districts plays a crucial role in creating a climate for growth. The opportunity to see the practices and models explained in a text is "worth a thousand words." Professionals see the ideas in practice ("it works") and can ask questions and debrief after the visit, reflecting on what they think might or might not work for them.

6. *E-mail and the Internet.* One of the most effective ways to involve all students in dialogue and reflection is through e-mail, Internet discussion boards, wikis, and blogs. These electronic sites can increase participation of some students who are more comfortable with the written than the spoken word. You can assign pairs of students to discuss reflections on e-mail, and you can set up a discussion board, wikis, or blogs through school or college media centers. Microlabs can be assigned on the discussion board, and students can share experiences and challenges with their colleagues. The whole realm of the Internet also is available to enrich discussion and knowledge.

7. *Distance learning and the virtual classroom.* The precise descriptions and directions for site practice and the companion video facilitate the use of this book for distance learning and the virtual classroom. In the distance learning classroom, students can practice the role plays and receive feedback from their colleagues and professors. The use of videos or DVDs for site assignments can provide the instructor with direct knowledge of the students' practice and progress. In the virtual classroom, videos and DVDs replace the university classroom experience. In addition, all the other technological resources—that is, e-mail, discussion board, wikis, blogs, and the Internet, among others—enrich learning and discussion in the virtual classroom. New and innovative interactive programs are continually introduced on the market. See Resource C for further information.

8. *Supervision in practice.* The professional development text that we have written, *Supervision in Practice,* can also serve as an instructional aid and a tool for students to turnkey the techniques and strategies they learn. Overheads and a detailed description of cycles of workshops are useful to instructors and students.

We have included some of the preceding suggestions in more detail in the text and in the Resources. Most chapters are replete with suggestions for reflections, microlabs, and class and site practices that expand on these ideas and offer others.

The Changing Context of Supervision 1

Democracy can provide the direction, goals, purposes, and standards of conduct that our profession and society desperately need. Clinical supervision can provide the means of translating democratic values into action, while strengthening teachers' teaching skills, conceptual understanding and moral commitment.

—Pajak, 2000, p. 292

Note: Before you begin reading this chapter, please complete the questionnaire in Figure 1.2 on pages 32–33.

CHAPTER OVERVIEW

1. Supervision Defined

2. The Influence of History

    a. Vignettes Within a Historical Context

    b. The History

3. Understanding the History of Supervision

    a. The Dilemma of Supervision vs. Evaluation

4. Assessing Belief Systems

    a. Developing a Personal Vision Statement

WHAT IS SUPERVISION?

Defining supervision has been a source of much debate for years (Bolin, 1987). Is supervision a function of administration, curriculum, staff development, action research, or a combination of these and other activities? Alfonso and Firth (1990) noted that the study of supervision lacks focus largely due to the "lack of research and continuing disagreement on the definition and purposes of supervision" (p. 188). In this volume, we view supervision as the center for the improvement of instruction. Supervision is the process of engaging teachers in instructional dialogue for the purpose of improving teaching and increasing student achievement. We believe that supervision for the improvement of instruction will continue to be the foremost concern of supervisors and other educational leaders well into the 21st century.

The Evolution of Supervision

Supervisory practice has evolved since its origins in colonial times, and its effectiveness as a means of improving instruction depends on the ability of educational leaders to remain responsive to the needs of teachers and students. An educational leader's resolve to remain adaptable also depends on an appreciation of the changing and evolving nature of supervision, especially in the new millennium. An educational leader who understands the history of supervision and how current demands are influenced by that history will be better able to confront the technological, social, political, and moral issues of the day. Educational leaders also will have to develop the requisite knowledge, skills, and dispositions that are the foundation for effective supervisory practice. This chapter explicates how supervision has evolved to its current state, how you might respond to ever-increasing supervisory needs and demands, and how your beliefs and attitudes affect how you react to daily challenges.

Vignette

Arlene Spiotta was recently appointed vice principal of Regional Valley High School, where she has worked as a teacher for three years. An affable, popular teacher, Arlene had been a teacher at Westfield High School, located in a neighboring township, for eight years. Prior to that, she was a teacher for five years in two schools in another state. She recently earned her supervisory certification and master's degree in administration and supervision at a local college.

Although Arlene received a warm welcome on the opening day of school in September, she noticed that teachers on the grade levels she supervises react much differently to her now. In one instance, she was passing the room of a former teacher-colleague, Linda Evans, who at the time was at her desk, assisting a student. When Linda noticed Arlene looking into the classroom, she stiffened in her chair and abruptly sent the pupil back to his desk. After receiving a stern and cold stare, Arlene proceeded down the hallway to her office. Arlene wondered why her colleague Linda acted so differently when she saw her now.

Reflection

Why do you think Linda reacted to Arlene the way she did? What factor(s) may have contributed to this situation? What dilemma is she facing in her new role?

Arlene Spiotta took for granted the fact that she was now in a position very different from that of Linda Evans. Although they were former colleagues and friends, Arlene was now a supervisor. As a supervisor, she was expected to assist and evaluate her former colleagues.

Linda Evans, on seeing Arlene apparently staring into the classroom (an assumption, we might add, that may or may not have been accurate), reacted as she had previously to other supervisors for whom she had worked. Her former supervisors were overbearing bureaucrats who looked for evidence of teacher incompetence at every turn.

Arlene, too, may have been influenced by what she considered to be behavior "expected" of a supervisor, that is, daily patrol or inspection of the hallways. After all, not only had Arlene been certified and trained as a supervisor in a state that mandates that all teachers be formally observed at least twice a year (eight times for nontenured teachers), but as an experienced teacher (of how many years? Right—16), she had been exposed to many supervisors who had conducted themselves in very autocratic and bureaucratic ways.

Had Arlene been cognizant of how past practices of supervision can affect current relationships between teachers and supervisors, she might have tried more earnestly to establish a spirit of mutual understanding and cooperation.

Reflection

How might Arlene establish this "spirit of mutual understanding and cooperation"?

One of the authors recalls a time when he confronted a similar situation and the difficulty he had in circumventing expected supervisory roles. An excerpt from Jeffrey's diary is instructive:

My first appointment as an assistant principal was at P.S. "Anywhere, USA." I arrived at the school in September. My predecessor's reputation was there to greet me.

Mr. Stuart Oswald Blenheim was known as a stickler for every jot, tittle, and iota inscribed in the Board of Ed's rules and regulations. He carried a tape measure, a portable tape recorder, and a stethoscope, and considered teachers to be one of the lower forms of sapient life. The others were nonprofessional staff members and students—in "descending" order.

This supervisor made his opinions abundantly clear by word and deed. Woe to the pupil caught wandering the halls without appropriate documentation. No excuses accepted. Period. End of message.

Furthermore, the offending miscreant's pedagogue was called on the carpet, raked over the coals, strung up by the thumbs, and subjected to a wide variety of other abusive clichés.

Stuart Oswald Blenheim was short; so short that it was difficult to see him among a group of eighth or ninth graders. He took full advantage of his camouflage, so that he could spy on his charges. He was known to walk up quietly to a room, place his stethoscope to the door, and gradually straighten his knees and stand on his toes so as to see through the small glass window. Teachers were constantly on the lookout for a bald head rising in their doors' windows.

Any teacher who observed this latter-day Napoleon lurking in the halls was honor bound to pass the information on to his or her neighbors. A note referring to "Pearl Harbor," "Incoming Scud Missiles," "Sneak Attack," or "Raid's Here" was enough to raise blood pressure and churn digestive juices.

Last spring, he was appointed as principal in a school on the other side of the city.

Such was Blenheim's repute that all the teachers whom I supervised avoided my presence like the very plague. On one occasion, I passed by a room and noticed a teacher caringly assisting a pupil at her desk. Suddenly, the teacher "felt" my presence, quickly straightened her posture, and proceeded nervously to the front of the room to resume writing on the board. I walked away bewildered. However, after ascertaining that I did not suffer from halitosis, dandruff, or terminal body odor, I realized the problem. Honestly, I couldn't blame them. After all, Blenheim's initials suited him perfectly.

Thus, I was forced to overcome these habits of fear and distrust and, somehow, to win my teachers' and students' trust.

During my first meeting with my teachers, I asked rather than told them not to think of me as their supervisor. I hoped that they would consider me a colleague with perhaps more experience and responsibility in certain areas. I wanted to work with them and learn about their own expertise, knowledge, interests, and ideas. . . . I was not going to spy on them. I was not going to humiliate them. I was a real human being, just like they were, just like the children were.

They had a difficult time accepting this. They had been abused for seven years by a petty tyrant and did not believe that any AP could think differently. After all, Blenheim had been rewarded for his fine methods. This had to be the AP road to promotion.

I promised that there would be no sneak attacks. We would do our best to cooperate and learn together. I would share my experiences and readily seek their expertise and ideas so that they could be effective teachers.

It took three to six months of hard work on my part and caution on theirs, but we've finally reached the point where we smile at each other when we meet in the hall. Several of them have come to me with professional and personal problems. They were a bit surprised at some of my proposed solutions. The word got around that Blenheim was really gone.

Stuart Oswald Blenheim is, of course, a caricature of an autocratic supervisor who occupied the position Jeffrey Glanz assumed many years ago. Yet the essential message is clear: Autocratic methods in supervision still prevail, and if changes are to be made, then understanding the antecedents for such practices is necessary. To understand the changing context of supervision, a brief excursion into the history of supervision is necessary.

THE INFLUENCE OF HISTORY

History can be understood as an attempt to study the events and ideas of the past that have shaped human experience over time; doing so informs current practice and helps us make more intelligent decisions for the future. How are prevailing practices and advocated theories connected to the past? How is what you currently do influenced, in any way, by previous practices and theories of supervision? How can an understanding of the past help us practice supervision today?

Our intention in this chapter is to indicate that past supervisory theory and practice influence what we believe about supervision and how we carry out our work with teachers and others. This chapter will help you identify your belief systems related to supervisory practice and how these beliefs are connected to history and the history of supervision. This identification will lay the initial foundation for the construction of a supervisory platform.

Guidelines for the creation of your own initial "personal vision statement" are a special feature of this chapter. As we indicate, what you believe about teaching and learning, for example, inevitably affects how you approach the practice of supervision. Subsequent chapters will encourage you to develop a "personal supervisory platform" that builds upon your personal vision statement.

> ### Reflection/Microlab*
>
> *Who or what in your personal or professional background influenced your present supervisory beliefs? What are some positive supervisory experiences you have encountered? What are some negative supervisory experiences you recall? Why did you feel that way? What does supervision look like in your school?*

Site Practice

1. Prepare five questions to ask two school supervisors about their beliefs and practices in relation to improvement of classroom instruction:
   - Record the questions and responses.
   - Reflect on each supervisor's answers. Describe consistencies and inconsistencies in the responses and compare the supervisors' actual practices to the responses given. Do they "walk the talk" (practice what they preach)?
   - What surprised you in their responses (positively or negatively)? Why?
   - Compare the two supervisors' responses and reflect on the similarities and differences between their answers.

   or

2. Ask two supervisors and two teachers what they consider to be the five most important tasks of instructional supervision.
   - Include a script of their responses.
   - What were the differences and similarities in the teachers' answers and in the supervisors' responses?
   - Compare the teachers' responses with those of the supervisors. Explain the differences and similarities. What surprised you in their responses (positively or negatively)?

   (Continued)

---

*See Resource A for microlab guidelines. Set up an Internet discussion board or wiki through your school or university media center to exchange reflections and hold electronic microlabs. Also, choose an e-mail partner and share reflections via e-mail between classes.

(Continued)

Shadowing Assignment: Shadow a supervisor of instruction for one day or on a few days when the supervisor is observing classes.

1. Provide a detailed log of the supervision of instruction that you observed. You may include *any* activities that you feel were related to supervision of instruction.

2. Describe the supervisory approaches and the process that the supervisor used.

3. What was effective in what you observed? Why? How will these effective practices improve classroom instruction? What did the teacher(s) learn?

4. Did the supervisor do anything that you would have done yourself? What and why or why not?

5. Were there supervisory practices that need improvement? Why? Did the supervisor do anything that you would NOT do? Were you surprised by anything the supervisor did? Why or why not? What would you do differently?

6. How did you feel about the "activities" before shadowing? After?

Source: The first and second sections of this site practice were adapted from Glickman et al. (1998).

The History

Supervision has medieval Latin origins and was defined originally as "a process of perusing or scanning a text for errors or deviations from the original text" (Smyth, 1991, p. 30). Later recorded instances of the word *supervision* established the process as entailing "general management, direction, control, and oversight" (see, e.g., Grumet, 1979). An examination of early records during the colonial period indicates that the term *inspector* is referenced frequently. Note the definition of supervision in Boston in 1709:

> Be there hereby established a committee of inspectors to visit ye School from time to time, when and as oft as they shall think fit, to Enform themselves of the methods used in teaching of ye Schollars and to Inquire of their proficiency, and be present at the performance of some of their Exercises, the Master being before Notified of their Coming, And with him to consult and Advise of further Methods for ye Advancement of Learning and the Good Government of the Schoole.
>
> —*Reports of the Record Commissions of the City of Boston,* 1709

The inspectors were often ministers, selectmen, schoolmasters, and other distinguished citizens. Their methods of supervision stressed strict control and close inspection of school facilities. As Spears (1953) explained, "The early period of school supervision, from the colonization of America on down through at least the first half of the nineteenth century, was based on the idea of maintaining the existing standards of instruction, rather than on the idea of improving them" (p. 14).

American schooling, in general, during the better part of the 19th century was rural, unbureaucratic, and in the hands of local authorities. The prototypical 19th-century school was a small one-room schoolhouse. Teachers were "young, poorly paid, and rarely educated beyond the elementary subjects"; teachers were "hired and supervised largely by local lay trustees, they were not members of a self-regulating profession" (Tyack & Hansot, 1982, p. 17). These local lay trustees (called ward boards) who supervised schools were not professionally trained or very much interested in the improvement of instruction (Button, 1961).

The tradition of lay supervision continued from the American Revolution through the middle of the 19th century or, as commonly referred to, the end of the Common Era. Despite the emergence during this period of a new "American system of educational thought and practice . . . the quality of supervision would not improve appreciably" (Tanner & Tanner, 1987, p. 10). With the advent of a district system of supervision and then state-controlled supervision beginning in the late 19th century, however, the character of supervision did, in fact, change dramatically.

> **Reflection**
>
> *School supervision originally referred to a procedure in which someone would "examine" a teacher's classroom "looking for errors." What impact or significance, if any, does this original meaning or intention of supervision have for you as a supervisor today?*

SUPERVISION IN THE LATE 19TH CENTURY

In general, unprecedented growth precipitated by the Industrial Revolution characterized the second half of the 19th century. The expansion of American education, which had started in the days of Horace Mann, whom Tanner and Tanner (1987) characterized as the "first professional supervisor," continued and assumed a new dimension in the latter decades of the 19th century. The schoolmen, specifically superintendents, began shaping schools in large cities into organized networks. Organization was the rallying cry nationally and locally. There was a firm belief that highly organized and efficient schools would meet the demands of a newly born industrialized age. That hierarchically organized public schools, as social institutions, would meet the crises and challenges that lay ahead was beyond doubt (Bullough, 1974; Cronin, 1973; Hammock, 1969; Kaestle, 1973; Lazerson, 1971).

The reform movement in education in the late 19th century was reflective of the larger, more encompassing changes that were occurring in society. Although rapid economic growth characterized the 19th century, reformers realized that there were serious problems in the nation's schools. In the battle that ensued to reorganize the nation's schools, sources of authority and responsibility in education were permanently transformed (Tyack, 1974). By the end of the 19th century, reformers concerned with undermining inefficiency and corruption transformed schools into streamlined, central administrative bureaucracies with superintendents as supervisors in charge. Supervision, during this struggle, became an important tool by which the superintendent legitimized his existence in the school system (Glanz, 1991). Supervision, therefore, was a function that superintendents performed to oversee schools more efficiently.

Supervision as inspection was the dominant method for administering schools. Payne (1875), author of the first published textbook on supervision, stated emphatically that teachers must be "held responsible" for work performed in the classroom and that the supervisor, as expert inspector, would "oversee" and ensure "harmony and efficiency" (p. 521). A prominent superintendent, James M. Greenwood (1888), stated emphatically that "very much of my time is devoted to visiting schools and inspecting the work." Three years later, Greenwood (1891) again illustrated his idea of how supervision should be performed: The skilled superintendent, he said, should simply walk into the classroom and "judge from a compound sensation of the disease at work among the inmates" (p. 227). A review of the literature of the period indicates that Greenwood's supervisory methods, which relied on inspection based on intuition rather than technical or scientific knowledge, were practiced widely.

Supervisors using inspectional practices did not view favorably the competency of most teachers. For instance, Balliet (1894), a superintendent from Massachusetts, insisted that there were only two types of teachers: the efficient and the inefficient. The only way to reform the schools, thought Balliet, was to "secure a competent superintendent; second, to let him 'reform' all the teachers who are incompetent and can be 'reformed'; thirdly, to bury the dead" (pp. 437–438). Characteristic of the remedies applied to improve teaching was this suggestion: "Weak teachers should place themselves in such a position in the room that every pupil's face may be seen without turning the head" (Fitzpatrick, 1893, p. 76). Teachers, for the most part, were seen by 19th-century supervisors as inept. As Bolin and Panaritis (1992) explained, "Teachers (mostly female and disenfranchised) were seen as a bedraggled troop—incompetent and backward in outlook" (p. 33).

The practice of supervision by inspection was indeed compatible with the emerging bureaucratic school system, with its assumption that expertise was concentrated in the upper echelons of the hierarchy. Many teachers perceived supervision as inspectional, rather than as a helping function.

Because supervision as inspection through visitation gained wide application in schools, it is the first model that characterizes early methods in supervision (see Table 1.1, Model 1).

Our brief examination of early methods of supervision indicates that (1) amid the upheavals of late-19th-century America, supervision emerged as an important function performed by superintendents, and (2) inspectional practices dominated supervision.

> **Reflection/Microlab**
>
> *What vestiges of inspectional supervisory practices remain today? To what extent do you or others you know function as "inspectors"? How do you feel about that? Would you feel comfortable "inspecting" classrooms? Why or why not? Do certain conditions in your school/district exist that involve an "inspectional mind-set"? Explain.*

The Emergence of the Distinct Position of Supervisor

In the first two decades of the 20th century, schooling grew dramatically. As the size and complexity of schools increased, greater administrative specialization was readily apparent. Supervisors gained in stature and authority in the early 20th century. In addition to the building principal, a new cadre of administrative officers emerged to assume major responsibility for day-to-day classroom supervision. Two specific groups of supervisors commonly were found in schools in the early 20th century (see Table 1.1).

First, a *special supervisor*, most often female, was chosen by the building principal to help assist less experienced teachers in subject matter mastery.

Special supervisors were relieved of some teaching responsibilities to allow time for these tasks, but no formal training was required. Larger schools, for example, had a number of special supervisors in each major subject area.

Second, a *general supervisor,* usually male, was selected not only to deal with more general subjects such as mathematics and science but also to "assist" the principal in the more administrative, logistical operations of a school. The general supervisor, subsequently called *vice principal* or *assistant principal,* prepared attendance reports, collected data for evaluation purposes, and coordinated special school programs, among other administrative duties.

Differences in functions between special and general supervisors were reflective of prevalent 19th-century notions of male-female role relationships. William E. Chancellor (1904), a prominent 19th-century superintendent, remarked, "That men make better administrators I have already said. As a general proposition, women make the better special supervisors. They are more interested in details. They do not make as good general supervisors or assistant superintendents, however" (p. 210). Representative of the bias against women in the educational workplace were notions espoused by William H. Payne (1875): "Women cannot do man's work in the schools" (p. 49). Payne, like many of his contemporaries, believed that men were better suited for the more prestigious and lucrative job opportunities in education.

It is also interesting to note that teachers readily accepted the special supervisors. Special supervisors played a very useful and helpful role by assisting teachers in practical areas of spelling, penmanship, and art, for example. In addition, these special supervisors did not have any independent authority and did not serve in an evaluative capacity, as did, for example, the general supervisor, who was given authority, albeit limited, to evaluate instruction in the classroom. Therefore, teachers were not likely to be threatened by the appearance of a special supervisor in the classroom. General supervisors, on the other hand, were concerned with more administrative and evaluative matters and, consequently, were viewed by the classroom teachers as more menacing. Special supervisors also probably gained more acceptance by teachers, most of whom were female, because they too were female. General supervisors were almost exclusively male and perhaps were perceived differently as a result. Frank Spaulding (1955), in his analysis of this period of time, concurred and stated that general supervisors "were quite generally looked upon, not as helpers, but as critics bent on the discovery and revelation of teachers' weaknesses and failures, . . . they were dubbed Snoopervisors" (p. 130).

The position of the special supervisor did not, however, endure for a very long period in schools. General supervisors gradually usurped their duties and responsibilities. The relative obscurity of special supervisors after the early 1920s can be attributed to discrimination based on gender. As a group comprising an overwhelming number of females, special supervisors were not perceived in the same light as were general supervisors, principals, assistant superintendents, and superintendents, who were, of course, mostly male. Gender bias and the sexual division of labor in schools go far toward explaining the disappearance of the special supervisor as such.[1] In short, general supervisors gained wider acceptance simply because they were men.

Reflection

How does gender affect your role and function as a supervisor today? Explain and provide an example.

Bureaucratic Methods in Supervision as Social Efficiency

Numerous technological advances greatly influenced American education after 1900. As a result of the work of Frederick Winslow Taylor (1911), who published a book titled *The Principles of Scientific Management,* "efficiency" became the watchword of the day. Taylor's book stressed scientific management and efficiency in the workplace. The worker, according to Taylor, was merely a cog in the business machinery, and the main purpose of management was to promote the efficiency of the worker. Within a relatively short period of time, *Taylorism* and *efficiency* became household words and ultimately had a profound impact on administrative and supervisory practices in schools.

Franklin Bobbitt (1913), a professor at the University of Chicago, tried to apply the ideas that Taylor espoused to the "problems of educational management and supervision" (p. 8). Bobbitt's work, particularly his discussion of supervision, is significant because his ideas shaped the character and nature of supervision for many years. On the surface, these ideas appeared to advance professional supervision, but in reality they were the antithesis of professionalism. What Bobbitt called "scientific and professional supervisory methods" (p. 9) were, in fact, scien*tistic* and bureaucratic methods of supervision aimed not at professionalizing but at finding a legitimate and secure niche for control-oriented supervision within the school bureaucracy.

In 1913, Bobbitt published an article titled "Some General Principles of Management Applied to the Problems of City-School Systems," which presented 11 major principles of scientific management as applied to education. Bobbitt firmly held that management, direction, and supervision of schools were necessary to achieve "organizational goals." Bobbitt maintained that supervision was an essential function "to coordinate school affairs. . . . Supervisory members must co-ordinate the labors of all, . . . find the best methods of work, and enforce the use of these methods on the part of the workers" (Bobbitt, 1913, pp. 76, 78). The employment of scientific principles in supervision, said Bobbitt, is a necessity for the continued progress of the school system.

Many supervisors were eager to adopt Bobbitt's ideas of scientific management for use in schools. However, a few did not readily accept his views. One of the more vociferous opponents of Bobbitt's ideas was James Hosic (1924), a professor of education at Teachers College, Columbia University. Hosic contended that Bobbitt's analogy was largely false:

> Teaching cannot be "directed" in the same way as bricklaying. . . . In education, the supervisor's function is not to devise all plans and work out all standards and merely inform his co-workers as to what they are. . . . [The supervisor] should not so much give orders as hold conferences. . . . His prototype is not a captain, lieutenant, or officer of the guard in industry, but chairman of committee or consulting expert. (pp. 82–84)

Despite Hosic's criticism, schoolmen of the day readily adopted the business model, as evidenced by William McAndrew (1922), who said about his role as supervisor in the school, "I am the captain of big business" (p. 91).

The criticisms against Bobbitt's methods, nonetheless, accurately stressed a number of disturbing ideas. First and foremost was the ill-conceived notion that "education in a school" is analogous to "production in a factory." Bobbitt claimed that "education is a shaping process as much as the manufacture of steel rails." Supervisors in the early 20th century were becoming aware of the fallacy of this logic as well as realizing the negative effects of bureaucracy in education. Bobbitt's "scientific management and supervision" found justification within a school organization that was bureaucratically organized.

Still, it remains clear that the significance of Bobbitt's work was in his advocacy of scientific and professional supervisory methods. Supervisors thought that their work in schools would be more clearly defined and accepted by adopting Bobbitt's principles of scientific management. Supervisors believed, as did Bobbitt, that "the way to eliminate the personal element from administration and supervision is to introduce impersonal methods of scientific administration and supervision" (p. 7). This was often translated into rating schemes. In a short time, supervision became synonymous with teacher rating.

In sum, just as "supervision as inspection" reflected the emergence of bureaucracy in education, so too "supervision as social efficiency" was largely influenced by scientific management in education (see Table 1.1, Model 2). Supervision as social efficiency was compatible with and a natural consequence of bureaucracy in education.

Democratic Methods in Supervision

Bureaucratic supervision, relying on inspectional methods and seeking efficiency above all else, dominated discourse in the field from 1870–1920. This sort of supervision attracted much criticism from teachers and others (Rousmaniere, 1992). Representative of the nature of this opposition were the comments of Sallie Hill (1918), a teacher speaking before the Department of Classroom Teachers, decrying supervisory methods of rating. Hill charged:

> There is no democracy in our schools. . . . Here let me say that I do not want to give the impression that we are sensitive. No person who has remained a teacher for ten years can be sensitive. She is either dead or has gone into some other business. . . . There are too many supervisors with big salaries and undue rating powers. (p. 506)

The movement to alter supervisory theory and practice to more democratic and improvement foci, while at the same time minimizing the evaluative function, occurred in the 1920s as a direct result of growing opposition to autocratic supervisory methods (see Table 1.1, Model 3). Consequently, supervisors tried to change their image as "snoopervisors" by adopting alternate methods of supervision. The following poem, quoted in part, indicates the desired change of focus to more democratic methods in supervision:

> *With keenly peering eyes and snooping nose,*
>
> *From room to room the Snoopervisor goes.*
>
> *He notes each slip, each fault with lofty frown,*
>
> *And on his rating card he writes it down;*

His duty done, when he has brought to light,

The things the teachers do that are not right . . .

The supervisor enters quietly, "What do you need? How can I help today?

John, let me show you. Mary, try this way."

He aims to help, encourage and suggest,

That teachers, pupils all may do their best.

—Anonymous, 1929

Influenced in large measure by Dewey's (1929) theories of democratic and scientific thinking as well as by Hosic's (1920) ideas of democratic supervision, supervisors attempted to apply scientific methods and cooperative problem-solving approaches to educational problems (Pajak, 2000). Hosic cautioned the supervisor to eschew his "autocratic past": "The fact that he is invested for the time being with a good deal of delegated authority does not justify him in playing the autocrat. . . . To do so is neither humane, wise, nor expedient" (1920, pp. 331, 332). Continuing to build a philosophic rationale for the supervisor's involvement in "democratic pursuits," Hosic explained that it was no longer viable to apply techniques of the past. Hosic believed, as did Dewey, that it was possible to reshape a school system that had originated with the idea of bureaucratic maintenance so that it would comply with the principles of democracy.

Democratic supervision, in particular, implied that educators, including teachers, curriculum specialists, and supervisors, would cooperate to improve instruction. Efforts by prominent superintendent Jesse Newlon reinforced democracy in supervision. In an article titled "Reorganizing City School Supervision," Newlon (1923) asked, "How can the ends of supervision best be achieved?" He maintained that the school organization must be set up to "invite the participation of the teacher in the development of courses." The ends of supervision could be realized when teacher and supervisor worked in a coordinated fashion. Newlon developed the idea of setting up "supervisory councils" to offer "genuine assistance" to teachers. In this way, he continued, "the teacher will be regarded as a fellow-worker rather than a mere cog in a big machine" (pp. 547–549). Participatory school management and supervision had their origins in the work of Newlon.

Scientific Supervision

In the 1930s and 1940s, educators believed that autocratic supervisory practices were no longer viable. They urged more scientific approaches to supervisory practice in schools. The early attempts to apply science via rating cards were now losing favor. Burton (1930), a prolific writer in supervision, explained that the use of "rating schemes from our prescientific days . . . would be wholly inadequate today." Although Burton recognized the usefulness of rating in some instances, he believed that "it is desirable and rapidly becoming possible to have more objectively determined items by means of which to evaluate the teacher's procedure" (p. 405).

One of the foremost proponents of science in education and supervision was A. S. Barr (1931). He stated emphatically that the application of scientific principles "is a part of a general movement to place supervision on a professional basis." Barr stated in precise terms what the supervisor needed to know:

> Supervisors must have the ability to analyze teaching situations and to locate the probable causes for poor work with a certain degree of expertness; they must have the ability to use an array of data-gathering devices peculiar to the field of supervision itself; they must possess certain constructive skills for the development of new means, methods, and materials of instruction; they must know how teachers learn to teach; they must have the ability to teach teachers how to teach; and they must be able to evaluate. In short, they must possess training in both the science of instructing pupils and the science of instructing teachers. Both are included in the science of supervision. (pp. x, xi)

Barr (1931) said the supervisor should first formulate objectives, followed by measurement surveys to determine the instructional status of schools. Then, probable causes of poor work should be explored through the use of tests, rating scales, and observational instruments. The results of supervision, continued Barr, must be measured. Most important, according to Barr, the methods of science should be applied to the study and practice of supervision. More concretely, Barr (1925) asserted that a scientific analysis of teaching is a necessary part of the training of a supervisor: "How can the scientific knowledge of the teaching process be brought to bear upon the study and improvement of teaching?" Barr contended that teaching could be broken down into its component parts and that each part had to be studied scientifically. If good teaching procedures could be isolated, thought Barr, then specific standards could be established to guide the supervisor in judging the quality of instruction. He based his scientific approach to supervision "upon the success of the professional student of education in breaking up this complex mass into its innumerable elements and to study each objectively" (pp. 360, 363).

Throughout the 1930s, 1940s, and 1950s, the idea that supervision involves improving instruction based on classroom observation gained momentum. Supervision as a means of improving instruction through observation was reinforced by the use of "stenographic reports," which were the brainchild of Romiett Stevens, a professor at Teachers College, Columbia University. Stevens thought that the best way to improve instruction was to record verbatim accounts of actual lessons "without criticism or comment." Stevens's stenographic accounts were "the first major systematic study of classroom behavior" (Hoetker & Ahlbrand, 1969).

Supervisors during this era advocated a scientific approach toward their work in schools (see Table 1.1, Model 4). Scientific supervision was considered to be distinct from social efficiency and entirely compatible with democratic practices (Dewey, 1929). Burton and Brueckner (1955) claimed that "a few individuals still speak, write, and supervise as if science and democracy were antagonistic, or at least not easily combined. The truth is that each is necessary in an integrated theory and practice" (p. 82).

Supervision as Leadership

Democratic and scientific supervision continued well into the 1950s. Democratic methods in supervision, however, clearly were expanded and clarified in the 1960s in the form of supervision as leadership (see Table 1.1, Model 5).

The political and social upheavals resulting from the urban plight, concerns for justice and equality, and antiwar sentiments dramatically affected education—and supervision, in particular. Virulent criticisms of educational practice and school bureaucracy were pervasive (e.g., Silberman's *Crisis in the Classroom*, 1970). Educators also took a serious look at supervisory practices in schools. The legacy of supervision as inspection that found justification in the production-oriented, social efficiency era was no longer viable. Bureaucratic supervision was not viable either. A new vision for the function of supervision was framed.

The work most representative of the 1960s was undoubtedly the anthology of articles that originally appeared in *Educational Leadership*, compiled by then editor and associate director of the Association for Supervision and Curriculum Development, Robert R. Leeper (1969). Leeper and the authors of this anthology maintained that supervisors must extend "democracy in their relationships with teachers" (p. 69). The way to accomplish this was to promulgate supervision as a leadership function.

Harris (1969) expressed the ideals of supervisory leadership this way:

The word *leadership* refers to showing the way and guiding the organization in definitive directions. New leadership is needed in this sense of the word. Two kinds are required:

1. Those in status positions must lead out with new boldness and find better ways of influencing the schools toward rationally planned, timed change.

2. New leadership positions must be created, and coordinated to facilitate the enormously complex job of leading instructional change. (p. 36)

Although issues of instructional leadership would not gain popularity for another 15 years, supervision as leadership essentially emerged in the 1960s.

The principal focus of supervision during this time was a concerted effort by those engaged in supervision to provide leadership in five ways: (1) developing mutually acceptable goals, (2) extending cooperative and democratic methods of supervision, (3) improving classroom instruction, (4) promoting research into educational problems, and (5) promoting professional leadership.

> **Reflection**
>
> *What does instructional leadership mean to you?*

Clinical Supervision

Uncertainty plagued the field of supervision by the 1970s. Markowitz (1976) stated,

> The supervisor in the educational system is plagued by ambiguities. His or her position in the authority structure is ill-defined and quite often vulnerable. There is a lack of clarity in the definition of his or her role and a lack of agreement on the functions associated with supervision. (p. 367)

Alfonso, Firth, and Neville (1975) described this role ambiguity in terms of a "power limbo;" that is, supervisors are "neither line nor staff, neither administration nor faculty, but somewhere in between" (p. 342). Wilhelms (1969) concurred that supervision had witnessed tremendous change: "Roles are changing; staff organization is swirling; titles and functions are shifting," said Wilhelms, "but whether his [sic] title is 'principal,' 'supervisor,' 'curriculum coordinator,' or what not, the person in a position of supervisory leadership is caught in the middle" (p. x).

Lacking focus, a sound conceptual base, and purpose, supervision explored alternative notions to guide theory and practice in the field. Efforts to reform supervision were reflective of a broader attempt to seek alternatives to traditional educational practice. Clinical supervision grew out of this dissatisfaction with traditional educational practice and supervisory methods. Goldhammer (1969), one of the early proponents of clinical supervision, stated that the model for clinical supervision was "motivated, primarily, by contemporary views of weaknesses that commonly exist in educational practice" (p. 1).

The premise of clinical supervision was that teaching could be improved by a prescribed, formal process of collaboration between teacher and supervisor. The literature of clinical supervision has been replete with concepts of collegiality, collaboration, assistance, and improvement of instruction. Bolin and Panaritis (1992) explained that clinical supervision "appealed to many educators" because of its "emphasis on 'collegiality.'" The rhetoric of clinical supervision favored collaborative practice over inspectional, fault-finding supervision.

Most researchers identify Morris Cogan (1973) as the progenitor of clinical supervision (Anderson, 1993), although Pajak (1989) credits Hill (1968) with incorporating a "lesser known version of the preconference, observation, postconference cycle" of supervision. Tanner and Tanner (1987), acknowledging Cogan's influence in developing the theory of clinical supervision, attributed the idea to Conant in 1936.

Clinical supervision, although advocated by professors and authors of textbooks, did not by any means gain wide acceptance in schools (see, e.g., Garman, 1997). Although clinical supervision received its share of criticism (e.g., Bolin & Panaritis, 1992; Tanner & Tanner, 1987), educators throughout the 1970s continued to argue that democratic methods of supervision should be extended and that vestiges of bureaucratic supervision should be excised. Supervision to improve instruction and promote pupil learning, instructional leadership, and democratic practices remained as prominent goals throughout the 1970s (see Table 1.1, Model 6).

Reflection

What are the chief characteristics of clinical supervision that distinguish it from other models of supervision? Have you ever used or been involved with clinical supervision? What obstacles might impede successful implementation of a clinical model in your school or district?

DEMOCRATIC METHODS AND SUPERVISION

During the early 1980s, public education continued to receive voluminous criticism for being bureaucratic and unresponsive to the needs of teachers, parents, and children (see, e.g., Johnson, 1990). One of the prominent proposals for disenfranchising bureaucracy was the dissolution of autocratic administrative practices where overbearing supervisors ruled by fiat. Favored was greater and more meaningful decision making at the grassroots level (Dunlap & Goldman, 1991). This idea translated into giving teachers more formal responsibility for setting school policies, thus enhancing democratic governance in schools (Glanz, 1992; Kirby, 1991). Johnson (1990) observed that "although schools have long been under the control of administrators, local districts are increasingly granting teachers more formal responsibility for setting school policies" (p. 337).

Criticism leveled at the educational bureaucracy has had consequences for school supervision (Firth & Eiken, 1982). Throughout this period, educators continued to consider alternative methods of supervision. In the early 1980s, developmental supervision, in which varied levels of teaching abilities were acknowledged, gained attention (Glickman, 1981). By the end of the decade, transformational leadership, which advocated that supervisors serve as change agents, became popular (e.g., Leithwood & Jantzi, 1990). Other writers advanced their notions of supervision as well (e.g., Bowers & Flinders, 1991).

Teacher empowerment (e.g., Darling-Hammond & Goodwin, 1993) gained attention as teachers became active participants in decision-making processes in schools. Pajak (2000) reviewed the literature on the "teacher as leader" during the previous five years. Peer supervision (e.g., Willerman, McNeely, & Koffman Cooper, 1991) appeared in the literature as an alternative to traditional supervision by "professionally trained supervisors," as did cognitive coaching (Costa & Garmston, 1997). Other collegial and democratic supervisory methods continued to receive notice (e.g., Smyth, 1991).

The publication of *Supervision in Transition* (Glickman, 1992) by the Association for Supervision and Curriculum Development marked a refinement in the changing conception of supervision as a democratic enterprise. Glickman, editor of the yearbook, clearly set the tone by stating emphatically that the very term *supervision* connoted a distasteful, even "disgusting" metaphor for school improvement. Instead of using the words *supervision* or *supervisor,* educators, or what Glickman called "risk-taking practitioners," were more comfortable with terms such as *instructional leadership* and *instructional leader.* The transition that Glickman and the authors of this comprehensive account of supervision envisioned was one that valued collegiality. Supervision, in the words of Sergiovanni (1992), was viewed as "professional and moral."

Other models and conceptions of supervision emerged in an attempt to extend democratic methods and to disassociate from bureaucratic and inspectional supervision. Clinical, developmental, and transformational supervision, among other models, had a common bond in that they emerged to counter the ill effects of supervision's bureaucratic legacy (see Table 1.1, Model 7).

Reflection/Microlab

From your experience, are collegiality and democratic supervision viable options for your school or district? Explain. Are you familiar with the implementation of any existing collegial or democratic processes? If so, which ones? How have staff and administration responded to them?

STANDARDS-BASED SUPERVISION

Although the democratic methods "changing concepts" model had an impact on supervision in the 1990s, over the past several years, especially since the turn of the new century, supervisory practice has been shaped and influenced by the general movement toward standards-based reform. Standards-based reform has affected supervision so greatly that we have identified a new and current model of supervision that has impacted and will in all likelihood continue to impact supervision as a field of study and practice. We call that model "Standards-Based Supervision" (see Table 1.1).

Although they are not new, standards-based teaching and learning have influenced curriculum, supervision, and teacher education in significant ways.

Supervisors and those concerned with supervision have been particularly challenged in the past several years to implement supervisory practices that ensure the technical competence of teachers. Receiving strong political backing from both state and national agencies, standards-based supervision has, in some quarters, relegated supervisors to relying on checklists to ascertain the extent to which teachers are meeting various curricular and instructional objectives embedded in core curriculum standards at various grade levels. Such supervisory practices thwart meaningful supervision aimed at fostering closer collaboration and instructional dialogue to improve teaching and learning. Pajak (2000) points to the compatibility problem of trying to use standards-based supervision with clinical supervision. He warns, "If we fail to provide empathy-based supervision, the current standards-based environment will ultimately prove stultifying for both teachers and their students" (p. 241).

To best understand standards-based supervision, some background knowledge on standards-based reform is necessary. The national movement toward standards-based education, including high-stakes testing, has served to legitimize and bolster local reform proposals that have influenced supervisory practices. Raising standards and promoting uniformity of curricular offerings to raise academic achievement has been an established reform proposal since the 1890s (Seguel, 1966).

During the first half of the 20th century, the College Entrance Examination Board (formed in the 1890s), the Scholastic Aptitude Test (the first SAT was administered in 1926), and the American College Testing Program (established in 1959) were the guardians of standards, as applied to the academic curriculum. As a result of the Russian launch of the first artificial satellite (Sputnik) in 1957, American education was attacked vociferously. Only months after the Sputnik launching, Congress passed the National Defense Education Act (NDEA), which poured millions of dollars into mathematics, sciences, and engineering. For several years following Sputnik, the postwar baby boom increased enrollments dramatically in high schools, and achievement scores in many academic areas also improved. Academic standards, up until this time, continued to be driven by levels of student achievement and assessed by national standardized tests (Ravitch, 1995).

After a lull in the tumultuous mid-1960s, the publication of the National Commission on Excellence in Education's 1983 report, *A Nation at Risk: The Imperative for Educational Reform*, drew attention to the assertion that schools had lowered their standards too much and that American students were not competitive with their international counterparts. The authors of this 1983 report were perturbed by the fact that American schoolchildren lagged behind students in other industrialized nations. The National Commission on Excellence in Education reported that among students from various industrialized nations, U.S. students scored lowest on 7 of 19 academic tests and failed to score first or second on any test. Similar results were reported by the Educational Testing Service (1992). Moreover, the study found that nearly 40% of U.S. 17-year-olds couldn't perform tasks requiring higher-order thinking skills.

Pressure to improve the quality of American education by articulating concrete standards for performance increased. Consequently, a spate of national and state reports continued through the 1980s, each advocating fundamental educational change. Commitment to democratic ideals and the influence of public education was reinforced once again in 1986 with the publication of the report, sponsored by the Carnegie Foundation, *A Nation Prepared: Teachers for the 21st Century* (Carnegie Forum on Education and the Economy, 1986) and the Holmes Group (1986) report. The national curriculum reform movement was catapulted into prominence and action with the Education Summit held in 1989 by then President George Bush and state governors. A year later, in his State of the Union Address, President Bush affirmed his commitment to excellence in education by establishing six national education goals to be achieved by the year 2000. Signed into law by Congress during the Clinton administration on March 31, 1994, *Goals 2000* proclaimed, in part, that by the year 2000 "U.S. students will be first in the world in science and mathematics achievement" and "Every school will be free of drugs and violence and will offer a disciplined environment conducive to learning" (http://www.nd.edu/~rbarger/and www7/goals200.html).

The adoption of national goals has been a major impetus for the increased attention to standards at the state level. More than 40 states have revised their curricula to reflect the standards they established.

Continuing in the tradition of standards-based education, President George W. Bush signed into law the No Child Left Behind Act of 2001, a reauthorization of the Elementary and Secondary Education Act Legislation of 1965. The purpose of the new legislation was to redefine the federal role in K–12 education and to help raise student achievement, especially for disadvantaged and minority students. Four basic principles were evident: (1) stronger accountability for results, (2) increased flexibility and local control, (3) expanded options for parents, and (4) an emphasis on teaching methods that presumably have been proven to work.

What can the history of standards-based education teach us about the practice of supervision? Pajak (2000) maintains that the "use of clinical supervision in standards-based environments is so recent that no clear consensus has yet emerged about whether this marriage is either desirable or successful" (p. 238). Our experiences and view of what is happening in the field tell us that a clear consensus is indeed apparent. The movement of standards-based education is indeed shaping supervisory practice by frequently compelling supervisors to incorporate a checklist approach to supervision. The pressure practitioners face to raise student achievement as measured on high-stakes tests is enormous. Principals and assistant principals are more accountable than ever to address prescribed core curriculum standards, promote teaching to the standards, and ensure higher student academic performance on standardized tests. Consequently, those concerned with supervision have been more inclined to incorporate supervisory practices that are a throwback to the 1930s, 1940s, and 1950s (Table 1.1, Model 4). Directive approaches of supervision find justification within a standards-based educational milieu.

UNDERSTANDING THE HISTORY OF SUPERVISION

Historically, the function and conception of supervision have changed. The earliest notions of supervision addressed the need for selectmen, committees, or clergymen to inspect the physical plant of schools and to ensure that children were receiving instruction as required by law. The legacy of inspectional supervision from the colonial period continued into the late 19th century as supervision became little more than an inspectional function local and city superintendents performed attempting to bureaucratize urban education. In the early 1900s, supervision as bureaucratic inspection was reinforced and strengthened as "social efficiency" became the watchword. Influenced by social and economic forces as well as by opposition to inspectional bureaucratic methods, supervision in the 1920s and 1930s embraced democratic theory; this trend would continue throughout the century, albeit in different forms.

What can we learn from this excursion into history? For some theorists and practitioners, a lesson learned is that authoritarian supervision aimed at faultfinding and suspecting the competence of teachers should not be compatible with the modern practice of supervision. Some view the evolution of the practice of supervision as a progression from crude, unsophisticated *bureaucratic inspectional* approaches to more refined democratic participatory techniques and methodologies.

For some theorists and practitioners, the legacy of inspectional supervision lives on in the form of evaluation. Democratic supervision is viewed as helping teachers improve instruction, whereas bureaucratic supervision is associated with accountability and judgments about teachers' efficiency. This conflict between the helping and evaluative functions of supervision is long standing. Tanner and Tanner (1987) asserted that this dilemma presents an almost insurmountable problem for supervisors: "The basic conflict between these functions is probably the most serious and, up until now, unresolved problem in the field of supervision" (p. 106).

Historically, the *evaluative* function of supervision is rooted in bureaucratic inspectional-type supervision. Maintaining an efficient and effective school organization as well as a sound instructional program mandates that teacher competency be evaluated. In other words, the evaluative aspect of the supervisory function emanates from organizational requirements to measure and assess teaching effectiveness. The origins of the *helping* or *improvement* function of supervision date back to democratic practices in the early 20th century. That is, helping teachers improve instruction and promote pupil achievement grew out of the democratic theory of supervision.

Supervisors or people concerned with supervision, however, have faced a basic role conflict, namely, the unresolved dilemma between the necessity to evaluate (a bureaucratic function) and the desire to genuinely assist teachers in the instructional process (a democratic and professional goal).

Table 1.1 Timeline

	Social/Cultural Markers of the Times	Models of Supervision
Pre-1900		
1893–1897 Grover Cleveland

1897–1901 William McKinley | • Debates about the Spanish-American War, territorial acquisitions, and the economy dominated thought and literature.
• Thorstein Veblen's *Theory of the Leisure Class* (1899) attacked predatory wealth and conspicuous consumption of the new rich.
• Jacob Riis in *How the Other Half Lives* (1890) documented gnawing poverty, illness, crime, and despair of New York's slums.
• Frank Norris's *The Octopus* (1901) condemned monopoly.

From REA U.S. History Review Book:
Teachers as the factory workers and the students as the raw material to be turned into the product that was to meet the specifications of the needs of the 20th century. (http://www.ux1.eiu.edu/~cfrnb/impbusin.html)

Education was conducted with military-like schedules and discipline, and emphasized farming and other manual skills. The daily schedule was split between academics and vocational training. (lcweb2.loc.gov/learn/community/NA_toolkit/overview.pdf) | **Model 1: Supervision as Inspection, Payne-Greenwood**

Payne (1875), author of the first published textbook on supervision. Greenwood's supervisory methods (1891), which relied on inspection based on intuition rather than technical or scientific knowledge.

Balliet (1894), a superintendent from Massachusetts, insisted that there were only two types of teachers: the efficient and the inefficient. |
| **1900–1919** | | |
| 1901–1909 Theodore Roosevelt

1909–1913 William H. Taft | • 1906: Upton Sinclair writes *The Jungle*, which depicts the poverty, absence of social programs, unpleasant living and working conditions, and hopelessness prevalent among have-nots in contrast with the corruption on the part of the haves. (wiki)
• 1906: Pres. Roosevelt wins Nobel Peace Prize for mediating the Russo-Japanese War.
• 1909: NAACP formed.
• 1914: World War I begins.
• 1917: United States declares war on Germany.
• 1917: Russian Revolution.
• 1919: Over 20% of U.S. labor force goes on strike.

Purpose of education was to prepare youth for jobs in factories. (http://tiger.towson.edu/users/rturnb1/ Education%20Presentation_files/frame.htm) | **Model 2: Supervision as Social Efficiency, Taylor-Bobbitt**

Taylor—author of *The Principles of Scientific Management*. Main point of management was to promote the efficiency of the worker.

Bobbitt—professor, University of Chicago, control-oriented supervision. |

	Social/Cultural Markers of the Times	Models of Supervision
1920s		
1913–1921 Woodrow Wilson	• 1920: 19th Amendment—Women's Suffrage ratified. • Literary Trends—reflected disgust with hypocrisy and materialism of American society: Hemingway's *The Sun Also Rises*; F. Scott Fitzgerald's *The Great Gatsby*; John Dos Passos's *Three Soldiers*.	**Model 3: Democracy in Supervision, Dewey-Hosic-Newlon** Teachers, curriculum specialists, and supervisors would cooperate to improve instruction.
1921–1923 Warren G. Harding	• Popular Culture—Movies—Introduction of Sound—*The Jazz Singer*; Major League Baseball—Babe Ruth; Boxing—Jack Dempsey. • Social Conflicts—the automobile, the revolution in morals, rapid urbanization with immigrants, and blacks inhabiting the cities.	
1923–1929 Calvin Coolidge	• 1920–1929: Roaring Twenties. • 1929: Stock market crashes in October. During the 1920s, when education turned increasingly to "scientific" techniques such as intelligence testing and cost-benefit management, progressive educators insisted on the importance of the emotional, artistic, and creative aspects of human development. (http://www.uvm.edu/~dewey/articles/proged.html)	
1930–1950s		
1929–1933 Herbert C. Hoover	• 1929–1933: Depression. Literary trends depicted the crushing poverty in America: James T. Farrell's trilogy *Studs Lonigan* about the struggles of lower-middle-class Irish Catholics in Chicago; Erskine Caldwell's *Tobacco Road* about impoverished Georgia sharecroppers; John Steinbeck's *The Grapes of Wrath* depicts "Okies" migrating to California in the midst of the Depression.	**Model 4: Scientific Supervision** Burton—writer. Barr—proponent of science in education—supervisors must possess expertise in instructing pupils and teachers.
1933–1945 Franklin D. Roosevelt	• 1939–1945: World War II. • 1949: NATO formed.	
1945–1953 Harry S. Truman	• 1954: *Brown vs. Board of Education* challenged the doctrine of separate but equal. • 1957: The launching of Soviet space satellite Sputnik created fear that America was falling behind technologically.	Stevens—professor, Teachers Coll., Columbia University; classroom observation through recording verbatim accounts of lessons was the first systematic study of classroom behavior.
1953–1961 Dwight D. Eisenhower	• 1957: National Defense Education Act—millions of dollars allocated to education for math, sciences, and engineering. Dramatic enrollments in high school. • 1959: James Conant in *The American High School Today* questioned the adequacy of American education. 1930s: Child-centered (progressive) education (http://www.brillion.k12.wi.us/hswebpage/Schools%20of%20the%201930's%20Lesson/index.htm)	

(Continued)

Table 1.1 (Continued)

	Social/Cultural Markers of the Times	Models of Supervision
	1940s: Progressive educational philosophy, influenced by John Dewey and New Deal liberalism predominant among educators. 1950s: New emphasis on science and technology emerges after 1957. (http://www.archives.nysed.gov/edpolicy/research/res_chronology1944.shtml)	
1960s		
1961–1963 John F. Kennedy 1963–1969 Lyndon B. Johnson	• Political and social upheavals resulting from urban plight, concerns for justice and equality, and antiwar sentiments. • American school curriculum shifted from academic to nonacademic. • 1964–1975: Vietnam War. • 1964: President Johnson announces war on poverty. • 1965: The Elementary and Secondary Education Act provided $1.5 billion to school districts to improve the education of the poor. 1960s: "Activity learning" (versus passive students and active teachers). Led to Jerome Bruner's *Man: A Course of Study (MACOS)* in 1962, calling for research-based curriculum stressing critical thinking, collaboration, and questioning of traditional thought and values. Met strong resistance and was never implemented. (http://www.archives.nysed.gov/edpolicy/research/res_chronology1960.shtml)	**Model 5: Supervision as Leadership** Leeper—Assoc. Dir. of Assoc. for Sup. and Curr. Dev. (1969). Supervisors must extend democracy in their relationships with teachers.
1970–1980s		
1969–1974 Richard M. Nixon 1974–1977 Gerald Ford 1977–1981 Jimmy Carter 1981–1989 Ronald Reagan	• 1964–1975: Vietnam War. • 1979–1983: New York Regents Action Plan for Improvement of Elementary and Secondary Education developed and approved. The nation's first comprehensive reform plan based on standards for student achievement and school and teacher accountability. • Political corruption: Watergate. • Feminism. • Environmentalism. • 1983: *A Nation at Risk: The Report of the National Commission on Excellence in Education.* President Reagan's Department of Education report finds inadequate or declining achievement scores, graduation rates, expectations of students, and focus on academics. Criticizes absence of standards and calls for major reforms.	**Model 6: Clinical Supervision, Goldhammer-Cogan** Formal process of collaboration between teacher and supervisor.

24

	Social/Cultural Markers of the Times	Models of Supervision
1981–1989 Ronald Reagan	• 1986: *A Nation Prepared: Teachers for the 21st Century*, sponsored by the Carnegie Corporation, calls for national teacher standards, restructuring of schools, increased teacher salaries, and aid for minorities becoming teachers. • 1989: National Education Summit convened by President Bush and the National Governors' Association at Charlottesville, VA. First statement of National Goals for Education approved. (http://www.archives.nysed.gov/edpolicy/research/res_chronology2000.shtml) Publication of Nat Hentoff's *Our Children Are Dying*, Jonathan Kozol's *Death at an Early Age*, Herbert Kohl's *36 Children*, and Charles Silberman's *Crisis in the Classroom*.	
1990s		
1989–1993 George Bush 1993–2001 Bill Clinton	• Clinton administration signed President Bush's *Goals 2000*—students will be first in world in math and science and every school will be drug and violence free. • U.S. Congress. National Council of Educational Standards—converted vague goals into curriculum standards. • 1994: Educate America Act: Goals 2000. Clinton administration adds two goals to the National Educational Goals: increased parental involvement and professional development for teachers. Provides support to states to develop standards and assessments. (http://www.archives.nysed.gov/edpolicy/research/res_chronology2000.shtml)	**Model 7: Changing Concepts Model of Supervision** Glickman's (1992) *Supervision in Transition*—set the tone by changing the word *supervision* to *instructional leadership* and *supervisor* to *instructional leader* Sergiovanni (1992) viewed supervision as professional and moral.
2000– Present		
2001–2009 George W. Bush 2009– Barack Obama	• President George W. Bush—No Child Left Behind—2001; a reauthorization of the El. and Sec. Ed. Act Leg. of 1965. Stronger accountability for results, increased flexibility and local control, expanded options for parents, emphasis on teaching methods that have been proven to work. • 2001: Requires: All students to be "proficient" in reading, mathematics, and science by 2014, with Adequate Yearly Progress measures to determine school success; annual standardized tests (developed by the states) in Grades 3–8 in reading and mathematics. (http://www.archives.nysed.gov/edpolicy/research/res_chronology2000.shtml) • 2003–2010: War in Iraq. • 2009: Barack Obama appoints Arne Duncan, CEO of Chicago schools, to lead U.S. schools as Secretary of Education during troubled economic times. • Mayoral control and charter schools proliferate in urban centers.	**Model 8: Standards-Based Supervision** Includes high-stakes testing. Accountability based on high-stakes testing and quantitative data thrives and influences supervision.

Catherine Marshall (1992), in a comprehensive study of assistant principals, described such role conflicts:

> An assistant principal might be required to help teachers develop coordinated curricula—a "teacher support" function. But this function conflicts with the monitoring, supervising, and evaluating functions. . . . The assistant may be working with a teacher as a colleague in one meeting and, perhaps one hour later, the same assistant may be meeting to chastise the same teacher for noncompliance with the district's new homework policy. . . . When they must monitor teachers' compliance, assistants have difficulty maintaining equal collegial and professional relationships with them. (pp. 6–7)

The field of supervision has attempted to resolve this basic conflict between evaluation and improvement (e.g., Hazi, 1994; Poole, 1994; Tsui, 1995). It clearly is evident throughout the history of supervision that efforts have been made to extricate supervision from its bureaucratic heritage. Nonetheless, advances in theory are not necessarily reflected in practice. Many, if not most, studies still conclude that teachers do not find supervision helpful (Zepeda & Ponticell, 1998).

We present, in brief, the rationales of the two camps and challenge you to take a stance. We definitely have an opinion on this issue, as you might discover with a careful read of this book. Still, we prefer not to indicate our view, but rather encourage you, especially in developing your vision, to address the issue in ways that make sense to you. Please e-mail us with your view, and we'd be happy, if asked, to indicate our own conception of the relationship between supervision and evaluation.

Camp 1 views supervision as a process that engages teachers as professional colleagues for the purpose of encouraging instructional dialogue so as to improve teaching practices. Judgments as to the competence of the teacher are eschewed during the supervision process. Supervisors serve, among other ways, as another set of eyes to help the teacher reflect on her teaching behaviors, for instance, in the classroom during instruction. Supervisors provide teachers with descriptions of what transpired during a lesson and then encourage teachers to make some observations and draw conclusions from the data presented. Supervisors function as a mirror for teachers. Through instructional dialogue teachers decide a course of action on their own, with facilitation by the supervisor. Maria, a fourth-grade teacher, for instance, might realize that she is asking questions that may be too complicated for her students. After examining Bloom's Taxonomy, she, in working with her supervisor, develops more appropriate lower-level questions for implementation next time. Evaluation, as opposed to supervision, is the process in which decisions are made about the competencies of a teacher and functions as an accountability measure. It is usually performed, in formal observation fashion, several times a year, with a summative evaluation report for the teacher's file at the end of the school year. Reappointment and tenure decisions are made as a result of such evaluations. Camp 1 adherents believe that the two processes are distinct and serve different purposes and should be kept separate for a variety of reasons. One such reason, according to adherents, is that teachers are unlikely to indicate any willingness to change teaching behaviors in a supervisory process when they know that disclosures may influence negatively on their formative or summative evaluative reports. "Supervision and evaluation are like oil and water; they don't mix," stated a supervisor who adheres to such a division between the processes.

Camp 2, on the other hand, maintains that the two processes, if implemented properly, are compatible and that a distinction or separation is artificial and impractical. Adherents maintain that trust is a necessary condition that must be established if supervision and evaluation are to work properly. Once established (that is, supervisors establish legitimacy in the eyes of teachers), a supervisor can easily work with teachers, wearing one hat, so to speak, in terms of working with them as colleagues to examine teaching in the classroom, and then, at some other point in time, serve as evaluator, when specified by legal mandates. Teachers are professionals who understand their role and importance in schools and should readily accept and expect that supervision and evaluation are employed to improve teacher performance so as to promote student learning and achievement.

We presented both views in caricature form for purposes of analysis. Finer distinctions exist as well as other rationales for their use and function. In addition, a good number of evaluation systems or approaches have been advocated in the literature that support each camp (Danielson & McGreal, 2000; Goldstein, 2007). We encourage you to consider this issue by reading some sources on the subject.

IMPLICATIONS FOR THE PRACTICE OF SUPERVISION

Present Context and Future Necessities

For most of the 20th century, schools retained features of the factory organizational model, a legacy of 19th-century industrial society. Schools relied on hierarchical supervisory control and representative democracy. We are now, however, undergoing major societal transformations into a postindustrial era (Ambrose & Cohen, 1997) characterized "by exponential information growth, fast-paced innovation, organizational change, and participatory democracy" (p. 20). As a result of these technological, political, economic, and social changes, schools (teachers and supervisors) are "being called on today to rethink and restructure how schools operate and how teachers relate to students. . . . We sorely need new ways of thinking about educational supervision and leadership" (Pajak, 1993, p. 159).

Attempts to restructure schools, classrooms, and practices (both teaching and supervisory) abound (see, e.g., Murphy & Hallinger, 1993). Over the past several years, alternative models or approaches to school and instructional improvement and teacher evaluation have gained prominence. Among these innovative ideas are site-based management, union-sponsored peer coaching, professional partnerships, reflective practice, and teacher self-evaluation. Based on our brief discussion of the history of supervision in this chapter,[2] these innovations can be seen as ways to extend participatory democracy in supervision.

The changing context of supervision necessitates that both prospective and practicing supervisors remain responsive to unprecedented demands and opportunities. Supervisors will need specialized knowledge and skills to meet organizational challenges in the 21st century. They will need to base their practice of supervision on a foundation of dispositions and beliefs. Supervisors will have to place a premium on initiative, flexibility, tolerance for ambiguity, collaboration, and an ethical mind-set. In the future, supervisors will be expected more and more to be collaborative and assist teachers in reflecting about classroom instruction in meaningful ways.

As we saw earlier in this chapter, with a firmly entrenched bureaucratic heritage, people have tried to reshape the image of supervision into a democratic enterprise aimed at instructional improvement. We maintain that your ability to facilitate teaching and learning depends as much on your belief system, because it requires knowledge and skills about instructional improvement. Much of this book is devoted to knowledge and skill development. The remainder of this chapter, however, is aimed at indicating how your beliefs might affect your response to daily instructional challenges. Are you more inclined to conceive of supervision as an inspectional, bureaucratic process, are you genuinely more concerned with developing collaborative relationships with teachers in an effort to improve instruction, or are you inclined to follow a path somewhere in the middle?

We make a bold assertion in this chapter: Bureaucratic inspectional supervision should have no place in schools in the 21st century. We must prepare supervisors who truly espouse participatory democratic values. We have found that some supervisors espouse collaboration when, in practice, they operate in rather autocratic ways. These supervisors are probably influenced very much by the traditional conceptions of supervision described earlier.

Case Study

Dr. William Jones believes that teachers need close scrutiny. "Many of the new teachers," explains Jones, "are generally weak. They have just been certified and need close supervision." He continues, "In fact, even experienced teachers continually need the guidance of an expert who can provide the needed instructional and managerial assistance."

Other supervisors are genuinely interested in working with teachers collaboratively, as evidenced by Elizabeth Gonzalez, a vice principal in Elmsville Elementary School, a suburban district in the Midwest.

Elizabeth Gonzalez believes in forging collaborative relationships with teacher professionals. "I think that every teacher should develop a unique style of teaching that is right for her or him," explains Gonzalez. "As a supervisor, I am really most effective as facilitator and guide, rather than an overseer."

Why does William Jones rely only on inspectional practices, yet Elizabeth Gonzalez acts in a much more collaborative way? We believe that each of these supervisors operates from a different belief system that inevitably affects how he or she approaches supervisory responsibilities.

ASSESSING BELIEF SYSTEMS

The bureaucratic model of schooling is based on what we believe are erroneous assumptions about how people work together most efficiently in schools.[3] There is a growing awareness that the key to successfully shifting to a collaborative educational paradigm is dependent on the degree to which we alter our thinking patterns, belief systems, and mind-sets, or as Sergiovanni calls them, "mindscapes" (Sergiovanni, 1992, p. 41). Our belief systems are intimately connected to the language we use to articulate and communicate meanings. The needed transformation in education requires a realignment of educational phraseology with an entirely different set of definitions, meanings, and purposes. For example, a reexamination of the metaphors we use is essential. Using supervision or reflective coaching not only clearly indicates "where we're coming from" but also defines human interactions in the workplace.

Yet a caveat about beliefs and actions or behaviors is in order. Reflective practice (see Osterman & Kottkamp, 2004) posits that our actions often are inconsistent with our intentions (or beliefs) and that new ideas do not necessarily lead to new behaviors. *Espoused theories* represent our conscious ideas, intentions, and beliefs. Following exposure to new ideas in graduate courses and workshops, we often believe that this information and the beliefs acquired through experience and formal education will guide our actions. Espoused theories, however, do not influence behavior directly. How many times have you thought after a leader's speech, "Why doesn't he or she practice what he or she preaches?" How many impressive workshops have we all attended with the best of intentions to implement our new knowledge, only to return to our old practices? How many supervisors preach active learning for all students and then conduct a feedback conference where they tell the teacher everything he or she must do without even thinking of asking for the teacher's input?

Although we may consciously adopt new ideas, these action theories are ingrained so deeply in our consciousness that we cannot change them easily. *Theories-in-use* build and crystallize over a long period of time and become such an integral part of our beings that we are unaware of the discrepancies between our beliefs and actions or between our actions and intended outcomes. Actual change in our behaviors will take place only when we become aware of the discrepancy between a predominant theory-in-use and an unacceptable practice or outcome. Figure 1.1 shows how theories-in-use directly impact behavior. Espoused theories do not directly influence behavior and may or may not be consistent with theories-in-use.

Nonetheless, we believe that it is essential to articulate our espoused theories in the form of vision statements. It is, however, through the use of reflective practice (which is presented in more detail in Chapter 2) that the new ideas we will be learning in this book and the beliefs we will develop will become theories-in-use.

Philosophy, at least indirectly, influences actions, which in turn affect behavior. How we think shapes the world in which we live. For example, our values and beliefs shape the kinds of experiences we want young children to have in classrooms. They also affect what adults do in schools and define role relationships among members of a school system. If our attitudes about how best to organize large groups of people focus on hierarchical notions of differentiation and classification, then we will tend to conceptualize supervision as, for example, didactic and evaluative. Conversely, if our view of school management stresses collaboration and shared leadership, we will not be willing to construct an educational environment where disempowered individuals become spectators of, rather than participants in, their own work. This worldview will define supervision as collegial and interactive.

Reflection

Compose a list of your beliefs about teaching and learning, about teachers, about supervision, and about yourself.

Figure 1.1   A Conceptual Framework Underlying Reflective Practice

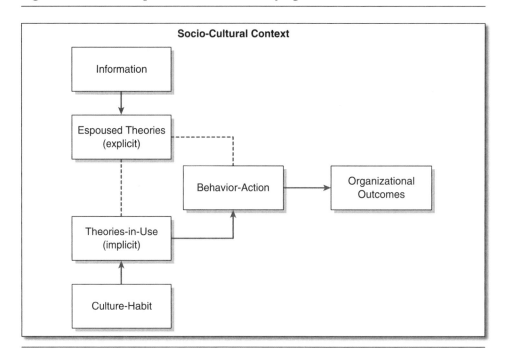

Source: K. F. Osterman and R. B. Kottkamp. (2004). *Reflective Practice for Educators: Professional Development to Improve Student Learning* (2nd ed.). Thousand Oaks, CA: Corwin.

Supervisory Beliefs Questionnaire

What are the qualities or dispositions we want future supervisors to possess? Are you willing and able to meet new supervisory challenges in the 21st century? The questionnaire in Figure 1.2 is designed to help you sort out your beliefs. More specifically, the survey is designed to assess your preference to function along the bureaucratic, inspectional, democratic, collegial continuum. You should have completed this questionnaire before you read this chapter. Make sure you retake the questionnaire when you have completed reading the book to assess whether any of your beliefs have changed.

Interpreting Answers to the Questionnaire

The following responses to each statement indicate that your supervisory preferences or inclinations operate along bureaucratic, authoritarian lines:

1. T	6. T	11. F	16. T	21. T	26. F	31. F	36. F
2. T	7. T	12. T	17. F	22. F	27. T	32. F	37. T
3. F	8. T	13. F	18. T	23. T	28. F	33. T	38. F
4. F	9. T	14. T	19. F	24. F	29. T	34. F	39. F
5. T	10. F	15. T	20. F	25. F	30. F	35. T	40. T

The following responses to each statement indicate that your supervisory preferences or inclinations operate along democratic, collaborative lines:

1. F	6. F	11. T	16. F	21. F	26. T	31. T	36. T
2. F	7. F	12. F	17. T	22. T	27. F	32. T	37. F
3. T	8. F	13. T	18. F	23. F	28. T	33. F	38. T
4. T	9. F	14. F	19. T	24. T	29. F	34. T	39. T
5. F	10. T	15. F	20. T	25. T	30. T	35. F	40. F

As we stated earlier, bureaucratic inspectional supervision should have no place in schools in the 21st century. For the future, we must prepare supervisors who truly espouse and practice participatory democratic values. Supervision that assumes that supervisors are experts and superior to teachers represents vestiges of control-oriented, inspectional practices. Although these kinds of practices were prevalent in early supervision, we argue that they should no longer be accorded attention.

(*Note:* In the ensuing discussion, statement numbers refer to the questionnaire in Figure 1.2.)

Bureaucratic thought essentially suggests that

- Supervision is inspectional (Statements 1 and 14).
- Hierarchy is necessary for organizational efficiency (Statements 5 and 6).
- Supervisors are experts and teachers are not (Statements 12, 18, 27, 29, 37, and 40).
- Teachers and supervisors are not equal partners (Statement 7).
- Teachers will not improve instruction on their own (Statements 16 and 33).

That hierarchy equals expertise and supervisors know more than teachers is axiomatic according to the bureaucratic belief system.

Furthermore, the following assumptions that, at first glance, might appear unproblematic also represent bureaucratic conceptions of supervision:

- Supervision is primarily about helping teachers improve instruction (Statements 8 and 9). This belief subtly implies that teachers are deficient, need help, and could not or would not seek improvement on their own.
- Supervisors help teachers change, as if teachers are deficient and necessarily need to change (Statements 15, 23, and 35). This belief implies that something is wrong with a teacher's teaching.
- Teachers at low levels need assistance (Statement 2). This belief implies that supervisors can identify with certainty that a teacher is deficient. It also implies that supervisors should *help* teachers because they cannot improve through collaboration or self-reflection.
- Supervisors are agents of improved instruction (Statement 21). This belief implies that supervisors, not teachers, are agents of improved instruction.

The aforementioned conceptions of supervision underscore the superordinate-subordinate relationship between teachers and supervisors. Bureaucratic conceptions of supervision imply that teachers don't know as much about teaching as do supervisors and, conversely, that supervisors possess greater teaching expertise than do teachers.

Democratic thought essentially suggests that

- Teaching is complex and not easily defined or understood (Statements 3 and 17).
- Individuals are more important than the organizations (Statements 4 and 32).

Figure 1.2 Questionnaire Beliefs About Supervision

Please answer *true* (T) or *false* (F) to each of the following statements. Be honest: Answer *true* if the statement generally describes a belief you once held or currently hold. If a statement represents a belief that holds true in most situations, although not in all, answer *true*. Answer *false* if the statement in no way describes a belief you once held or currently hold. If a statement represents a belief that is false in most situations, although not in all, answer *false*. There is no need to share your responses with anyone.

T	F	1.	When it comes down to it, supervision, as I conceive of it, is essentially about looking for errors.
T	F	2.	Guided directed approaches to supervision are most appropriate for teachers at low levels of personal and professional development.
T	F	3.	Teaching is a highly complex, context-specific, interactive activity.
T	F	4.	Organizational concerns are almost always secondary to individual needs.
T	F	5.	The supervisor's position in the hierarchy, as compared to the teacher's, is unproblematic.
T	F	6.	Hierarchy of offices is necessary for organizational efficiency.
T	F	7.	I am not comfortable participating with teachers as partners.
T	F	8.	Supervision is about offering teachers specialized help in improving instruction.
T	F	9.	Supervision is about examining and analyzing classroom teaching behaviors so that recommendations can be made with regard to the course of action teachers should take instructionally.
T	F	10.	Teachers can help supervisors improve their performance.
T	F	11.	Most teachers are self-directed.
T	F	12.	Supervisors should be expert diagnosticians.
T	F	13.	Supervision is primarily a collaborative process in which teachers and supervisors talk about ways to improve instruction.
T	F	14.	Supervision is about looking for errors and then engaging teachers in dialogue so that they realize these deficiencies on their own.
T	F	15.	The focus of supervision should be about helping teachers change and improve instruction.
T	F	16.	Without assistance, teachers generally will not make changes.
T	F	17.	Reality in classrooms is essentially subjective, not objective, and teaching is a complex endeavor that requires continual study.
T	F	18.	Although supervisor-teacher collaboration is important, a supervisor's judgment must ultimately hold sway.

#	T	F	Statement
19.	T	F	Schools are centers of inquiry in which teachers themselves must assume responsibility for instructional excellence.
20.	T	F	Teacher self-evaluation plays a prominent role in instructional improvement.
21.	T	F	The supervisor is the agent of improved instruction.
22.	T	F	Qualitative approaches to instructional improvement are just as valid as quantitative approaches.
23.	T	F	Supervisors help teachers change.
24.	T	F	Reflective dialogue is an integral component of supervision.
25.	T	F	Instructional improvement activities include peer coaching, action research projects, and problem-solving groups, as well as more traditional development activities.
26.	T	F	Supervision is primarily about asking questions that facilitate the examination of teacher practice in the classroom.
27.	T	F	When I offer teachers constructive criticisms, I expect they will consider them carefully.
28.	T	F	Experienced, high-functioning teachers should have complete control over their professional development.
29.	T	F	The supervisor ultimately should determine what and how a teacher should teach.
30.	T	F	Teachers should be encouraged to carry out their own educational goals and curricular decisions.
31.	T	F	Teachers should be given options on how they want to teach.
32.	T	F	Teachers should disobey official regulations if they feel that they interfere with the welfare of students.
33.	T	F	Teachers don't spend enough time thinking about ways to improve instruction.
34.	T	F	Supervisors should create opportunities for teachers to make professional and personal choices, not shape their behavior.
35.	T	F	Supervisors should attentively listen to the teachers' concerns and offer critical assessment and constructive ideas for change.
36.	T	F	Schools will improve primarily when a norm of collegiality exists in which shared discussion and shared work among all staff members exist.
37.	T	F	The knowledge base of a supervisor is generally superior to that of a teacher.
38.	T	F	Supervisors actively should seek input from teachers, parents, and students about ways to improve instruction.
39.	T	F	Most teachers don't need specific instructions on what to teach and how to teach.
40.	T	F	Supervisors should have more expertise than teachers with respect to teaching and learning.

33

- Most teachers are self-directed, responsible, and competent (Statements 10, 11, 19, 20, 28, 30, 31, and 39).
- Supervision is a truly collaborative process (Statements 13, 34, 36, and 38).
- Qualitative approaches to classroom improvement are just as valid as quantitative ones (Statements 22 and 24).
- Alternative approaches to traditional supervision are viable (Statement 25).
- Supervisors function at their best when they pose questions for critical analysis by teachers (Statement 26).

The aforementioned conceptions of supervision underscore the empowering nature of supervisor-teacher relationships. Teachers and supervisors work as collaborative inquirers for the benefit of students. The telling-and-prescribing nature of traditional supervision has no place in such a paradigm for school improvement.

Developing a Personal Vision Statement

Examining your beliefs about supervision and related areas is crucial if you are to function effectively as a supervisor in the 21st century. We think that developing a personal vision statement that articulates your beliefs about teachers and supervision is critical (Osterman & Kottkamp, 1993). This section challenges you to begin this process, which will be refined continually throughout this book. Now that we understand how supervision has evolved and realize that our beliefs are influenced, in part, by that history, our challenge will be to construct a personal supervisory vision statement that supports the view that supervision remains a potent process for facilitating instructional improvement.

What are your beliefs about teaching and learning, about teachers, about supervision, and about yourselves as supervisors?

In courses that we teach, we expect our prospective supervisors to develop such a vision statement. We, of course, review the contents of this chapter with them and have them take and interpret the Beliefs About Supervision questionnaire. We also expose them to other theories and surveys that help them to uncover their often hidden assumptions about supervisory work.[4]

Although we advocate a participatory democratic orientation to supervision, we believe that traditional types of supervision such as directive informational approaches (see Chapter 2) are useful. These practices should be employed with teachers who need substantial support. Use of this form of directive informational supervision "does not necessarily mean that the supervisor acts in an authoritative or arbitrary fashion" (Daresh & Playko, 1995, p. 333). Offering some direct assistance to teachers in need is necessary only when the situation calls for it. In our questionnaire, Statement 2 is indicative of a generalization often made by supervisors without input and agreement from other parties, including perhaps lead teachers. Therefore, this book does include one traditional, directive approach that should be used judiciously.

- Let's begin to develop your personal vision statement. This vision statement is a personal statement that allows you to present your views regarding education and educational administration, your philosophy, your values, your beliefs, your vision of the way schools should be, and your view about what you as a school leader would do to realize this vision. In short, the vision statement that will lead to a supervisory platform is a way for you to say what you stand for as an educational leader.

Guidelines and Questions for Writing Your Vision Statement

Writing a position statement is a powerful way to reflect. It's a way to purposely articulate a leadership stance that can guide one's practice as a leader. Reflection leads to more reflection as we refine our position or vision for leadership and school improvement.

As you are about to frame your vision statement, simply follow these general guidelines:

- Think deeply about the factors that have influenced your professional work and view of leadership.
- Keep in mind that the vision statement you're about to frame is a personal statement that allows you to present your views regarding education and educational leadership, your philosophy, your values, your beliefs, your vision of the way schools should be, and your view about what you as a school leader would do to realize this vision. In short, the vision statement is a way for you to say what you stand for as an educational leader.

We offer specific questions to stimulate your thinking. We include questions based in part on the Interstate School Leaders Licensure Consortium (ISLLC) standards that can also help frame your statement. For a complete listing of the current ISLLC Standards, consult http://www.ccsso.org/publications/details.cfm?PublicationID=365. Where possible,

- Support your ideas with examples and theories from the literature on leadership.
- Use examples that have inspired or influenced you.

Please remember that this activity is intended to help you articulate your own personal feelings and ideas. It is not a test of what you know, and there are no right answers. The guiding questions that follow are meant to stimulate thought. Although your statement should address the "big" ideas implied in these questions, you do not have to answer each one in sequence or at all. Allow them to guide your thoughts. Read them all and then start writing.

Guiding Questions:

1. What has influenced your vision of leadership? (ISLLC Standard 1)

2. What are your goals or hopes for your students? (ISLLC Standard 1)

3. What are the types of skills, attitudes, and feelings you want students to possess? (ISLLC Standard 1)

4. What type of climate is needed to support the student outcomes you identified above? (ISLLC Standard 2)

5. What can you do to help establish that climate? (ISLLC Standard 2)

6. What are your views about teaching and learning? (ISLLC Standard 2)

7. How should instruction be organized and delivered to support the type of climate and student outcomes you desire? (ISLLC Standard 2)

(Continued)

(Continued)

8. How would you promote a positive school culture, providing an effective instructional program, applying best practice to student learning, and designing comprehensive professional growth plans for staff? (ISLLC Standard 2)

9. What is your philosophy on leadership? (ISLLC Standard 5)

10. What can leaders do to create effective schools? (ISLLC Standard 6)

11. How will you exercise leadership in your building? (ISLLC Standard 3)

12. How would you facilitate the development, articulation, implementation, and stewardship of a school vision of learning supported by the school community? (ISLLC Standard 4)

13. How would you manage the organization, operations, and resources in a way that promotes a safe, efficient, and effective learning environment? (ISLLC Standard 4)

14. What are your responsibilities as a leader? (ISLLC Standard 5)

15. What are your ideas for collaborating with all families and other community members, responding to diverse community interests and needs, and mobilizing community resources? (ISLLC Standard 4)

16. How would you seek to understand, respond to, and influence the larger political, social, economic, legal, and cultural context? (ISLLC Standard 6)

17. What is your ideal school? (ISLLC Standard 6)

Be sure to offer a concluding statement.

Three sample vision statements developed by our students appear at the end of this chapter; you can use these as a guide to inspire you in developing your own. These statements vary in length and style as well as content. Two pages may suffice to elucidate one person's ideas, whereas another may require ten. These differences illustrate the idiosyncratic and essentially personal nature of visioning.

Class Practice

Bring three copies of the first draft of your vision statement to class. In groups of three, read each other's vision statements, one at a time.

Please note that as you read others' statements, do not be critical or judgmental. Simply raise questions for discussion as there is no one "right" response. The purpose of these sharings is to stimulate discussion, reflection, and personal refinement of vision statements. Therefore, offer descriptive, not evaluative, feedback to others. Here are a few guidelines to consider as you read others' statements:

- What are the underlying assumptions?
- Are the statements in the platform internally consistent? For instance, if one attributes her or his current emphasis on nontraditional teaching methods to progressive teaching methods in the 1970s and 1980s, does she or he indicate similar inclinations in individual learning styles?
- Are there apparent inconsistencies? For instance, problematic is one who advocates constructivist teaching and then relies on directive methods in

one's personal classroom. Remember, don't criticize but merely ask, "I've noticed you said such and such, how does _____ relate to what you've said earlier?"

- Take notes on the writer's perspective and value orientation to clarify your own positions and values.[5]

Realize, of course, that as you share your statements with others, revisions are inevitable. Incorporate your colleagues' feedback and further reflections into your revisions. Share your draft with your supervisor(s) and ask them for feedback. We have found that we can also test our vision statements through simulated role plays (Osterman & Kottkamp, 1993, pp. 95–99). In these situations, we provide students with realistic situations or case studies and have them role-play.[6] The following section outlines three examples.

Case Studies

In each of the following situations, put yourself into the role of a supervisor who makes sense to you in your particular situation. It may be the role of building principal or assistant principal, department chairperson, or some other kind of district supervisor. Write down what you hope to accomplish in the role play. The class can divide into pairs, or volunteers can present each scenario. On completion of the role play, you reveal your intentions by reading your planning notes and sharing what you think you have achieved. The supervisee then describes how he or she felt, tells what he or she is going to do as a result of the interchange, and reflects on his or her perceptions of the supervisor's perspective.

1. You have been invited into Mrs. Sanchez's classroom to observe a high school social studies lesson on censorship in the media. You've spent 40 minutes observing the lesson and taking detailed descriptive data. At the feedback conference, Mrs. Sanchez feels the lesson was great. You have some reservations, however.

2. You are new to your supervisory position, and teachers are eager to find out more about you. At a grade or faculty conference, you are introduced to the faculty, at which time you make a 2-minute introductory statement. After the meeting, several teachers warmly welcome you to the school, but two teachers in particular inform you that your "lofty" ideas will fail "in our school."

3. A teacher has been late to school and to homeroom. The situation first came to your attention when you observed students standing by the classroom doorway after the last bell had rung. You questioned the students and discovered that there was a pattern to the teacher's late arrival. You have left a note in the teacher's mailbox requesting that he or she see you after school. In the current situation, the teacher has just arrived.

Reflection

How did you respond to these situations? What do you think is the value of a personal vision statement in handling difficult supervisory situations?

EXAMPLES OF PERSONAL VISION STATEMENTS[7]

Sample 1

The education of children is the most important job a country undertakes, and the one most crucial for its growth. The investment in education reaps untold rewards as the nation forges ahead as a global leader in technology, the arts, industry, and in the development of humanity itself. In the 21st century, the schooling of children has become the single most important job America does, and those who engage in this crucial profession—teachers and administrators alike—are the innovators of our time. A school leader, then, is a facilitator who efficiently organizes the many resources necessary for a comprehensive and sustained learning environment. As a prospective school leader, I will strive to nurture the growth of students into becoming thoughtful human beings who care about America, ready at a future time to work for its betterment.

Educating the whole child—mind and body—into becoming a kind scholar concerned with the welfare of people will be the centerpiece of my vision. Social justice, then, will be the overarching goal with which our school will concern itself. Our school's purpose will be to educate the child not just for the purpose of getting a good job, but to gain, through an intellectually rigorous curriculum, an appreciation for the delightful diversity and amazing structure of the world itself—and by appreciating it, the child will be troubled by the many difficulties afflicting it. We will ask this crucial question: How can we bring knowledge of English, mathematics, history, science, and the arts to bear on the problems within our community and our great country? Our learning community will strive to create rich, engaging lessons that will answer this question, and, in the process, not only comply with the standards but go beyond them in encouraging thoughtful scholars who can think critically, analyze rigorously, and synthesize usefully.

Junior high school students need stability in order to grow, indeed, to flourish. Therefore, whenever possible I will implement teacher looping from sixth to eighth grade as a means of ensuring that each class feels it has a concerned adult who oversees its middle school experience. Done properly, looping has the potential to foster a bedrock foundation of trust between student and teacher—an important component of any type of learning process—leading to new heights of learning and expectations in the classroom. I believe students and adults will rise to the challenges presented to them once confidence is established among all participants.

The principal leads by example and must derive forward-thinking ideas based on data and research gleaned directly from classroom practice. My vision includes myself as teacher and learner. To gain legitimacy as a school leader, I plan to conduct constant professional development, modeling successful instruction through time-tested and research-backed methodologies that encourage student interest. Furthermore, when time is available, I aim to model these lessons in the classroom, teaching the most "at risk" students, those who may be seen as unteachable.

Through this, I will promote and encourage a learning culture where the question is not, "Why isn't this child learning?" but, rather, "What can we do to have this child learn?" Every child has enormous potential for learning, potential that may at times be largely untapped until he or she meets the right teacher in the right school. I aim to model this philosophy by jumping right into the midst of instruction, bridging the gap that so often divides administrator from teacher. The principal as teacher, then, does a number of things: She or he (1) combats the perception that administrators are ex-teachers who grow tired of the classroom; (2) leads through collaboration among teachers, but as an equal, practicing and understanding effective instruction; and (3) shows commitment to his or her firmly held belief that all students can learn by teaching those who are too often left along the wayside.

The instructional climate is one where teachers are partners, not just participants, in the planning of curriculum, the development of new instructional programs, and the creation of a school culture that has high standards for its children as well as its adults. My vision includes collaborative teams where decisions are made democratically so that every faculty member feels vested in the process and the outcome. This includes, but is not limited to, teams that analyze data and use them to guide instructional decisions, school leadership teams that assess the effectiveness of schoolwide instruction, and community outreach teams that identify segments of the community that can benefit from student involvement.

My vision of leadership includes a large technological component. Teaching in the 21st century must embrace what technology has to offer in the form of engaging subject lessons, student collaboration, teacher-parent communication, streamlining of organizational procedures, and much more. The role of a school leader will be to keep abreast of new technologies, share them with the staff, model their efficiencies, and put into action ongoing and effective professional development to sustain implementation. Learning new technology can be daunting for many people, and it is crucial that the school leader show the kindness of technology in making the job of a teacher much more exciting and efficient. Therefore, a school leader needs to model standards-based lessons where technology plays a central role in eliciting and encouraging student interest. Furthermore, the school leader must show how technology endows student assessment with laserlike focus, enabling teachers to plan lessons around the instructional needs of their classes.

Parental support is crucial if a child and, by extension, a school are to succeed. Parents are partners in the education process and must be brought in to the equation of student learning if there is to be continued student growth and success. A mutual relationship—the central purpose of which is our students' intellectual, social, and moral growth—must be based on respect, trust, and the development of our children. A school leader must act in the highest ethical manner with integrity and sensitivity to the needs of parents. Once trust is established, a school leader can foster a culture where everyone, parents and teachers alike, are focused on student achievement. Rapid and plentiful communication, then, is central to creating this plan. My vision for effective parent-school communication would entail creating a Web site that would function as a platform for extensive and up-to-date school information. Additionally, every class will have a Web site account in which to facilitate teacher-student-parent interaction and information. Fast and efficient communication is the hallmark of the 21st century. My vision for a school will have that as a cornerstone.

The role of the community in strengthening the school both financially and socially is essential for the growth of a successful learning institution. As a school leader, I will facilitate community relationships, solicit private and nonprofit services, and engage and invite parent volunteers. My vision includes encouraging members of the community to feel a vested interest in the welfare of the school and the children attending it and, thus, look out for those children when they aren't in school. This would include working with local government and community organizations to create fun, educational afterschool activities to sustain student development.

A school leader bears a sacred trust, one not to be taken lightly. Thus, my vision statement aims to incorporate the ideas necessary for what I see as a successful, vibrant school where teaching and learning flourish, and where, through education, children's and adults' possibilities become filled with new and ever-widening horizons. Surely the position of a school leader, then, is the greatest job in the world!

Sample 2

One hundred years from now it will not matter what kind of car I drove, what kind of house I lived in, how much money I had in my bank account, or what my clothes looked like. But one hundred years from now the world may be a little better because I was important in the life of a child.

—Dr. Forest E. Witcraft
(http://www.pgcps.pg.k12.md.us/~kworth/1046/within.html)
October 1950 issue of *Scouting* magazine (p. 2)

In crafting a personal vision, it is important to reflect on what matters most in one's life. What matters to me is that I make a difference in this world, hopefully one child at a time. Children are the future of our country, and as such, there is no job more important than educating them. As educators, we play a critical role in molding the world in which we live. We get to leave our mark on society through our development of minds. There is no other profession in society that has been entrusted with this responsibility, and I can think of no greater honor I shall receive in my lifetime.

If you give a man a fish, he eats for a day; if you teach a man to fish, he will be able to eat for a lifetime. When thinking about my philosophy of education, this saying often comes to mind. It has long been my goal to develop independence in my students. I perceive my role as an educator as one that gradually decreases over time. Initially, I provide strong guidance to students, then over time, scaffolding. In a sense, I am like the training wheels on a bicycle that can be removed when no longer needed. A job well done should leave my students ready to drive away, not with a road map, but rather with a compass they can use to navigate their way through life.

All children have the right to an education. This education should develop the child socially, emotionally, academically, and ethically. Recognizing that each member of the school community possesses unique gifts and talents will enable us to build on strengths rather than focus on weaknesses. Using Stephen Covey's *7 Habits of Highly Effective People* will enable the school community to create an environment that allows every individual to feel valued. Recently Covey (2005) revised his work to add an eighth habit, and one that fits particularly well with my educational values—"Find your voice, and inspire others to find theirs." It is my hope that as an educational leader, I can help people find their voices and use them to have a positive impact on society. My vision will be to embed Dr. Covey's principles into the culture of the school, and use them to guide the faculty and students as they create a shared vision. In addition, as part of this collaboration, I would invite the PTA, community members, and families to participate in this process. Through establishment of these cooperative relationships, I hope to develop a strong community of learners.

As the school's leader, I have the responsibility of creating an effective learning environment. This environment will include several crucial team members—students, teachers, and parents. Students come to school to learn and should be engaged and excited about their learning. Teachers come to school to teach and should be given administrative support to meet the needs of the students in their care. Parents send their children to school with the hope that we will educate, mold, and care for them, and should find comfort in the knowledge that their child is in good hands. Peter Senge states that "A shared vision is not an idea. . . . It is, rather, a force in people's hearts. . . . At its simplest level, a shared vision is the answer to the question 'What do we want to create?'" (http://www.leading-learning.co.nz/famous-quotes.html#culture).

I believe that this question can be the focal point for all team members in the learning community. Given this opportunity, what is it that we want to create, and how will we go about creating it? The infusion of Covey's habits can give us an organizational structure and a starting point for our work.

Using the habit *begin with the end in mind* will lead to reflection about school goals. The overall goal of the school will be to provide a safe, engaging learning environment that meets the needs of all participants. The curriculum will be rigorous and will provide opportunities to discover and build on individual strengths. Integrated into our academic curriculum will be strong character development, using Covey's model by which we will teach leadership skills, tolerance, respect, and responsibility. Developing leadership in students empowers teachers to provide individualized instruction that meets diverse needs. Further, it empowers students to construct their learning in the manner that best suits their individual learning style. Moving away from a one-size-fits-all model, I would like to empower all stakeholders, our children, our teachers, and our parents, to construct a learning community that will challenge them all to reach their potential.

In order to accomplish these ideals, we will need to have strong professional development for all the stakeholders. Covey's habit *seek first to understand, then to be understood* fosters the idea that the stakeholders first have to understand themselves what they are trying to accomplish. Training everyone involved about Covey's leadership model will enable us to develop consistency in our mission, build community, and develop strong links between home and school.

In developing a strong leadership curriculum, it will be important for teachers and students to meet with and understand common characteristics of strong leaders. These characteristics will be embraced by all: strong work ethic, perseverance, hard work, and being goal oriented. Modeling how leaders work together collaboratively with diverse members of our population will be critical to developing tolerance and respect for others. Classrooms will be structured so that teamwork can occur daily. Curriculum developed will foster collaborative learning activities that teach the value of others' opinions and the idea that you are working for the betterment of a group. No longer will students hold themselves accountable to only themselves, but rather they will now be accountable to others as well. It will be through creation of *synergy* that great ideas will be born.

Being *proactive* will enable us to tie leadership training into our efforts to strengthen academic performance. Using data, we can set attainable goals for all members of our school community. I will meet with all teachers at the beginning of the school year to discuss their personal goals for the year. What is it that they would like to accomplish, and how can I support them in achieving their goal? Follow-up meetings will occur throughout the year to monitor progress in reaching individual goals and to discuss any additional support they feel is needed. In the same manner, students will set individual goals based on personal needs. For example, if students achieved a Level 4 (the highest level) on the state exam, we can discuss scale scores and help them set personal goals. Using the scale score, we can determine how much room they have to grow within the year and ask them what they think is an attainable goal. All students will set personal and academic goals quarterly, enabling us to monitor their progress over time. Goal setting will also take place at the classroom level with each class creating a mission statement. Students will construct collaboratively with their teacher a mission statement for the work they will do throughout the year. In addition, older students will be taught to write personal vision statements and reflect on them as the year progresses. Action plans such as goal setting will enable us to grow as professionals and learners because we have systems in place that provide ongoing support to all involved. These are also life skills that will support each participant in his or her personal development.

While we will strive to meet the learning standards of our state, I do not foresee these as boundary setting. Rather, I believe we can go beyond the basic competency levels outlined in the state and city standards through implementation of a rigorous curriculum. Integrating curriculum using the differentiation model created by Carol Tomlinson (1999) will allow us to deliver instruction that is standard and concept based, student centered, and relevant to the world. As a school leader, I will support the development of concept-based units in grade-level teams. The figure below illustrates the organizational structure we will use as we develop our units of study.

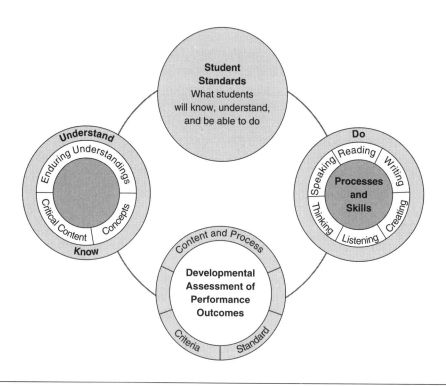

From *What Students Need to Know, Understand, and Do* by Carol Tomlinson, an unpublished PowerPoint presentation.

In breaking down planning like this, we are *beginning with the end in mind.* Reflecting on key understandings we begin by asking, What is it the students need to understand and/or be able to do, and what broader concept is that learning a part of? This dialogue will lead to development of an essential understanding, or essential question, that will guide the learning. Instruction will be differentiated to meet the needs of all learners, and teachers will be provided with strong professional development to ensure that they understand this process.

Schools should be the hub of the community, or the place people gather. It is my hope that I can partner with community-based organizations to open the school beyond normal school hours. I envision a school that offers programs after school and on weekends, providing students with a safe haven. By offering organized activities, we will provide additional means by which students can develop leadership qualities. Students will be offered opportunities to work collaboratively for social action on causes they select. In addition, participation in team sports can afford students the opportunity to foster identified leadership characteristics such as hard work, perseverance, and working toward betterment of the group. Funding for such activities will likely be needed, and I plan to reach out to community-based organizations through grant writing to achieve this goal.

Any worthwhile goals require sacrifice and hard work; however, when you love what you do, the work is easy. Becoming an educational leader is something I have wanted for a long time. I have strived to learn as much as I could in my field and now feel ready to take those next steps. It is my hope that I will get to make a difference in the lives of the teachers, children, and families in my care. I believe I will be a true constructivist leader who, to paraphrase John Dewey, will seek to make my school fit the child.

Sample 3

Leadership Platform

A school is a community of individuals who are committed to a set of guiding principles, and who take personal responsibility for the success of each member of the community. As the educational leader of this school community, my mission is to support the development of an educational environment that addresses the intellectual and developmental needs of the middle school child, that acknowledges individual variability while maintaining a high level of expectations for all, and that provides a variety of forums for individual and collective reflection and self-assessment.

Central to the creation of a school culture that reflects my vision are four interrelated components: student outcomes, instructional climate, philosophy of instruction, and governance and leadership. Culture is defined as the habits, routines, and behaviors (conscious and unconscious) that reveal the beliefs, norms, and values that build up over time within a school. Within this definition are four subcategories: (1) interpersonal culture, or the philosophy and level of collegiality among members of the school community; (2) organizational culture, or the philosophy and level of internal support for practices and programs; (3) teaching culture, or the philosophy and level of belief in student achievement; and (4) external culture, or the philosophy and level of external support for practices and programs. The art of the principal lies in her ability to orchestrate each element in the environment into a unified culture of shared expectations and accountability. To better understand my vision of leadership, it is necessary to define each component and demonstrate how each is integrated into the overarching school culture.

Student Outcomes

The cornerstone of any educational vision is student outcomes. Viewed holistically, students need to develop the academic, social, and personal levels of competence that will prepare them to be productive members of society and contributors to the workforce. All children have the potential to reach high standards of personal competence. My vision is to create a culture that supports all students in realizing their potential by creating an instructional program that supports high academic achievement and that encourages the development of self-discipline, positive self-image, strong personal values, and unilateral respect for all school community members.

Academically, students would develop literacy skills in written and spoken English and apply these skills to the mastery of content-area material. This is critical in light of the implementation of the performance standards and the new promotional policy. They would have access to technology and develop the skills necessary to locate, utilize, and evaluate electronic information. Students would have extensive exposure to the arts, so as to develop an appreciation for the richness and diversity of cultures. Learning would be interactive, with ample opportunities for students to experience "real world" applications of knowledge, so as to see the connections between content-area materials and between the classroom and life.

Concurrently, students would develop social consciousness and civic responsibility. They would have opportunities to participate in school and community-based service projects whose focus is the development of student awareness of social and political issues, and the relevance of these issues to their lives, the lives of their families, and the life of their community. Ideally, these opportunities would be intergenerational and multicultural, so as to engage students in meaningful and sustained relationships with adults and younger children from all cultural and economic groups, as well as with their peers. In this way, students would be able to develop sensitivity to the needs of others, recognize their similarities, appreciate their differences, and thereby develop a sense of mutual respect. Integral to these service projects should be connections to their classroom content-area learning to reinforce the connections between school and life.

Academic and service-learning outcomes are intrinsically connected to the developmental outcomes for students. These are crucial for all students, but particularly for adolescents who are grappling with issues of identity and self-worth. Integrated into student outcomes for academic and social learning would be outcomes for personal development and growth. Students should have multiple opportunities to develop self-awareness, self-competence, and self-esteem. Educational experiences would be varied and allow for individual differences, learning styles, and rates of development. Opportunities for student self-expression would abound within the context of social and personal accountability. Character education would be a key component of the educational program and support the development of students who strive to achieve their personal best.

Instructional Climate

The realization of student outcomes is inextricably tied to the instructional climate. My vision is of the school as a safe harbor or sanctuary in which students, staff, and parents feel safe and nurtured, and in which there is an atmosphere of personal responsibility and mutual respect. The culture of the school would support collaboration, foster reflection, and celebrate accomplishment. Multiple opportunities for celebration of individual and schoolwide success in all areas of achievement would be developed. Student work would be prominently displayed throughout the building, and efforts to acknowledge each student's strengths would be encouraged. Classrooms would be print and material rich, and students would have daily access to technology. A code of appropriate behavior would be developed, agreed on, and modeled by all. Consequences for inappropriate behavior would be clear and consistently enforced by all members of the school community.

The school climate would also support professional development that is an outgrowth of self-assessment and reflection and that supports collaboration and collegiality. All staff have the capacity for professional growth. My vision is to create a culture that supports teachers in fulfilling this capacity by providing new-teacher training, leadership opportunities, meaningful staff development, and experience in innovative educational practices and strategies. Opportunities for staff to develop and refine their instruction would be organic, teacher directed, and sustained throughout the year. Flexible programming would provide time for teachers to participate in weekly study groups to examine student work and teacher practice in the context of the standards. Each study group would follow specific protocols and be facilitated by a peer coach, teachers would participate in weekly peer observations, and classrooms would serve as demonstration sites for specific organizational and instructional practices. Structured opportunities for daily interaction among staff around instructional issues, and ongoing reflection among colleagues about student work and outcomes, would replace one-day trainings and workshops. Ample professional resources would be housed in the professional library so as to support all aspects of the professional development program.

Time and funding for teachers to participate in professional conferences would be provided, with the expectation that they would turnkey this training. In this way, a cadre of in-house specialists would be developed to build schoolwide capacity and foster the development of a community of learners.

Parents would also have ample opportunities to develop the capacity to be partners in their children's education. All parents have the responsibility to be active members in their children's educational experience. My vision is to create a culture that supports parents in exercising this responsibility by fostering a dynamic school-family partnership whose focus is active parental involvement in the educational decision-making process and shared, constructive evaluation of learning policies. A parent center with extensive resources in multiple languages would be established. Parent workshops on a wide spectrum of topics, ranging from parenting skills, to literacy strategies, to leadership teams, would be offered throughout the day, as well as in the evening and on weekends to encourage participation. Translators would be provided to facilitate interaction. Parents would be encouraged to participate in the daily activities of the school, to serve on committees and leadership teams, to become volunteers and tutors, and to participate, with teachers and administrators, in study groups around student work. They would be viewed as full and equal partners in the educational process and in the daily life of the school.

Instructional Program

The instructional climate is the framework that supports the instructional program. Students would have a variety of learning experiences within and outside of the classroom that focus on the development of the habits of mind of the lifelong learner. The schedule would be divided into instructional blocks that are interdisciplinary in focus and that are taught by a team of teachers. These teachers would be a combination of generalists and specialists, and they would develop curriculum that explores the connection between content areas and between the classroom and the world. This curriculum would reflect multiple instructional strategies, so as to accommodate diverse student learning needs and styles. Students would be grouped heterogeneously, and teachers would follow their classes from grade to grade to support instructional and interpersonal continuity. Curriculum would include authentic, project-based learning, and opportunities for community mentorships. Class groupings and scheduling would be flexible to allow for reconfiguration of students and blocks of time as needed. Each student would have an adult adviser and a minimum of 20 minutes of advisory per day.

Opportunities for enrichment, intervention, and extracurricular activities would be offered before and after the school day. Parents and members of the community would be encouraged to offer courses during the extended day, as well as to serve as tutors and mentors. The assessment model would incorporate a spectrum of tools to support a holistic approach to evaluation. Foremost among these tools would be student portfolios and student exhibitions. Rubrics for assessing student growth toward the standard, and the tools to assess this growth, would be developed by students and their teachers with the input of the school community. Every aspect of the instructional program would focus on the diverse needs of the students; on their academic, social, and personal growth; and on high standards for student achievement. The school community would be committed to maintaining the same high level of expectations for all students, while acknowledging the individual differences among students in meeting the standards and encouraging and nurturing student enthusiasm for learning.

Governance and Leadership

Essential to the realization of my educational vision is a model of governance and leadership that supports collaboration and a sense of personal accountability to a set of guiding principles, and that includes and encourages multiple perspectives. In this model, the principal would be responsible for providing the time and the structure for students, staff, parents, and other school community members to openly participate in some aspect of the governance process. This would require identifying specific issues and constituencies and creating multiple governance forums, as well as ensuring that all stakeholders are involved at some point, as appropriate. This includes not only teachers, parents, and students but also custodial and cafeteria staff, health providers, and members of community-based organizations. The principal would also create an environment that fosters open dialogue among the various stakeholders and that provides training in the new paradigm of the shared decision-making process. In this environment, the goals of the school would be developed collaboratively with student achievement as the focus, and the progress toward the goals would be assessed through a process of ongoing reflection. The specific structure of the assessment component would be developed by the school community and would incorporate multiple assessment models, both formal and informal. Responsibility for student achievement would be shared by all stakeholders, and finger-pointing and blaming would be replaced by an atmosphere of collegiality and collaboration in which each member of the school community would take responsibility for the successes and the failures.

As the leader in this school culture, I would model the values, beliefs, and behavior I sought to engender. My leadership style would be proactive, flexible, and reflective. I would be genuine in my commitment to a collaborative approach to leadership and sustain a constant focus on the fundamental belief that student achievement must drive all aspects of the educational process. I would maintain an open-door policy, seeking input from members of the school community and participating in the reflective process. I would actively work to secure the resources needed to support the instructional process and to develop and sustain a supportive and open relationship with the district and the community. I would lead by example and demonstrate those qualities of integrity, focus, and mutual respect that are fundamental to my vision of a school community. I would share in both the joys of our successes and in the struggles of our setbacks. I would be coach, facilitator, and exemplar, sustaining the vision and holding the guiding principles continually in the forefront of all our endeavors.

CONCLUSION

The supervisory landscape has evolved since the early inspectional practices of supervisors in the 19th and early 20th centuries. Supervision in a postindustrial society requires a new breed of supervisor, one who advocates and affirms participatory democratic practices. Who are these supervisors? What kind of supervisors do we want to attract into the field? Are you more inclined to encourage teachers in ongoing, meaningful dialogue about instructional improvement, or do you feel more comfortable suggesting to teachers ways to improve their teaching?

We have suggested in this chapter that supervision in postindustrial times requires that supervisors develop a personal vision statement so that they begin to consciously affirm their beliefs about teaching and supervision. Such reflective practice is a powerful way to enhance professional development.

Confronted by complex and seemingly perplexing social, political, technological, and moral issues, educational supervisors, perhaps more than ever before, play a crucial role in developing sound educational programming that is both educative and meaningfully relevant. Considering these awesome and challenging responsibilities, we believe educational supervision can play a vital role in promoting excellent instruction.

NOTES

1. Although the special supervisor as a specific title disappeared, a host of other supervisors later emerged, such as supervisors of curriculum, instruction, and reading, among others.

2. For a more in-depth historical analysis, see Glanz (1998).

3. This section is informed by the work of Reitzug (1997).

4. Favorite surveys that we use include the Myers-Briggs Type Indicator (Myers & McCaulley, 1985), the Personal Values Questionnaire and Managerial Style Questionnaire from McBer and Company (1994), the Let Me Learn Learning Combination Inventory Professional Form (Johnston & Dainton, 1997), Assessing Your Natural Leadership Qualities (Glanz, 2002), and the Natural Life Energy Survey (Null, 1996). We also encourage our students to read *The Reflective Supervisor* by Calabrese and Zepeda (1997).

5. For a more in-depth discussion of descriptive feedback, see Osterman and Kottkamp (1993), pp. 91–95.

6. This exercise has been adapted from Osterman and Kottkamp (1993), p. 96. See pp. 96–99 for a more detailed discussion of the process.

7. Special thanks to Laura Kump (Sample 2) and Fran Macko (Sample 3) for giving us permission to share their vision statements. The first one is the vision statement of a leadership candidate.

Three 2
Interpersonal
Approaches to
Supervision

A barrier to communication is something that keeps meanings from meeting. . . . Because so much of our education misleads people into thinking that communication is easier than it is, they become discouraged and give up when they run into difficulty. Because they do not understand the nature of the problem, they do not know what to do. The wonder is not that communicating is as difficult as it is, but that it occurs as much as it does.

—Howe, 1963, pp. 23–24

CHAPTER OVERVIEW

1. Interpersonal Skills

   a. Listening, Reflecting, and Clarifying Techniques
   b. Barriers to Communication

2. Approaches to Providing Feedback

   a. Directive Informational Approach
   b. Collaborative Approach
   c. Self-Directed Approach

3. Guidelines for Reflective Practice

   a. Reflective Practice Process
   b. Reflector's Feedback Guidelines

In the previous chapter, you became acquainted with the historical framework of supervision and began to examine your present personal beliefs within the current context of supervision. This chapter explores and develops the interpersonal skills that we believe are a prerequisite to all effective supervisory practice. After a brief introduction to the philosophical principles underlying the supervisory beliefs and methods presented in this book, we briefly discuss the various communication techniques that are essential for all effective interpersonal relationships: listening, nonverbal clues, and reflecting, clarifying statements. We then offer exercises that hone these techniques. A description of the three interpersonal approaches that we believe are most effective in working with teachers follows. Before practicing each of the three interpersonal approaches in a group, we introduce a reflective practice model and provide guidelines for reflective practice that are used throughout this book to build and reinforce skills. This chapter concludes with two exercises that permit you to begin to internalize these approaches prior to implementing them on-site.

HOW WE LEARN

People learn best through active involvement and through thinking about and becoming articulate about what they have learned. Processes, practices, and policies built on this view of learning are at the heart of a more expanded view of teacher development that encourages teachers to involve themselves as learners—in much the same way as they wish their students would.

—Lieberman, 1995, p. 592

How many lectures have we all sat through during which the speaker expounded at great length about the importance of student-centered learning in the classroom? How many workshops have we attended where the presenter talked on and on about student-centered practices? A district superintendent recently hired one of us to facilitate a teacher-centered retreat, which he began with a 2-hour speech. Ann Lieberman (1995) pointed out that "what everyone appears to want for students—a wide array of learning opportunities that engage students in experiencing, creating, and solving real problems, using their own experiences, and working with others—is for some reason denied to teachers when they are learners." The main goal of this book is to "walk the talk": to enable students of supervision not only to learn teacher-centered supervisory methods but also to have the opportunity to practice the skills and experience the perspectives as they are exposed to them.

The approaches to providing feedback outlined in this chapter and the methods presented for becoming proficient in their use are based on constructivist principles. In the Preface to *In Search of Understanding the Case for Constructivist Classrooms,* Catherine Twomey Fosnot (1993) draws on a synthesis of work in cognitive psychology, philosophy, and anthropology to define constructivism as a theory not about teaching but about knowledge and learning.

Knowledge is defined as temporary, developmental, socially and culturally mediated, and nonobjective. Learning is "a self-regulated process of resolving inner cognitive conflicts that often become apparent through concrete experience, collaborative discourse, and reflection" (Fosnot, 1993, p. 2). In other words, meaningful knowledge and learning are centered around the learner and are best constructed through collaboration and reflection around personal experience.

This belief has ramifications for the two principal focuses of this chapter: interpersonal approaches for providing feedback and the use of reflective practice in working with teachers and in learning supervisory skills. With respect to working with teachers, no matter what the developmental level of the staff member or the interpersonal orientation of the supervisor, the person receiving feedback should be involved in generating ideas and solutions for the situation under discussion. With regard to learning how to provide feedback, it is only through practicing the skills and reflecting on their development that students of supervision will internalize and personalize what they have learned.

LISTENING, REFLECTING, AND CLARIFYING TECHNIQUES

Before we begin learning and practicing the three different approaches to providing feedback, it is important to incorporate skills that promote communication as well as to become aware of those that create barriers. Table 2.1 provides three types of skills that foster bridging the interpersonal gap. Each category can be integrated into any of the feedback approaches. In each approach, we want to encourage the teacher to provide as complete a picture of his or her perspective as possible. The listening techniques and the nonverbal clues are key means to promote open responses. The reflecting and clarifying techniques also are crucial to all the approaches because they facilitate avoiding or clearing up potential misunderstandings and miscommunications. They provide verbal techniques for separating the supervisor's understandings and perceptions from the teacher's without accusing or putting the other person on the defensive. To remind you of appropriate responses, we recommend that you use the crib sheets that summarize the key techniques and steps for practice and actual implementation. Detachable cards for these techniques are provided on a perforated page at the back of the book.

Table 2.2 contains a summary of common communication spoilers and high-risk responses culled from the interpersonal skills literature. We refer to them as "high-risk" responses because their impact is frequently negative, and as a general rule, they should be avoided. Nonetheless, a few of them can be effective in special circumstances.[1]

The communication techniques and barriers to avoid are critical components of feedback. Effective and appropriate responses are difficult to develop because the barriers to communication are engrained in our language and habits. For these reasons, it is important to practice the communication techniques in class and in your professional and personal lives as much as possible

Table 2.1   Communication Techniques

Listening	Nonverbal Clues	Reflecting and Clarifying
"Uh-huh."	Affirmative nods and smiles	"You're angry because . . ."
"OK."	Open body language, e.g., arms open	"You feel . . . because . . ."
"I'm following you."		"You seem quite upset."
"For instance,"	Appropriate distance from speaker—not too close or too far	"So, you would like . . ."
"And?"		"I understand that you see the problem as . . ."
"Mmm."	Eye contact	
"I understand."	Nondistracting environment	"I'm not sure, but I think you mean . . ."
"This is great information for me."	Face speaker and lean forward	"I think you're saying . . ."
"Really?"	Barrier-free space, e.g., desk not used as blocker	
"Then?"		
"So?"		
"Tell me more."		
"Go on."		
"I see."		
"Right."		

before proceeding to the feedback approaches. As the communication techniques begin to be a part of your repertoire, they will enhance the feedback approaches. The following exercises are an introduction to the type of reflective practice role plays that you will find throughout the book.

Reflective Practice

Class Practice

Everyone in the class should find a partner and face that person. Each student will take a turn listening and responding to his or her partner. The goal is to use the communication techniques to foster an effective interchange and to avoid falling into any of the barrier traps. Keep Tables 2.1 and 2.2 handy to facilitate the learning process.

Table 2.2   Barriers to Communication

Barrier Type	Examples

1. Judging
   • Criticizing
   • Name calling and labeling
   • Diagnosing—analyzing motives instead of listening
   • Praising evaluatively
	1. Judging
	   • "You are lazy; your lesson plan is poor."
	   • "You are inexperienced, an intellectual."
	   • "You're taking out your anger on her."
	   • "I know what you need."
	   • "You're terrific!"

2. Solutions
   • Ordering
   • Threatening
   • Moralizing or preaching
   • Inappropriate questioning or prying
   • Advising
   • Lecturing
	2. Solutions
	   • "You must . . ." "You have to . . ." "You will . . ."
	   • "If you don't . . ." "You had better or else."
	   • "It is your duty/responsibility; you should."
	   • "Why?" "What?" "How?" "When?"
	   • "What I would do is . . ." "It would be best for you."
	   • "Here is why you are wrong . . ." "Do you realize . . . ?"

3. Avoiding the other's concerns
   • Diverting
   • Reassuring
   • Withdrawing
   • Sarcasm
	3. Avoiding the other's concerns
	   • "Speaking of . . ." "Apropos . . ." "You know what happened to . . ."
	   • "It's not so bad . . ." "You're lucky . . ." "You'll feel better."
	   • "I'm very busy . . ." "I can't talk right now . . ." "I'll get back to you . . ."
	   • "I really feel sorry for you."

Step 1. Each partner should take a minute to think of a current personal or professional dilemma.

Step 2. Partner No. 1 will recount his or her dilemma.

Step 3. Partner No. 2 will show interest in the speaker's situation by using the listening and nonverbal techniques and avoiding the barriers (Tables 2.1 and 2.2).

Step 4. Partner No. 2 will choose reflecting and clarifying techniques to verify what he or she heard and show understanding of the feelings expressed.

Step 5. Partner No. 1 will give feedback on how well partner No. 2 used the techniques.

Change partners and repeat the cycle. Each cycle should take no more than 5 minutes.

Site Practice

During the next week, target someone who is going to share an experience, problem, or dilemma with you. It can be a spouse, a child, a colleague, or a student. Have your cards with Tables 2.1 and 2.2 on hand, and practice your listening and communication techniques. When the interchange is completed, reflect on what worked well and what areas need improvement. Jot down notes so that you can share your reflections on the experience with your colleagues, first in an e-mail, a discussion board, a wiki, or a blog, and then in class. You may feel a little uncomfortable at first using these techniques. Remember that because the listeners are involved in their virtually uninterrupted sharing, they won't be aware of your novice status as active listeners.

APPROACHES TO PROVIDING FEEDBACK

With communication techniques now in hand, we can introduce and discuss approaches that are fundamental to providing effective feedback.[2] Some textbooks suggest that individual behavior can be divided into four major groups that require four styles of responses (Glickman, Gordon, & Ross-Gordon, 2004). For example, in his developmental model, Glickman recommends four approaches to working with individuals:

1. Directive control

2. Directive informational

3. Collaborative

4. Self-directed

These approaches range from almost total supervisor control to primarily teacher control. The approach the supervisor chooses is supposed to match the specific teacher's level of development. In reality, many of us tend to favor one approach in our interactions with others. In the directive control approach, the supervisor makes the decision and tells the individual or group how to proceed. The supervisor who uses the directive informational approach frames the choices for the group or individual and then asks for input. In the collaborative approach, the supervisor and the individual or group share information and possible solutions as equals to arrive at a mutual plan. In the fourth approach, the supervisor facilitates the individual or group in developing a self-plan or in making its own decision. Glickman et al. (2004) believe that the teacher's level of development, expertise, and commitment and the nature of the situation determine the choice of approach. We agree that "different folks need different strokes" and that varying school circumstances call for a range of approaches; however, *we believe that meaningful learning is dependent on the learner's involvement in constructing that knowledge and so there is no need for the directive control approach.* Many supervisors over the years have used this approach, many continue to follow it, and you may favor it yourself. Nonetheless, we think that the collaborative and self-directed models are the most effective, with the occasional application of a modified directive informational approach.

Elena's Dilemma

To illustrate the use of the three approaches, we will present three variations of the same dilemma and offer suggestions on how the different models could be applied to the scenarios (see Table 2.3 for a summary and comparison of the three approaches).

Elena Santiago was appointed principal of New Hope Middle School in September. New Hope Middle School is a large urban school that has a reputation for lax discipline, an unruly atmosphere, and has recently seen significant population changes. Over the past ten years, an increasing number of English language learners (ELL) have been entering the school. The range of their language and academic skills is vast. This new group of students has created new challenges for the faculty and staff and a very recent district "needs improvement" citation. In Elena's previous position as an assistant principal, also in a demanding environment with a large ELL student body, she had gained the confidence of the staff through her high expectations, blended with excellent interpersonal skills and a collaborative manner. She had also effectively addressed the ELL needs through teamwork. The school district's awareness of her effectiveness led to her appointment as principal of New Hope Middle School. In her first weeks at the school, she has been working closely with all constituencies to address the ELL challenge.

In her daily classroom visits, Elena has noticed some consistent ELL issues. Elena has decided to discuss one issue individually with three teachers she has observed who have struggling ELL students.

Scenario I

Elena approaches Martha before school one morning. Martha also joined the New Hope faculty in September as a seventh-grade Language Arts teacher. New Hope is her first teaching job, and despite a solid academic background and an assigned mentor, she seems somewhat overwhelmed.

Elena: Good morning, Martha. How are you doing?

Martha: OK, I guess.

Elena: As I've been visiting classes, I've noticed some newer ELL students who seem to be struggling. A couple of them, Jorge and Carlos, are in your third period Language Arts class. How do you feel they are progressing?

Martha: I honestly haven't had time to focus on them. It takes all my energy to plan and deliver my lessons and of course to keep the class's attention. I have noticed that Jorge and Carlos don't participate in class and haven't been handing in their assignments.

I get so bogged down toward the end of class. I can't seem to make it through what I've planned for the class; students come up to talk to me at the end of the period and I'm left with assignments I've either not collected or new homework sheets that I haven't had time to distribute. So, everyone is gathered around me at the end of class, and my next class appears before I get out from behind my desk.

Elena: I remember those first days of teaching. It took me quite a while until I could begin to see the forest for the trees. I think there are a few initial steps you can take to help Jorge and Carlos that will not add to your classroom stress. First, it is important to call their homes to determine what kind of family support they have. Second, you can meet with the ESL teacher to find out their language skills and knowledge levels. With this information, you can then meet with your mentor and grade colleagues to discuss strategies for Jorge and Carlos. Could these suggestions work for you? I figured out an end-of-class system that worked for me. What I did first was to post a sign-up sheet for students to talk to me outside of class so that they didn't bombard me at the end of every period. That way they knew I was accessible but didn't keep me pinned to the front of the classroom. Then I created a system for collecting homework and distributing assignments. I set up individual files, and I made sure I stopped active work 5 minutes early to allow the class to hand in their homework and pick up new assignments. During those few minutes, I was able to pull myself together and take care of an occasional individual emergency. Could any of these ideas work for you?

Martha: I like the idea of having students sign up to talk to me. There's always a group anyway that comes to see me after school. A sign-up sheet might help organize the afterschool chaos, too. I also have to pay attention to ending the lesson before the bell rings so that I can take care of business and get to the door. Maybe I could set a timer that would ring 5 minutes before the end of the period. I have so many students that I don't think I could set up a filing system. I appreciate your bringing Carlos and Jorge to my attention and I will focus on them, especially with so many people to turn to for support. Is it OK if I ask Ana to assist in the phone call in case no one speaks English in their homes?

Elena: Of course. It could be very helpful. Since you see Jorge and Carlos every day, do any other ideas come to mind that you could implement while you are obtaining more information? Do you have any ideas for an end-of-period system that might work for you?

Martha: What if I appointed two monitors each month in every class to collect homework and distribute assignments at the end of each period? With respect to Jorge and Carlos, there are two Spanish-speaking girls in the class whose English is quite good. What if I seat one next to each boy and put them in the same cooperative groups for now? I can ask the girls before class if it's OK with them.

Elena: That sounds like a good idea. Let's go over your plan. First, you will contact Jorge's and Carlos's homes to ascertain what kind of family support they have. Second, you'll meet with the ESL teacher to find out their language and knowledge levels. With this information in hand, you will meet with your mentor and your grade-level teachers to discuss strategies. In the meantime, you will seat the two Spanish-speaking girls in the class with Jorge and Carlos and put each pair in the same group. And you will post a sign-up sheet for students to talk to you instead of coming up to you at the end of the period. Second, you'll set a timer so that you end 5 minutes before the passing bell to allow time for homework distribution and collection. Finally, you will appoint two monitors in each class to take care of the homework. How does that sound to you? Do you want to restate the plan to make sure we're on the same page?

Martha: Sure. I'll call Jorge's and Carlos's homes today and set up a meeting with the ESL teacher. As soon as I have family and ESL information, I'll meet with my mentor and the grade teachers to brainstorm strategies to assist Jorge and Carlos. I'll also seat Jorge and Carlos with the Spanish-speaking girls, at least until I have other strategies. I'm going to get a timer so I can end class 5 minutes early to take care of homework. I'm going to appoint monitors to collect homework and distribute new assignments, and I'm going to post a sign-up list so that the students don't detain me at the end of the class.

Elena: Sounds like a plan. Terrific! How about setting up a time for us to meet and see what transpires over the next couple of weeks and decide how this system works for you? I can meet with you at the same time in two weeks so we can catch any glitches that may have surfaced.

Martha: OK. I'll see you before school on Thursday, September 23, when I will have attended my Wednesday grade-level meeting.

> ### Reflection
>
> *How does Elena approach Martha? How does she foster Elena's "buy-in" of her suggestions? What does she do to ensure that the suggestions don't just remain suggestions?*

I. The Directive Informational Approach

Key Steps: Directive Informational Approach

1. Identify the problem or goal and solicit clarifying information.

2. Offer solutions. Ask for the teacher's input into the alternatives offered and request additional ideas.

3. Summarize chosen alternatives, ask for confirmation, and request that the teacher restate final choices.

4. Set a follow-up plan and meeting.

This approach is used primarily for new teachers or those who are experiencing difficulties that they don't have the knowledge, expertise, or confidence to resolve on their own or collaboratively. These teachers are seeking or need direction and guidance from a supervisor who can provide expert information and experienced guidance. Nonetheless, the supervisor wants the teacher to seek solutions and generate ideas so as to feel at least some ownership of the final choices. Therefore, the supervisor is the initiator of suggestions and alternatives, which the teacher can then revise and refine and to which he or she can add ideas.

1. *Identify the problem or goal and solicit clarifying information.* Avoid small talk and focus immediately on the problem or goal in question. Ask the teacher for clarification of the situation so that you are both sure that you are addressing the same problem or goal.

2. *Offer solutions.* Ask for the teacher's input into the alternatives offered and request additional ideas. Even though the new teacher might feel overwhelmed, the supervisor's ideas will probably stimulate his or her thinking. Offering input and requesting additional ideas will give the teacher a feeling of ownership and allow him or her to begin constructing a personal perspective. Separating the alternatives from the request for additional ideas allows the teacher to think through the suggestions and then come up with modifications or new possibilities.

3. *Summarize chosen alternatives, ask for confirmation, and request that the teacher restate final choices.* Verification that both supervisor and teacher have the same understanding of the final choices is crucial. Two people can easily interpret the same words differently or hear different words. Therefore, if each party repeats his or her understanding, any misunderstandings or differences in perceptions can be cleared up before action is taken.

4. *Set up a follow-up plan and meeting.* A concrete plan (written is preferable) and a scheduled meeting are the only ways that two very busy professionals can be sure of the follow-through that is crucial to the success of any plan.

Scenario 2

Ann has been teaching at New Hope for 10 years. Her reputation is that of a cooperative, collaborative, and effective teacher. Elena is therefore surprised to notice in her daily walk-around that Jorge and Carlos, two new ELL arrivals, don't seem involved in the class. Elena decides to stop by during Ann's free period to find out what has been preventing her from providing support to Jorge and Carlos.

Elena: Hi, Ann. How's it going? I know that you are already aware of our need to focus on our ELL students. I've been discussing with faculty how they are doing with their new arrivals. I noticed that Jorge and Carlos are in your math class. How are they doing?

Ann: I'm happy you stopped by. With the start of classes, I haven't been able to focus on Carlos and Jorge as much as I would like to. Since Carlos has stronger English skills, I thought he might be able to assist Jorge, whose English knowledge is very limited. Carlos seems to be more interested in socializing than in math, and rather than helping Jorge, he seems to be distracting him. Given that it is a very social class, I have been looking mostly at whole-class strategies. One of the reasons for my negligence is that I've been having difficulty with a couple of students in two classes.

Elena: So what you're saying is that the combination of new scholastic year adjustments and monitoring the whole class's socializing has limited your individual involvement with Carlos and Jorge. There seem to be a few discipline problems that are preoccupying you. Is this accurate?

Ann: Sounds right to me.

Elena: Well, I'm pleased that you have been addressing the "lively" socializing of this class. Tell me more about Carlos and Jorge and the disruptive students. Maybe we can figure out something together.

Ann: Jorge is lost and now Carlos is making the situation worse. I called their homes—to no avail. No one speaks English. I spoke to the ESL teacher, who confirmed what I already knew. He also mentioned that their actual math skills are pretty good. There are two Spanish-speaking girls in the class whose English skills are stronger, but whose math skills are not at grade level. Maybe if I seat them together, the girls can assist the boys with their English skills and the boys can help with the girls' math. Mercedes is very quiet and probably wouldn't respond to Carlos's antics. Alma's English is solid, so she can work with Jorge. The other problem is two special needs students in two of my math classes. I haven't discussed the problem with the rest of the team because the students aren't in anyone else's classes. The decision was made at their elementary school to include them in the general ed math classes, and they are having a great deal of difficulty adjusting.

Elena: Those ideas seem like an effective first step. Since Alma and Mercedes need math support, I can place all four of them together in the extended-day program. That way we can also make sure that their homework gets completed. Let's ask Ana if she can call their home. The family may be able to support more if they can communicate with a Spanish-speaking person. Have you talked about the special needs students' behavior with their special ed teachers?

Ann: I'm sure that both of those strategies will help. I also think that if I am having difficulty with Carlos and Jorge, the less experienced teachers in our grade also need ideas. I can ask if we can devote a part of our next grade-level meeting to discussing our ELL students.

Communication between the special ed and regular teachers hasn't been what it should be. So much of this inclusion is so recent that we just haven't had time to develop proper communication channels. We've had so many initiatives this fall that I can barely keep up with what I have to do.

Elena: Your suggestion is very important. If you address your ELL students at the grade level, I will tackle the problem at the school level. Would you like me to attend your next meeting? I hear what you're saying. However, if two of your classes are being affected by this problem, we have to address it. Do you have any ideas?

Ann: I hate to suggest it, but I can think of one possibility. The school-based planning team might organize a subcommittee of representatives from regular ed and special ed to figure out what kind of communication we need and how to set it up. In the meantime, I've got to figure out how to handle the short-term dilemma.

Elena: The subcommittee is an excellent idea. I'll bring it up at the next school-based planning meeting. I hope you'll be willing to serve on the committee. In the meantime, I can arrange to free up the special ed teachers and you to meet together to discuss these particular students. Would you mind if I sat in on the meeting to get a clearer picture of what's involved in the realities of inclusion?

Ann: I'd prefer meeting with them on my own the first time. Two of our grade-level teachers are new and might feel intimidated if you're there. I'd like to get as much honest information as possible.

Elena: Fine. Just provide me with written or verbal feedback following the meeting to help me address the problem schoolwide. So, let's see what we've agreed on. First, you'll pair up Carlos with Mercedes and Jorge with Alma. They will all go to the extended-day program to work on math and English skills. Ana will call Carlos's and Jorge's families to seek support in Spanish. You will also request that at least part of the next grade-level meeting be devoted to ELL students. And, you'll provide me feedback so that I can incorporate your results into a school plan. I'll free up you and the special ed teachers so that you can talk about the students with special needs. You'll provide me with feedback on that meeting. I'll request to set up a generalized and special ed committee at the next school-based planning meeting and you will serve on it. How does this plan sound to you?

Ann: I'm glad to meet with the special ed teachers and report back to you afterward. I'm not so sure about the committee. I feel like I'm already on overload and am afraid of making another commitment. I wouldn't mind attending one meeting to provide my perspective, but I'm not ready to offer to become a charter member of the committee. Let's hold on that one.

Elena: I understand. Can we look at some times for you to meet with the special ed teachers and to give me feedback on that meeting before I leave?

Ann: Sure. I can stop at your office after school to schedule my meeting with the special ed teachers for sometime next week, and we can meet at this same time the following week, if it's OK with you. Sounds like a go for me. Our grade-level meeting is next Wednesday.

Elena: I'll set up the afterschool program today and ask Ana to get in contact with you. Could we meet here during your prep on Thursday so that you can give me feedback on your grade-level meeting?

Ann: Sure. My prep is third period on Thursday. See you then.

> **Reflection**
>
> *How does Elena make sure she understands what Ann explains? Does Elena approach Ann differently than she approaches Martha? If so, how? How do Ann and Elena deal with their differences?*

II. The Collaborative Approach

> **Key Steps: Collaborative Approach**
>
> 1. Identify the problem from the teacher's perspective, soliciting as much clarifying information as possible.
>
> 2. Reflect back on what you've heard for accuracy.
>
> 3. Begin collaborative brainstorming, asking the teacher for his or her ideas first.
>
> 4. Problem solve through a sharing and discussion of options.
>
> 5. Agree on a plan and follow-up meeting.

In the collaborative approach, the goal is to resolve a problem or reach a goal through shared decision making. The supervisor encourages the teacher to develop his or her ideas first to allow maximum ownership. Nonetheless, the brainstorming and problem solving are shared, and disagreement is encouraged, with assurances that a mutual solution will be reached. The conference always ends with a restatement of agreed-on plans and the setting up of a follow-up meeting. Unresolved issues can be included in the planning process and revisited at the follow-up session.

   1. *Identify the problem from the teacher's perspective, soliciting as much clarifying information as possible.* With the exception of some new teachers and those with problematic practices, the supervisor wants the teacher to

initiate the discussion from his or her perspective. The more information provided, the clearer the situation for both parties. Therefore, a more complete description can be drawn out with prompts, that is, eye contact and encouraging open body language and nonverbal cues, paraphrasing, probing questions, and phrases such as "Tell me more," "Uh-huh," "I see," and "I understand."

2. *Reflect back on what you've heard for accuracy.* It is crucial that you verify that you've heard accurately the content and perspective of the teacher. A summary of what you understood, with the teacher's verification of what you heard, can avoid many misunderstandings and problems down the road. You may feel like you sound silly repeating; rest assured that the teacher is hanging on your every word to be sure that you heard and understood.

3. *Begin collaborative brainstorming, asking the teacher for his or her ideas first.* If the supervisor proposes options first, the teacher might not try to develop his or her own ideas and might just follow what the supervisor suggests. Because the teacher is the one most familiar with the situation, it is important to allow him or her to build on that knowledge or to decide to construct a different or new resolution.

4. *Problem solve through a sharing and discussion of options.* One of the greatest challenges to a supervisor in a collaborative approach is to encourage disagreement convincingly. Few teachers are accustomed to administrators fostering challenges and encouraging risk taking. Asking for the teacher's suggestions is a first step. Promoting an open dialogue about the options is the second step.

5. *Agree on a plan and follow-up meeting.* In the complex lives of teachers and administrators, a written plan on agreed-on solutions and those yet to be resolved will save a lot of time in the long run. What often seems time consuming can be cost effective in the final analysis. Taking the time to write out a plan and set up the next appointment is the essential concluding step.

Scenario 3

Will has been teaching for many years. He has his routines down to a science. He teaches in a traditional manner, peppering his well-organized lectures with amusing anecdotes. He tends to avoid new initiatives and believes that if "it ain't broke, don't fix it." As the new kid on the block, Elena wants to solicit cooperation from this veteran teacher without him feeling imposed upon. For this reason, she chooses the self-directed approach to try to encourage him to become involved with the ELL challenge.

Elena: How's it going so far, Will?

Will: It's always fine behind my closed door. It's what goes on outside of my room that can infiltrate my classroom.

Elena: So, you feel that your classroom is under control, but outside events are having an effect on your teaching. Do you want to explain that a little further for me?

Will: As you know, we've had an influx of non-English-speaking students. I believe in maintaining the same high standards for all students, but if these new arrivals aren't learning English fast enough in their ESL classes, I'm left in the lurch.

Elena: I understand what a challenge it is to maintain your standards with such a varied student body. As I've been visiting the seventh-grade classes, I've been particularly concerned with the difficulties that Jorge and Carlos seem to be having.

Will: I'm ready to give up on them. I've told them to come after school for extra help, but they don't come. I even called their homes, but either no one answered or no one spoke English. Their ESL teacher must not be doing much with them. You should speak to him.

Elena: I hear your frustration with their lack of response and your inability to communicate with their families. I commend you for extending yourself. Since you are an experienced, effective teacher, do you have any other suggestions that might work for you and perhaps for all the teachers?

Will: Since it has become a schoolwide problem, I think that the initiative has to come from you, our new leader. We have so many new teachers in the seventh grade, I don't think they could be much help. The only thing that I can think of is that I could meet with Ann and we might be able to lead a discussion at our grade-level meeting.

Elena: Great minds think alike! That is exactly what Ann suggested. Could you talk to her about planning for the meeting? I could release both of you for an hour prior to the grade-level meeting so that you could create an agenda.

Will: I guess we could. What are *you* going to do about the influx of ELL students?

Elena: I'm hoping to get feedback from grade-level meetings like yours and devote our next faculty meetings to professional development on ELL learners. I also think that sharing the strategies the different grade teams come up with will be another initial step. Addressing our new arrivals will be a long-term goal. I look forward to the support of experienced teachers like yourself to help get this initiative off the ground.

Will: Just don't make me the head of any committee. I'm not really into this collaborative stuff. I just want to keep getting the results I am used to getting.

Elena: I hear you. Can you, Ann, and I meet after your grade-level meeting next week to see what you come up with that I can incorporate into the faculty meeting?

<table>
<tr><td>

Reflection

Why doesn't Elena start out mentioning to Will the problems with ELL students? What does Elena do to avoid negativity? What specific words and phrases does she use to encourage Will's participation?

</td><td>

Will: I think that Ann and I have a common prep on Thursday. We could meet then.

Elena: Thanks so much for your assistance. I really look forward to hearing the ideas that emerge from the grade-level meeting.

</td></tr>
</table>

III. The Self-Directed Approach

Key Steps: Self-Directed Approach

1. Listen carefully to the teacher's initial statement.

2. Reflect back on your understanding of the problem.

3. Constantly clarify and reflect until the real problem is identified.

4. Have the teacher problem solve and explore the consequences of various actions.

5. The teacher commits to a decision and firms up a plan.

6. The supervisor restates the teacher's plan and sets up a follow-up meeting.

The goal of the self-directed approach is to enable the teacher to reflect on the problem, draw conclusions, and construct his or her own alternatives. The supervisor serves more as a coach who does not express his or her point of view or ideas unless the teacher specifically requests them. The supervisor functions as the facilitator of the teacher's development of his or her own ideas. The outcome should always be the teacher's autonomous decision. This approach is appropriate for a very knowledgeable and often experienced teacher. It also can be successful in providing a sense of ownership when the teacher is the primary person responsible for carrying out a decision or when the decision or problem at hand has limited ramifications. A less experienced, but creative, promising teacher can also benefit from the guided ownership that this approach affords.

1. *Listen carefully to the teacher's initial statement.* As in the collaborative approach, the starting point is the teacher's perspective of the situation. The techniques and prompts are the same as in the collaborative approach: eye contact, body language, paraphrasing, verbal cues, and probing questions.

2. *Reflect back on your understanding of the problem.* Again, as in the collaborative approach, verification that you have clearly and accurately understood the teacher's perspective is essential. Reflecting back on what has been heard begins to accomplish this task. In addition, paraphrasing can clarify any uncertainty the supervisor may have about

what has been expressed and can even allow the teacher to distance himself or herself from what was said and reflect on it from the outside.

3. *Constantly clarify and reflect until the real problem is identified.* The crucial prerequisite to solving a problem is to conceptualize accurately what the problem is. Solutions often are hidden in the identification of the problem, thereby limiting the range of resolutions. Thus, the real need must be ascertained. For example, your husband says he's taking the car, and you have a meeting. Your need is not necessarily to take the car but to find a way to get to the meeting. The facilitator's role is to use the reflecting/prompting/questioning process judiciously to permit the teacher to arrive at a crystallization of the need.

4. *Have the teacher problem solve and explore the consequences of various actions.* Once the need has been identified, simply ask the teacher to think of possible alternatives. Assist the teacher in walking through the steps, process, and consequences of each action. Ask questions such as "What would happen if . . . ?" or "How would you . . . ?" Then ask the teacher to explore the advantages and disadvantages of the alternatives. At this point, the teacher may be ready to respond to concluding questions, that is, "Which do you think will work best? Why? In what ways would it be better?"

5. *The teacher commits to a decision and firms up a plan.* Once the teacher makes a choice, you can request a plan and encourage a walk-through of the next steps. "What, who, when, how, where" may be part of the plan, or the provision of simple planning forms that the teacher can complete.

6. *The supervisor restates the teacher's plan and sets up a follow-up meeting.* It is important for the supervisor to restate the teacher's plan before ending the meeting. This verification will avoid future misunderstandings. In addition, even though the teacher owns the plan, the scheduling of a follow-up meeting to see how it's working should always conclude the session.

Table 2.3 includes a summary of each of the three interpersonal approaches to supervision.

GUIDELINES FOR REFLECTIVE PRACTICE

We believe that learning is most effective when the learner is actively involved in the learning process, when it takes place as a collaborative activity (Bridges, 1992), and when reflection is the means of observing, analyzing, considering, and reconceptualizing the experience. As we mentioned in Chapter 1, the process used in reflective practice can guide our development of new skills and change ingrained behaviors that may be inconsistent with internalization of the new skills. We first look at the stages of reflective practice and then discuss how they guide our development of supervisory skills.

Table 2.3 Approach Comparison

Direct Informational	Collaborative	Self-Directed
1. Supervisor identifies problem, then solicits clarifying information.	1. Supervisor seeks to identify problem from teacher's perspective.	1. Supervisor asks teacher to identify problem.
2. Supervisor offers solutions and then requests input.	2. Collaborative brainstorming for solutions.	2. Clarification and reflection until teacher identifies problem.
3. Supervisor summarizes and then asks for confirmation.	3. Problem solve through sharing and discussion.	3. Teacher problem solves and explores consequences.
4. Teacher restates final choices.	4. Joint agreement on plan.	4. Teacher commits to decision.

Reflective practice is based primarily on two learning theories:

- Experiential learning theory, popularly associated with Dewey and Piaget, maintains that learning is most effective and likely to lead to behavior change when it begins with experience, especially problematic experience (Osterman & Kottkamp, 2004).
- The situated cognition perspective that Bridges (1992) popularized in problem-based learning argues that learning is most effective when the learner is actively involved in the learning process, when it takes place as a collaborative rather than an isolated activity, and when it is in a context relevant to the learner. This dialectic and cyclical process consists of four stages: experience, observation and reflection, abstract reconceptualization, and experimentation (Kolb, 1984).

In reflective practice, the first stage is to identify a problematic situation; the second is to reflect on the problem or experience—preferably in a collaborative, cooperative environment; the third is to consider alternate ways of thinking and acting; and the fourth is to test the reconceptualized behavior and assumptions. The cycle can begin again with the new concrete experience (see Figure 2.1).

Reflective practice serves two principal purposes in this book:

1. Every idea, tool, and technique to foster internalization of the new learning is accompanied by directions for reflective practice in the course classroom and on-site.

2. We hope to instill the ongoing experience of reflecting individually and collaboratively on developing skills as a habit that you carry with you in your personal and professional lives and that you model as an educational leader.

Before you try out your new skills in a classroom or with another teacher, it is important that you have the opportunity to experience and reflect on them in a safe environment. We have developed a method for you to role-play all the interpersonal skills in this book. This method also can serve as a model for experiencing and reflecting on any communication skills or problematic situations you might want to rehearse. The only tools you need are two people who interact and a reflector with a watch or timer. We recommend that you use the "Fishbowl" method outlined in Resource B to model each role play. This method involves student volunteers who model each approach before the whole class attempts each role play. View the accompanying video that models the role plays before practicing.

For the purposes of developing supervisory skills, the model presented is limited to the roles of a supervisor and a teacher. We first outline the roles and responsibilities in the process (see Table 2.4) and then provide specific feedback guidelines for the reflector (see Table 2.5).

Reflective Practice

Class Practice

During the next three weeks, each of you is going to create three scenarios. If possible, model the scenarios on existing challenges or dilemmas currently occurring in your school or in real-life situations with which you are familiar.

- The first scenario involves a supervisor and either a new teacher or a teacher in difficulty for whom the directive informational approach is appropriate.
- The second scenario takes place between you and a colleague who is an experienced and/or effective teacher with whom you feel comfortable using the collaborative approach.

Figure 2.1   Experiential Learning Cycle

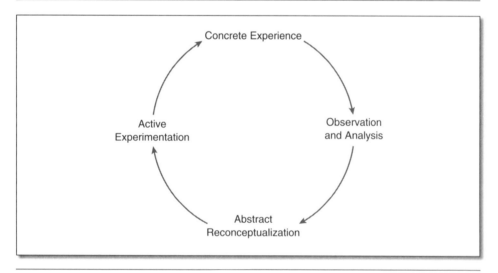

Source: K. F. Osterman and R. B. Kottkamp. (2004). *Reflective Practice for Educators: Professional Development to Improve Student Learning* (2nd ed.). Thousand Oaks, CA: Corwin.

Table 2.4   Reflective Practice Process—Three Steps, Three Responsibilities

Steps	Supervisor (Person Practicing)	Teacher	Reflector
1. Setting the scene (5 min.)	• Describes situation • Describes other person and possible reactions • Reviews steps on card and mentally rehearses	• Listens carefully • Asks clarifying questions • Mentally rehearses responses	• Starts monitoring time • Takes notes on key points • Reviews steps on card
2. Practice (10 min.)	• Practices each step	• Responds based on the description of the other person	• Observes practice • Takes notes • Keeps practice on track • Monitors time
3. Feedback and reflections (10 min.)	• Provides personal reflections first • Follows reflection guidelines	• Expresses personal feedback and reflections second • Follows reflection guidelines	• Facilitates reflections and feedback • Provides personal feedback and reflections last • Gives notes to person practicing

Source: Adapted with permission from AchieveGlobal, Inc. © 1999 AchieveGlobal, Inc. All rights reserved.

• The third scenario involves an interaction with a teacher who is so knowledgeable that he or she just needs prompting to come up with solutions or when you feel it would be beneficial for the teacher to solve the problem on his or her own.

Each week, you should practice a different approach in the course. Observe the appropriate role play on the video. Then, three volunteers will model the approach in front of the class before breaking into groups of three. Videotaping at least the three volunteers is recommended. It is very useful for other groups to volunteer to be videotaped so they can observe themselves on tape in the privacy of their homes. All students will have the opportunity to role-play the supervisor observer for each approach.

Site Practice

Each week, after you have practiced an approach, try it out by solving a site-based challenge. Where feasible, look for classroom-based problems as the basis of communication. Keep your cards available so that you can refer to them when the occasion arises. Be certain to reflect on how the interchange worked. What went well? What could be improved? What would you do differently next time? Take notes to facilitate class discussion of your experiences.

Table 2.5   Reflector's Feedback Guidelines

1. Ask the supervisor:

   - What went well in each of the steps?
   - What needs improvement?
   - What would you do differently next time?

2. Ask the teacher:

   - What do you feel the supervisor did effectively?
   - What areas do you feel need improvement?
   - What suggestions do you have for future interactions?

3. Reflector's feedback and conclusion of process:

   - Offer your reflections on what went well.
   - Provide your suggestions or alternatives.
   - Ask the supervisor for questions or comments.
   - Give your written reflections to supervisor.

Note: To promote self-reflection, make sure that the reflector asks the person role-playing the supervisor for input first. Also, separate carefully the response to "What needs improvement?" from suggestions. The problematic areas need to be thought out before solutions are addressed.

Source: Adapted with permission from AchieveGlobal, Inc. © 1999 AchieveGlobal, Inc. All rights reserved.

SUMMARY

In this chapter, we began to lay the groundwork for developing the interpersonal skills that are a prerequisite for all effective supervisory practice. Case studies introduced the three interpersonal approaches for providing feedback: the directive informational approach, the collaborative approach, and the self-directed approach. Before actually learning and practicing these approaches, the listening skills integral to the three approaches were outlined: phrases that show attentive listening, nonverbal cues, and reflecting and clarifying techniques. Class- and site-based exercises for practicing the listening and feedback approaches were accompanied by the introduction of the reflective practice process and guidelines that will be used throughout the book. With these skills and techniques under our belts, we can now tackle the observational tools and techniques for observing classroom teaching and learning that will be presented in Chapter 3.

NOTES

1. *People Skills* by Robert Bolton (1979) is an excellent source of many communication skills.

2. The approaches in this section are adapted from Glickman et al. (2004).

3 Observation Tools and Techniques

You can observe a lot by watching.

—Yogi Berra

CHAPTER OVERVIEW

1. Supervision Case Study

2. Ten Guidelines of Observation

3. Summary of Tools and Techniques
   a. By Approach
   b. By Content

4. Twenty-two Quantitative Observation Tools

5. Ten Qualitative Observation Tools

6. Summary
   a. Reflective Clinical Supervision in a Standards-Based Environment

7. Conclusion

A major assumption of the authors is that judicious use of reliable and easy-to-use observation techniques can increase a teacher's awareness of classroom behavior and therefore become instrumental in improving the teaching and learning process. To this end, a variety of teaching tools and techniques for use in the classroom are included in this chapter. These tools are by no means a complete compilation; rather, they are a sampling. The authors encourage you to begin thinking about your individual needs in the classroom and creating your own tools. This chapter will help you begin the process.

Teaching is a challenging art and science. Complicating matters are the incredibly fast-paced interactions between teachers and students as well as between students and students. Given the complex nature of classroom life (Jackson, 1990), tools for systematically recording classroom interactions are especially useful to assist teachers in understanding classroom behavior more fully and becoming aware of it (Good & Brophy, 2002). The use of observation instruments, however, has been criticized because of its presumed directive, behaviorist, and positivist orientation (e.g., Eisner, 1994). We heartily agree that use of observation instruments is problematic when directly connected to evaluation. We believe that "life in classrooms" is context bound, situationally determined, and complex. The supervisor is not and should not be the overseer or prescriber but rather the guide, facilitator, or collaborator. Relying on enhanced communication and shared understandings, the supervisor can effectively use observation instruments to encourage interpersonal and collegial relationships.

A major assumption of this chapter is that judicious use of reliable and easy-to-use observation techniques can increase a teacher's awareness of classroom behavior. Moreover, we would be negligent if we didn't include observation instrumentation in a volume devoted to instructional improvement. Through the use of these observation tools and techniques, supervisors and others involved with the supervision process will work more ably with teachers to improve instruction and, hence, promote student achievement.

Another major assumption in this chapter is that instructional improvement is best encouraged through instructional dialogue. Supervision, as a reflective process, is essentially concerned with enhancing teacher thought and commitment to improving instruction. Through the use of observation instruments, supervisors or those concerned with supervision are able to promote such improvement.

Many books or parts of books are devoted to describing various observation instruments, strategies, and techniques (e.g., Acheson & Gall, 1997; Boehm & Weinberg, 1997; Borich, 2002; Pajak, 2000; Willerman et al., 1991). From our experience, we have found that some of these systems are difficult to implement. We have selected for this chapter only those observation tools and techniques that we have personally experienced as easy to implement and effective toward promoting that all-important instructional conversation between supervisors and teachers.[1]

> **Microlab**
>
> *Think of different kinds of observation instruments or strategies you have personally experienced. Which seemed most effective? Which seemed least effective? What did you learn from these experiences? What was the impact on students?*

We should note again that many observation instruments are not discussed in this chapter. The reader interested in an overview of other systems should consult Pajak (2000). We also strongly encourage you to develop new tools or adapt the ones we have included to meet your specific needs.

You can view additional tools by clicking on the following link: http://www.naeyc.org/. This link will connect you to the site of the National Association for the Education of Young Children where you will find many reproducible forms to be used as observation tools.

After you access the site, type the words *self study* at the search bar, click on the first option (Self-Study Resources—National Association for the Education . . .), and select Complete Observation Tool under Tools for Self Assessment. This form offers you a tool that can be used for overall assessment.

This chapter begins with a transcript of an actual sixth-grade lesson that will be referred to throughout the chapter. Quantitative and qualitative observation instruments highlight the remainder of the chapter. Each instrument is discussed in detail, and completed examples are provided for implementation in the chapter, and practice sheets can be found in Appendix D. Reflective practice activities will enhance your skill development.

SUPERVISION SCENARIO

Mario Tommasi has just completed his advanced certificate program at a local college and received his state certification as a school administrator and supervisor. A teacher for 10 years, Mario applies to a nearby township for a vice principalship. The board is impressed with his extensive teaching experience and letters of recommendation, as well as his keen insight into instructional improvement. Mario is hired.

The school to which he is assigned is William Heard Kilpatrick Middle School, which has a population of 1,200 pupils in Grades 6 through 8. The school is located in an urban section of the Northeast, and the ethnic makeup of the student body is 45% African American, 40% Hispanic American, 10% Asian American, and 5% others. Mario discovers that teacher morale is quite low, in large measure due to the autocratic practices of the former vice principal, who used strict traditional methods of teacher evaluation and frequently observed teachers without notice. The former supervisor would write lengthy, albeit well-written reports criticizing the teachers' methods and urging them to comply with his recommendations.

Mario is sympathetic toward their resentment of the supervisory practices they have experienced. Initially, he decides to establish rapport with his teachers.

He begins by communicating a vision. He acts in a manner that is representative of an inclusive leader; he listens, validates teachers' feelings, includes teachers in the decision-making process, and collaborates. He sets goals that meet the needs of both supervisor and teachers.

Once trust in the form of a collegial relationship is established, he believes that instructional matters, such as observation and the improvement of teacher performance, will follow naturally.

Six months pass, and Mario feels proud of the rapport and mutual respect he has developed with his teachers. Teachers, too, are happy that the former assistant principal is gone, and they consider Mario to be congenial, articulate, and trustworthy. Mario is ready to model instruction.

At a recent sixth-grade conference, Mario presents an overview of his supervisory approach: "Student achievement can be enhanced only when we, as colleagues, discuss matters of instruction in an open, forthright manner." Mario continues,

The first step toward instructional improvement is for us to describe what is happening in the classroom when we teach. I'd like to present several observation tools and techniques that can help us begin to dialogue about instruction in a nonjudgmental, cooperative way. I'd like to introduce some of these tools to you and then conduct a demonstration lesson in which you will have the opportunity to observe me. You can use any of these techniques you want.

Teachers enthusiastically listen to Mario, and several teachers welcome him into their classrooms.

Over the course of the next year and a half, Mario makes great progress in demonstrating that supervision is less about highlighting teacher deficiencies and more about collegial discussion of instructional matters. Both the principal and associate superintendent remark that a "culture of improvement" is clearly evident in the sixth grade. Teacher morale is high, pupil behavior is markedly improved, and test scores are on the rise.

Not all teachers, however, are partaking of Mario's "quiet revolution" at Kilpatrick Middle School. Clara Weingarten, a tenured social studies teacher with more than 28 years of classroom experience, is conspicuously absent during Mario's many staff development sessions and instructional workshops. At a recent afterschool faculty conference, however, she lamented the change in the student body, claiming that "these kids today aren't the same as before. They're rowdy, lazy, and disrespectful of authority."

Clara, realizing Mario's growing popularity and effectiveness, finally confides to him that she is at her wits' end. "Can you help?" she asks Mario in a genuine manner. Mario and Clara meet several times during her prep periods to discuss not only instructional strategies but the changing student population and demographics of the community. Their informal chats continue over the next several weeks. Discussions include many different topics, such as observation techniques and teaching strategies. They share their experiences and expertise. Fully cognizant of the fact that Clara has 18 more years of teaching experience than he, Mario nevertheless suggests one day that Clara tape-record a lesson on her own. Never having done so, she could then listen to the tape recording, and if she feels she would like "another ear," she is free to call on him. Call on Mario she does. After listening to the tape, Mario feels it wise to transcribe the tape before he meets with Clara.

The transcription follows (visual descriptions are added to enhance readability):

> **Reflection**
>
> *Can you think of other ways to build trust and confidence with teachers? What do you think of Mario's approach to supervision?*

Class: Sixth grade; 16 girls and 16 boys; reading scores are on grade level

Teacher: Clara Weingarten, tenured with 28 years of experience

Description of room: Movable desks are arranged in concentric arcs for this lesson. Student work is exhibited around the room with headings for each topic. A daily plan is outlined on the right panel of the chalkboard. A map of the world is hanging from the center of the wall above the chalkboard.

(Continued)

(Continued)

Curriculum area: Social studies

Topic: The United Nations; lesson in current events given on December 10, 2005

Mrs. Weingarten:	What famous place in New York City is having its 60th birthday this year?
Ronald:	(volunteering) The United Nations.
Mrs. Weingarten:	What do you think we should discuss about the United Nations in class today?
Juanita:	(volunteering) Where it's located?
Warren:	(calling out) What it's supposed to do?
Mrs. Weingarten:	Class, what is it supposed to do?

(At this point she writes on the board: "Can the United Nations Prevent War?")

Huan:	(volunteering) I visited the U.N. with my class when I was in the fourth grade in the school that I came from.
Mrs. Weingarten:	What did you see there?
Huan:	It was a tall, flat building with a lot of windows. There was a smaller, round building, too.
Kevin:	I saw the Assembly on television when the president spoke to them on the 60th birthday of the U.N. It was on a news program.
Mrs. Weingarten:	Good. But let's get back to the question I wrote on the board at the beginning of the lesson.

(She asks the class to read the question aloud, which they do.)

Jessie:	(raising his hand) When countries want to go to war, they talk about it in the Assembly. I guess then they vote on what to do about it in the Security Council.
Natasha:	(raising her hand) But when Russia and the United States talk to each other about keeping the peace, they don't speak to each other at the United Nations. Like at Geneva. I saw that on television, too!
Mrs. Weingarten:	That's an excellent observation, Natasha. Class, what's the answer we could give for Natasha's question? (No one responds.) Because problems can be settled in many ways, including the United Nations. (pause) So what do we know about the United Nations? Do you think it can really prevent World War III?
Susan:	(volunteering) Yes, when it gets countries who want to go to war to stop.
Mrs. Weingarten:	That's right, when it gets countries that want to go to war to stop.
George:	(raising his hand) So how come Israel was at war with the Arabs? And what about Bosnia and other places?
Mrs. Weingarten:	Yes, but it's still not World War III. (pointing to the question on the chalkboard) Let's see whether we can answer this question today. How can we go about doing this?
Warren:	(volunteering) Well, we've had World War I and World War II, but so far we haven't had World War III.
Mrs. Weingarten:	Very good. World War I happened between 1914 and 1918, and World War II took place between 1939 and 1945. How do you know that World War II ended in 1945? We have all been given a clue to this question at the beginning of this lesson today.

(Teacher looks around the room, waits a short while, with no response forthcoming.) Because it was 60 years ago. Don't you remember what we talked about at the beginning of the lesson? (raising her voice) What did we talk about? Let's try to summarize what we have spoken about up to now.

Kevin: (volunteering) The United Nations is 60 years old this year.

Mrs. Weingarten: Rochelle, can you tell us what that means?

Rochelle: I don't know.

Mrs. Weingarten: It means that the United Nations got started at the end of World War II to make sure that World War III would never happen.

Tim: (raising his hand) How can they do that?

Mrs. Weingarten: They have two sections—the Security Council and the General Assembly. Their job is to try to make sure that we don't have World War III. (She then writes "Security Council" and "General Assembly" on the board.) Does anyone know how many members there are in the Security Council?

Tatiana: (volunteering) Russia and the United States, because they are the two biggest nations and they are the ones that could start World War III by attacking each other. I heard someone say that on television.

Mrs. Weingarten: No, there are 15 members in the Security Council, and 5 of them are there permanently, forever. The other 10 get elected by the General Assembly from time to time. The General Assembly has all the members, 159, each one of them having one vote. (pause) Class, class, which one—the General Assembly or the Security Council—votes on preventing war? Paul, we haven't heard from you yet.

Paul: I guess it's the General Assembly, because all the members are in it.

Mrs. Weingarten: No, it's the Security Council, because 5 of the 15 members are the great nations: the United States, Russia, China, England, and France. (She writes these countries' names on the board under the title "Permanent Members of the United Nations.") If one of these five says, "No," the United States can't take action against a nation that is making trouble. That is called the veto power. (pause)

Here is an assignment to be done at home. I want you to look through newspapers and magazines and clip pictures and articles about the United Nations. You have one week to do this, and next Monday, when we have our next weekly current events lesson, we'll go over your clippings. You see, there is much more to learn about what the United Nations has done for the world. There are many other things it gets into besides trying to keep the peace. (pause)

Now, let's sum up what we learned today.

Vivian: That the United Nations could stop World War III before it begins.

Mrs. Weingarten: Thank you. Good. Now, let's turn to the homework that was assigned to you last night. Take out your textbooks, as well as your homework.

Microlab

How do you think the former assistant principal would have handled the feedback conference with Clara? What would he have said?

How do you think Mario will handle the feedback conference with Clara? What will he say? What concrete steps would he take to engage this teacher in instructional dialogue for improvement?

How would you handle the feedback conference?

Analysis

Based on our view of supervision, we maintain that Mario is not likely to make subjective judgments about Clara's style of teaching. She has been reluctant to engage in instructional improvement discussions, but now, for the first time she has requested some assistance. Mario sees this as an invaluable opportunity to encourage this teacher to become more reflective about her teaching practice. His goal is to facilitate Clara's reflection on her lesson—to focus more on her lesson aim, questioning techniques, or motivational strategies rather than attributing student lack of motivation and achievement to demographic changes in the community.

The next step Mario takes is to enable Clara to become aware of how her behavior and teaching style contribute to her classroom effectiveness. Mario realizes that this experienced teacher will view any feedback he might offer with suspicion and, possibly, resentment.

> **Reflection**
>
> *How would you recommend that Mario approach Clara? Would you use audiotapes? Why or why not? What other ways could the tapes be used?*

Seeing a film or listening to an audiotape of oneself teaching is certainly an eye-opening experience. If you haven't had the opportunity to do so recently, we suggest you do.

Practice

Tape-record or videotape your next lesson and listen to the tape or watch the video at home. What's your reaction? After you get over the initial shock, listen to or watch the tape the following week. Imagine that this lesson was not your own. What aspects of the lesson were effective and which areas need improvement? What strategies would you employ to enable this teacher to help herself or himself? Record your reflections and share them in small groups in class. Please note that after you read the later chapters in this book, you'll have a better idea of how to analyze your lesson. Still, this activity is useful at this point.

Watching a video or listening to an audiotape of your lesson, however, may not be very productive. Interactions in the lesson occur too quickly and are too complex for you or anyone else to pick up teaching subtleties such as effective use of wait time, number of higher-level questions asked, or distribution of questions to all ethnic groups in the class. We believe that videos and audiotapes are useful to enhance instructional improvement only if specific teaching behaviors can be highlighted, analyzed, and discussed.

Being familiar with the use of various observation tools and techniques, Mario encourages Clara to choose an observation tool to increase her awareness of what is occurring in her classroom. The ultimate goal is for Clara to be able to monitor herself.

Before Clara is able to become self-monitoring, she will have to learn how to collect data, know what behaviors to look for, and have a conceptual framework to guide her analysis. The remainder of this chapter is devoted to introducing observation instruments that Mario could use with Clara, or with any teacher for that matter. Each observation tool is presented, applied to Clara's lesson, if applicable, and practiced through the use of reflective activities and practice sessions.

Before we introduce and explicate each tool, several guiding principles about observation should be kept in mind:

Figure 3.1 Ten Guidelines of Observations

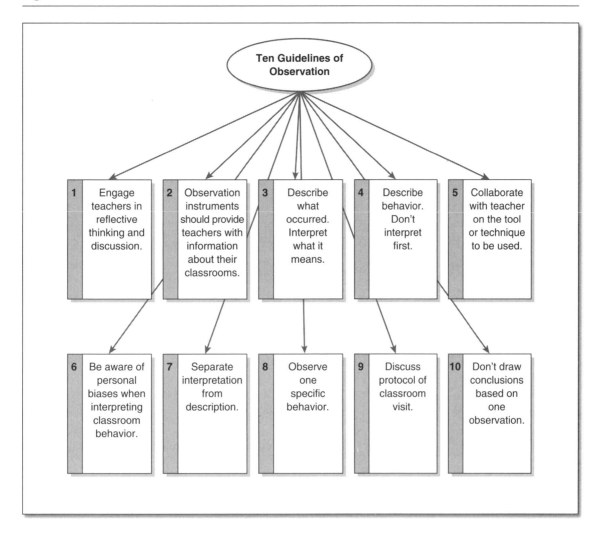

THIRTY-TWO TOOLS AND TECHNIQUES FOR OBSERVATION

As we mentioned earlier, many excellent observation systems exist. Our intention is not to review all the systems for observation; rather, it is to introduce those tools for observation that we personally have used and think can be incorporated easily into almost any classroom situation. The teachers in our classes constantly adapt the tools provided and create new ones, often during the planning conference in collaboration with the teachers they are observing for the course.

Two major categories of observation tools exist: quantitative and qualitative. *Quantitative* approaches reveal the *number* and the ratios of teacher-student behaviors; *qualitative* approaches reveal the *nature* of the observed behaviors. In other words, one category of tools reduces data into fixed or preestablished groups, and the other category describes a situation so that common themes may emerge. In fact, we sometimes offer a qualitative and a quantitative tool for the same focus.[2]

Both approaches are valid. Each provides a different and unique lens to view a situation or a classroom. Look at Figure 3.2. What do you see? . . . Ah, so there may be more to "see" and "understand" from a different perspective! Well, that's what each approach offers—just a different, not better, perspective from which to view a classroom.

Figure 3.2   Do you see a musician or a girl's face?

From Girl or Musician, http://www.sandeepkejriwal.com/illusions.htm. Used with permission.

Table 3.1 provides an outline of the tools and techniques we discuss next.

QUANTITATIVE OBSERVATION TOOLS

There are several types of assessment instruments that fall under the umbrella of quantitative tools; for example, categorical frequency, performance indicator, visual diagramming, and tailored.

Categorical frequency tools define certain events or behaviors that can be checked off at frequency intervals and counted. Tables 3.2 through 3.5 are examples of categorical frequency tools.

Performance indicator tools allow the observer to record whether or not an action or activity listed on the instrument has been observed. Tables 3.6 through 3.8 are examples of performance indicator tools.

Visual diagramming tools portray what happens visually in the classroom. The use of videotaping and audiotaping are particularly useful here to provide visual and/or auditory evidence. Look at Figures 3.3 and 3.4 for visual diagramming tools.

Table 3.1 Summary of Observation Tools

Tool #	Table or Figure	Description of Tool
Quantitative Tools		
1	Table 3.2	Teacher Verbal Behaviors
2	Table 3.3	Teacher Questions Using Bloom's Taxonomy
3	Table 3.4	Teacher Questions Using Webb's Depth of Knowledge
4	Table 3.5	Student On-Task and Off-Task Behaviors
5	Table 3.6	Gardner's Multiple Intelligences
6	Table 3.7	Hunter's Steps in Lesson Planning
7	Table 3.8	Johnson and Johnson's Cooperative Learning Criteria
8	Table 3.9	Group Performance: Assessment of Individual Participation
9	Figure 3.3	Diagram of Verbal Interactions
10	Figure 3.4	Diagram of Teacher Space Utilization
	Figure 3.5	Diagram of Student Space Utilization
11	Figure 3.6	Feedback
12	Table 3.10	Teacher-Pupil Interaction
13	Table 3.11	Indicators of Culturally Diverse Learners
14	Table 3.12	Strategies for Diverse Learners
15	Table 3.13	Accommodations and Modifications for English Language Learners
16	Table 3.14	The Differentiated Classroom
17	Table 3.15	Guided Reading
18	Table 3.16	Read-Aloud/Story Time
19	Table 3.17	National Council of Teachers of Mathematics (NCTM) Standard 3—Geometry
20	Table 3.18	National Council of Teachers of Mathematics (NCTM) Process Standards (Standards 6–10)
21	Table 3.19	Teacher Behaviors Keyed to Accountable Talk
22	Table 3.20	Student Behaviors Keyed to Accountable Talk
Qualitative Tools		
23		Detached Open-Ended Narrative
24		Participant Open-Ended Observation
25		Child-Centered Learning Observation

(Continued)

(Continued)

Tool #	Table or Figure	Description of Tool
26	Table 3.21	Nonverbal Techniques
27		Questioning Techniques
28		Strategies for Diverse Learners
29		Differentiated Instruction
30	Table 3.22	Guided Reading
31		Team Teaching in the Inclusion or General Education Classroom
32		Classroom Assessment in the Differentiated Classroom

Summary of Observation Tools by Focus

I. Categorical Frequency Tools

 1. Teacher Verbal Behaviors (Table 3.2)
 2. Teacher Questions Using Bloom's Taxonomy (Table 3.3)
 3. Teacher Questions Using Webb's Depth of Knowledge (Table 3.4)
 4. Student On-Task and Off-Task Behaviors (Table 3.5)

II. Performance Indicator Tools

 5. Gardner's Multiple Intelligences (Table 3.6)
 6. Hunter's Steps in Lesson Planning (Table 3.7)
 7. Johnson and Johnson's Cooperative Learning Criteria (Table 3.8)
 8. Group Performance: Assessment of Individual Participation (Table 3.9)

III. Visual Diagramming Tools

 9. Diagram of Verbal Interactions (Figure 3.3)
 10. Diagram of Teacher or Student Space Utilization (Figures 3.4 and 3.5)

IV. Tailored Tools

 11. Feedback (Figure 3.6)
 12. Teacher-Pupil Interaction (Table 3.10)
 13. Indicators of Culturally Diverse Learners (Table 3.11)
 14. Strategies for Diverse Learners (Table 3.12)
 15. Accommodations and Modifications for English Language Learners (Table 3.13)
 16. The Differentiated Classroom (Table 3.14)
 17. Guided Reading (Table 3.15)
 18. Read-Aloud/Story Time (Table 3.16)
 19. National Council of Teachers of Mathematics (NCTM) Standard 3—Geometry (Table 3.17)
 20. National Council of Teachers of Mathematics (NCTM) Process Standards (Standards 6–10) (Table 3.18)
 21. Teacher Behaviors Keyed to Accountable Talk (Table 3.19)
 22. Student Behaviors Keyed to Accountable Talk (Table 3.20)

V. Qualitative Approaches

 23. Detached Open-Ended Narrative
 24. Participant Open-Ended Observation

25. Child-Centered Learning Observation
26. Nonverbal Techniques (Table 3.21)
27. Questioning Techniques
28. Strategies for Diverse Learners
29. Differentiated Instruction
30. Guided Reading (Table 3.22)
31. Team Teaching in the Inclusion or General Education Classroom
32. Classroom Assessment in the Differentiated Classroom

VI. The Differentiated Classroom

5. Gardner's Multiple Intelligences (Table 3.6)
13. Indicators of Culturally Diverse Learners (Table 3.11)
14. & 27. Strategies for Diverse Learners (Table 3.12)
15. Accommodations and Modifications for English Language Learners (Table 3.13)
31. Team Teaching in the Inclusion or General Education Classroom
32. Classroom Assessment in the Differentiated Classroom

VII. Student-Centered Tools

4. Student On-Task and Off-Task Behaviors (Table 3.5)
8. Group Performance: Assessment of Individual Participation (Table 3.9)
10. Diagram of Student Space Utilization (Figure 3.5)
22. Student Behaviors Keyed to Accountable Talk (Table 3.20)
25. Child-Centered Learning Observation

VIII. Math and Literacy Tools

16. & 28. Guided Reading (Tables 3.15, 3.22)
18. Read-Aloud/Story Time (Table 3.16)
19. National Council of Teachers of Mathematics Standard 3—Geometry (Table 3.17)
20. National Council of Teachers of Mathematics Process Standards (Standards 6–10) (Table 3.18)

IX. Questioning Tools

2. Teacher Questions Using Bloom's Taxonomy (Table 3.3)
3. Teacher Questions Using Webb's Depth of Knowledge (Table 3.4)
27. Questioning Techniques

Note: All of the other tools and techniques are either teacher centered or interactions between students and teachers.

Practice

Using any of the tools,

- Find a colleague who will allow you to observe him or her for at least 15 minutes.
- Choose a chart together and keep a record of the results.
- Share the information with your colleague.
- What was his or her reaction?
- How did you find the experience of actually using the tool?
- What did you learn?
- Will you make any changes in your own instructional practices based on what you have learned?

Tailored tools are those that are specially developed based on a teacher's unique concerns. The teacher, in other words, wants the observer to focus on a specific area or areas. See Figures 3.5 and 3.6 for examples.

Tool 1: Teacher Verbal Behaviors

Materials. A watch with a second hand; a Teacher Verbal Behaviors chart (see Table 3.2).

Explanation. Supervisor and teacher collaboratively develop a list of no more than seven teacher behaviors that will be checked off as they occur at frequency intervals of, for example, 1 minute. In Table 3.2, seven teacher behaviors have been agreed upon: information giving, questioning, teacher answering own questions, praising, direction giving, correcting, and reprimanding. You'll notice that during

Table 3.2 Teacher Verbal Behaviors

Class: 3-1

Date: 5/10

Time began: 9:25

Time ended: 9:41

Min.	Information Giving	Questioning	Teacher Answering Own Questions	Praising	Giving Direction	Correcting	Reprimanding
1	X	X	X			X	
2	X	X			X		
3		X			X		X
4	X			X	X		X
5	X				X		
6		X				X	
7	X						
8	X	X			X		
9							X
10	X						
11	X				X	X	

Min.	Information Giving	Questioning	Teacher Answering Own Questions	Praising	Giving Direction	Correcting	Reprimanding
12							X
13							X
14	X						
15	X		X				
16	X				X		

Source: C. D. Glickman, S. P Gordon, and J. Ross-Gordon, *SuperVision and Instructional Leadership: A Developmental Approach* (6th ed.). Copyright © 2004 by Allyn & Bacon. Reprinted/adapted by permission.

the first minute, the teacher gave information, questioned, answered her own questions, and reprimanded. Note that the frequency of each behavior is not recorded, merely the fact that the teacher behavior occurred within the time frame.

Postnote. Note that the observer and teacher may collaboratively decide on any kind of teacher verbal behavior, not just the ones listed in Table 3.2. Also, some teachers and observers like to note student questions to ascertain teacher-student interaction. Some observers prefer checking the total number of behaviors over a time period, not just checking if a behavior occurred during brief intervals during a time period.

Tool 2: Teacher Questions Using Bloom's Taxonomy

Materials. A watch; a Teacher Questions Using Bloom's Taxonomy chart (Table 3.3).

Special Prerequisite Knowledge. Familiarity with Bloom's Taxonomy. Click on the following link to learn more about Bloom's Taxonomy: http://projects.coe .uga.edu/epltt/index.php?title=Bloom%27s_Taxonomy#Revised_Bloom.27s_ Taxonomy_.28RBT.29.

Explanation. Supervisor and teacher collaboratively decide to focus on only the number and quality of questions posed during a specified time period. In the case presented in Table 3.3, both teacher and supervisor agree that Bloom's Taxonomy will be used as the principal guide. The six levels of Bloom's revised Taxonomy are listed: remembering, understanding, applying, analyzing, evaluating, and creating. A tally is kept for each instance in which a question is posed. The observer listens to the question and decides into which of Bloom's categories the tally mark should be made. If your knowledge of Bloom's Taxonomy is rusty, the aforementioned Internet site and several others can refresh your and the teacher's memory. Just Google "Bloom's Taxonomy." Bring to the observation a copy of the categories, their definitions, and sample questions. At the completion of the observation, totals are computed and percentages are calculated, as noted

Bloom's Original Taxonomy	**Bloom's New Taxonomy**
Level 6: Evaluation	Level 6: Creating
Level 5: Synthesis	Level 5: Evaluating
Level 4: Analysis	Level 4: Analyzing
Level 3: Application	Level 3: Applying
Level 2: Comprehension	Level 2: Understanding
Level 1: Knowledge	Level 1: Remembering
(Level 1 is the lowest level)	(Level 1 is the lowest level)

From http://www.odu.edu/educ/roverbau/Bloom/blooms_taxonomy.htm. Used with permission.

Table 3.3 Teacher Questions Using Bloom's Taxonomy

Class: 7-2

Date: 3/11

Time began: 10:15

Time ended: 10:45

Number of questions asked: 24

Question Category	Tally 5 min.	Tally 10 min.	Tally 15 min.	Total	Percent	Comments
Creating				0	0	Where could you have developed creative questions?
Evaluating		✓✓		2	.08	Discuss placement of evaluation questions.
Analyzing				0	0	Discuss possible analysis questions and where they could be placed.
Applying	✓✓✓	✓✓✓	✓✓	8	.33	How could some of these become analyzing questions?
Understanding	✓✓✓	✓✓	✓✓✓	8	.33	How could some of these be made higher-level questions?
Remembering	✓✓✓	✓✓	✓	6	.25	How could some of these be made higher-level questions?

Source: C. D. Glickman, S. P. Gordon, and J. Ross-Gordon, *SuperVision and Instructional Leadership: A Developmental Approach* (6th ed.). Copyright © 2004 by Allyn & Bacon. Reprinted/adapted by permission.

in Table 3.3. Note that the frequency of each type of question is recorded, but the question itself is not. In addition, many teachers and observers want to observe if there is a progression in the level of questioning during the time period. If the teacher prefers a running record of each question posed and/or a record of the progression in the level of questioning, a tape recorder could be used.

Tool 3: Teacher Questions Using Webb's Depth of Knowledge

Materials. A watch; a Teacher Questions Using Webb's Depth of Knowledge chart (Table 3.4).

Special Prerequisite Knowledge. Familiarity with Webb's Depth of Knowledge. To view an interesting Depth of Knowledge chart, click on the following link: www.dese.mo.gov/divimprove/sia/msip/DOK_Chart.pdf.

Explanation. Supervisor and teacher collaboratively decide to focus on only the number and quality of questions posed during a specified time period. In the case presented in Table 3.4, both teacher and supervisor agree that Webb's Depth of Knowledge will be used as the principal guide. Four of Webb's levels are listed: recall, basic application of skill/concept, strategic thinking, and extended thinking. A tally is kept for each instance in which a question is posed. The observer listens to the question and decides into which of Webb's categories the tally mark should be made. If your knowledge of Webb's Depth of Knowledge is rusty, the above-mentioned site and several other Internet sites can refresh your and the teacher's memory. Just Google "Webb's Depth of Knowledge." Bring to the observation a copy of the categories, their definitions, and sample questions. At the completion of the observation, totals are computed and percentages are calculated, as noted in

Table 3.4 Teacher Questions Using Webb's Depth of Knowledge

Class: 7-1

Date: 5/21

Time began: 11:20

Time ended: 11:50

Question Category	Tally 5 min.	Tally 10 min.	Tally 15 min.	Total	Percent	Comments
Extended Thinking		✓✓	✓✓	4	.15	What additional questions would result in extended thinking?
Strategic Thinking				0	0	What kind of question would have resulted in strategic thinking, and where in the lesson would you have put it?

(Continued)

Table 3.4 (Continued)

Question Category	Tally 5 min.	Tally 10 min.	Tally 15 min.	Total	Percent	Comments
Basic Applications of Skill/Concept	✓✓✓✓✓	✓✓✓	✓	10	.35	How could some of these become strategic thinking questions?
Recall	✓✓✓✓✓	✓✓✓	✓✓✓✓	14	.50	How could these be made higher-level questions?

Table 3.4. Note that the frequency of each type of question is recorded, but the question itself is not. In addition, many teachers and observers want to observe if there is a progression in the level of questioning during the time period. If the teacher prefers a running record of each question posed and/or a record of the progression in the level of questioning, a tape recorder could be used.

Reflect and Practice

Activity. Refer back to the lesson transcript at the beginning of this chapter. Using the Teacher Questions chart, record the *level* of Clara's questions using either Bloom's Taxonomy or Webb's Depth of Knowledge Categories. You can also choose to record her Verbal Behaviors. Discuss your findings with a colleague. Did your recordings match your colleague's observations?

Postnote. Note that this type of categorical frequency tool doesn't necessarily have to deal with teacher questions. Any behavior that can be tallied may be observed using this format. For a comparison of Bloom's Taxonomy and Webb's Depth of Knowledge categories, click on the following link: http://uwadmnweb.uwyo.edu/wyhpenet/WAHPERDhandouts/COGNITIVE%20COMPLEXITY.doc.

Tool 4: Student On-Task and Off-Task Behaviors

Materials. A watch with a second hand; a Student On-Task and Off-Task Behaviors chart (Table 3.5).

Special Prerequisite Skills. Although using Tool 2 or 3 is relatively easy without much practice, we suggest that you practice identifying student on-task and off-task behaviors (Tool 4) prior to actually using it in a classroom with a class. We suggest you memorize and practice using the key prior to any real observation.

Explanation. Supervisor and teacher collaboratively decide to focus on student on-task and off-task behaviors. A list of student names is made as noted in Table 3.5. The students' names are listed according to their seat order beginning from the front row or table and going down each row or table. The observer should be situated to the side of the front of the room. Because the observer will be seen readily by the students, we suggest that the observer come into the class a couple of times prior to the observation to sit up front and make believe that he or she is taking notes to acquaint students with the observer's presence.

Observations are made in 5-minute intervals (depending on the number of students observed). In our case, 15 students are being observed. Thus, each student will be watched for 20 seconds (5 minutes = 300 seconds divided by the number of total students being observed [15] = 20 seconds per student). In a large class, the novice observer may need to reduce the number of behaviors observed. Often, the teacher will choose to focus on a small number of specific students. The observer records what he or she sees using the key at the bottom of the chart. Again, familiarity with student on-task and off-task behaviors is essential for this technique to work properly. By the way, the precise on- and off-task behaviors also should be collaboratively developed between observer and teacher.

Table 3.5 Student On-Task and Off-Task Behaviors

Class: 3-2

Date: 9/9

Time when sweep began: 9:00

Time ended: 9:35

Student	9:00	9:05	9:10	9:15	9:20	9:25	9:30	9:35	Observations
Tania	A	A	A	A	A	A	O	A	
Manuel	A	A	A	A	A	O	A	A	
Vivian	A	TK	TK	A	A	TK	A	TK	
Nurit	O	O	P	P	OT	O	O	OT	
Joseph	OT	OT	A	P	A	A	P	P	
Michael	OT	OT	A	P	0	A	A	TK	
Loi	A	P	P	A	P	P	P	OT	
Helen	A	A	A	A	A	A	A	A	
Mari-Celi	A	A	A	A	O	A	A	A	
Wayne	P	P	A	A	P	P	O	O	
Virginia	P	A	A	A	P	A	A	A	

(Continued)

Table 3.5 (Continued)

Student	9:00	9:05	9:10	9:15	9:20	9:25	9:30	9:35	Observations
Colleen	O	A	A	A	TK	O	A	A	
Hajime	OT	OT	OT	OT	OT	OT	OT	OT	
Kahlid	TK	A	A	TK	TK	TK	A	A	
Maria	O	A	A	A	TK	A	A	A	

Key: A = at task; TK = talking (social); P = playing; O = out of seat; OT = off task

Source: C. D. Glickman, S. P. Gordon, and J. Ross-Gordon, *SuperVision and Instructional Leadership: A Developmental Approach* (6th ed.). Copyright © 2004 by Allyn & Bacon. Reprinted/adapted by permission.

Reflect and Practice

Our video *Supervision in Practice* has three classroom scenes that you can use to practice this and other techniques. The New Teacher Center in Santa Cruz, California, also has a number of classroom DVDs designed to foster the development of coaching and observation skills. Contact: products@newteachercenter.org for further information.

In addition, the Association for Supervision and Curriculum Development (1990) video *Another Set of Eyes* has a number of classroom scenes that you can use to practice this technique. You might also ask a colleague to videotape your own class. Practice and report your ability and comfort in using this technique.

Postnote. Note that this type of categorical frequency tool refers to student behavior, whereas the previous two formats referred only to teacher behavior. What are other examples of student behaviors for which this technique can be used?

Tool 5: Gardner's Multiple Intelligences

Materials. A performance indicator chart keyed to Gardner's nine intelligences (see Table 3.6).

Explanation. Well versed in Gardner's intelligences theory, both observer and observee have collaboratively decided to record the extent to which Gardner's intelligences are incorporated in a fifth-grade science lesson. A specified period of time to observe the lesson is agreed upon. The observer merely checks off whether or not the teacher addressed in any way each of Gardner's intelligences. The observer may comment on the nature or extent to which each intelligence was introduced and applied. Naturalistic and emotional intelligences are sometimes added to the list of multiple intelligences.

To learn more about Gardner's Multiple Intelligences or to find out what your own intelligence(s) is/are, click on: http://www.businessballs.com/howard gardnermultipleintelligences.htm.

Table 3.6 Gardner's Multiple Intelligences

Class: 3-310

Date: 6/28

Time: 1:15 p.m.

Elements	Response Yes	No	N/A	Observations
Logical/mathematical	☑	☐	☐	Mathematical equation examples on board
Bodily/kinesthetic	☐	☑	☐	No references made
Visual	☑	☐	☐	Overhead transparencies used
Musical	☐	☑	☐	No references made
Interpersonal	☑	☐	☐	Small-group work
Intrapersonal	☐	☑	☐	No references made
Linguistic	☑	☐	☐	Problem-solving examples
Naturalistic	☐	☑	☐	No references made
Emotional	☐	☑	☐	No references made

Source: C. D. Glickman, S. P. Gordon, and J. Ross-Gordon, *SuperVision and Instructional Leadership: A Developmental Approach* (6th ed.). Copyright © 2004 by Allyn & Bacon. Reprinted/adapted by permission.

Reflect and Practice

Postnote. Howard Gardner's theory is only one example for which a performance indicator tool may be applied. What is another example of how you might use this tool?

Tool 6: Hunter's Steps in Lesson Planning

Materials. A performance indicator chart keyed to Hunter's lesson plan steps (see Table 3.7).

Explanation. Well versed in Hunter's lesson plan model, both observer and observee have decided collaboratively to record the extent to which Hunter's steps are incorporated into a 12th-grade foreign-language lesson. A specified period of time to observe the lesson is agreed upon. The observer merely checks off whether or not the teacher in any way addressed each of Hunter's steps. The observer may comment on the nature or extent to which each of Hunter's steps were introduced and applied.

To read up on Hunter's Steps in Lesson Planning, click on: www.humboldt.edu/~tha1/hunter-eei.html.

Reflect and Practice

Postnote. Hunter's steps are applicable to many current classroom strategies. To which ones can you apply these steps?

Table 3.7   Hunter's Steps in Lesson Planning

Class: 10-406

Date: 5/18

Time: 11:15 a.m.

Elements	Response Yes	No	N/A	Comments
Anticipatory set	☐	☑	☐	No references made
Objective and purpose	☐	☑	☐	Unstated, unclear
Input	☑	☐	☐	Group discussion employed
Modeling	☐	☑	☐	No references made
Checking for understanding	☐	☑	☐	Teacher asked "Do you understand?" but did not check
Guided practice	☑	☐	☐	Teacher circulates
Independent practice	☑	☐	☐	Sample sheets distributed

Source: C. D. Glickman, S. P. Gordon, and J. Ross-Gordon, *SuperVision and Instructional Leadership: A Developmental Approach* (6th ed.). Copyright © 2004 by Allyn & Bacon. Reprinted/adapted by permission.

Tool 7: Johnson and Johnson's Cooperative Learning Criteria

Materials. A performance indicator chart keyed to the criteria applied to cooperative learning (see Table 3.8).

Explanation. Well versed in Johnson and Johnson's cooperative learning format, both observer and observee have decided collaboratively to record the extent to which the criteria of cooperative learning are incorporated in a 12th-grade foreign-language lesson. A specified period of time to observe the lesson is agreed upon. The observer merely checks off whether or not the teacher in any way addressed each of the cooperative learning criteria. The observer may comment on the nature or extent to which each cooperative learning criterion was introduced and applied. To read up on Johnson and Johnson's Cooperative Learning, click on: http://www.co-operation.org/.

Reflect and Practice

Postnote. We are providing only some examples for which a performance indicator tool may be applied. Can you think of another example for which this tool may be applicable?

Table 3.8 Johnson and Johnson's Cooperative Learning Criteria

Class: 4-417

Date: 3/15

Time: 9:15 a.m.

	Response			
Elements	*Yes*	*No*	*N/A*	*Comments*
Explanation of academic and social objectives	☐	☑	☐	No explanation of either occurred—just went into lesson
Teaching of social skills	☐	☑	☐	Teacher merely said, "Cooperate"—no instruction
Face-to-face interaction	☑	☐	☐	Students sitting quietly facing each other
Position interdependence	☑	☐	☐	One set of responses required from each group
Individual accountability	☐	☑	☐	None evident—teacher walked around classroom minimally
Group processing	☑	☐	☐	Students rated their performance

Source: C. D. Glickman, S. P. Gordon, and J. Ross-Gordon, *SuperVision and Instructional Leadership: A Developmental Approach* (6th ed.). Copyright © 2004 by Allyn & Bacon. Reprinted/adapted by permission.

Tool 8: Group Performance: Assessment of Individual Participation

Materials. A performance indicator chart keyed to individual performance in cooperative learning groups. The observer and observee have decided to record the extent to which the agreed-upon criteria of individual participation are incorporated into an elementary school class. A specific period of time to observe the groups is agreed upon. Specific students or groups may be targeted. The observer checks off the level of participation of the individual students and adds comments to situate the involvement of the student and clarify the quality of the interaction.

Reflect and Practice

Postnote. We are providing a cooperative learning context for this tool. Can you think of how you could modify this tool for another use in the classroom? How could the use of videos enhance or impede this observation?

Table 3.9   Group Performance: Assessment of Individual Participation

Student: Jamal

Class: 5-3

Date: 4/9

Time: 9:20–11

	Regularly	Sometimes	Rarely	Comments
A. Contribution to group goals				
1. Participates in the group's activities	X			
2. Does his or her share of work		X		Sometimes allows the more assertive students to control work
B. Staying on the topic				
3. Pays attention; listens	X			
4. Makes comments to help group get back on topic			X	Again, lets the more dominant students control
5. Stays on topic	X			
C. Offering useful ideas or information				
6. Gives helpful ideas & suggestions		X		
7. Offers helpful feedback & comments		X		Reticent to criticize
8. Influences group decisions & plans		X		
D. Consideration of others				
9. Makes positive, encouraging remarks about group members & their ideas			X	Reserved
10. Shows & expresses sensitivity to the feelings of others	X			Considerate of others
E. Involving, working, & sharing with others				
11. Tries to get the group working together to reach group agreements			X	Lets others lead the group
12. Considers the ideas of others; exchanges, rethinks, defends ideas		X		Participates at times
F. Communicating				
13. Speaks clearly; easy to hear & understand	X			When he participates, he speaks clearly, though softly
14. Expresses ideas clearly & effectively		X		Tries hard; seems to think before speaking

Source: Modified from the Connecticut State Department of Education; sponsored by the National Science Foundation.

Tool 9: Diagram of Verbal Interactions

Materials. A verbal interaction chart outlining the seating arrangement of the particular class being observed (see, for example, Figure 3.3).

Explanation. A specified period of time to observe the lesson is agreed upon. For purposes of analysis in this case, both supervisor and teacher have agreed on a 30-minute observation period. Six copies of Figure 3.3 in Resource D should be made for the observer to record verbal interactions in 5-minute increments, that is, one chart for *each* 5-minute period. Cross-hatching facilitates the recording of multiple interactions. One of our students effectively used multiple transparencies of the seating chart as overlays for each 5-minute interval. The clear plastic sheets can be superimposed later. She also used different colors of ink to represent each observation interval.

Each arrow indicates a complete statement directed to another individual, and the arrows are numbered in sequence. The observer should have extensive experience applying this technique so that recording can proceed smoothly and accurately. Figure 3.3 is provided as a training tool to interpret the verbal interaction provided.

Figure 3.3 Diagram of Verbal Interactions

Class: 10-517

Date: 11/15

Time: 10:15 a.m.

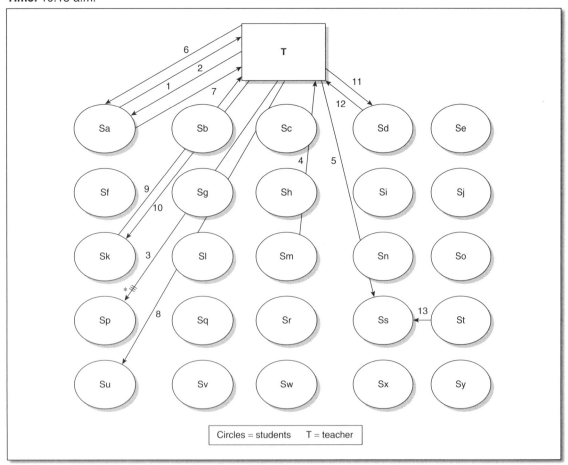

Source: C. D. Glickman, S. P. Gordon, and J. Ross-Gordon, *SuperVision and Instructional Leadership: A Developmental Approach* (6th ed.). Copyright © 2004 by Allyn & Bacon. Reprinted/adapted by permission.

Reflect and Practice

Postnote. How might the use of audiotaping assist or hinder interpretation of the nature of verbal interactions in a lesson?

Tool 10: Diagram of Teacher or Student Space Utilization

Materials. A teacher or student space utilization chart outlining the room arrangement of the particular class being observed (see, for example, Figures 3.4 and 3.5).

Explanation. A specified period of time to observe the lesson is agreed upon. The observer charts teacher or student movement around the room and, at the same time, records the times.

Site Practice

Find a colleague who will allow you to observe him or her or one of his or her students for an appropriate length of time. Using the Diagram of Space Utilization, keep a record of the teacher's or student's movements during the lesson. Share information with your colleague. What was her or his reaction? How did you find the experience of actually using this technique?

Figure 3.4   Diagram of Teacher Space Utilization

Class: 1.3

Date: 4/16

Time: 9:10–10:00

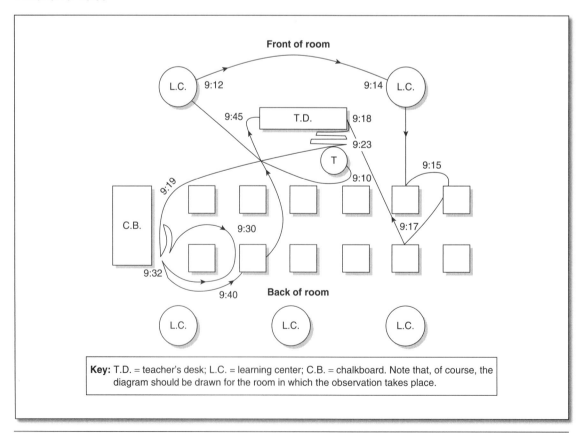

Postnote. How might the use of videos assist or hinder interpretation of the nature of teacher space utilization?

1. A gets pillow, puts it on his head, moves it to sling it over his shoulder, crawls on knees to bookshelf.

2. Stops at bookshelf, chooses a book, stands and walks back to corner.

3. Reads quietly for about 3 minutes.

4. Crouches on knees and slides back and forth, glances around and spots E, another student.

5. Stands and walks over to bookshelf next to E, throws his book into a book bin, and sits next to E. E moves to the rug with a book, A grabs one and follows.

6. A lays down next to E, who is reading and watches him read. E stands up and returns book. A crawls on knees toward the closet.

7. A lays down again with book. E rejoins him. A closes his book and reads the back cover, then looks at E as he reads. They begin whispering—many interchanges. They begin reading after about 4 minutes. Seven minutes later class is asked to do a reading response in individual reading logs.

8. A crawls on knees while hugging pillow. Three boys come and try to pry him from pillow. E comes to lay next to him on it. Three boys return to tug pillow. Teacher redirects. A still does not move. Two girls come and pull pillow away from A. A stays on rug, others leave.

9. A stands and goes to sit in corner of rug where other pillows are kept.

Figure 3.5   Diagram of Student Space Utilization

Class: 3-402
Date: April 18
Start Time: 9:05
End Time: 9:35

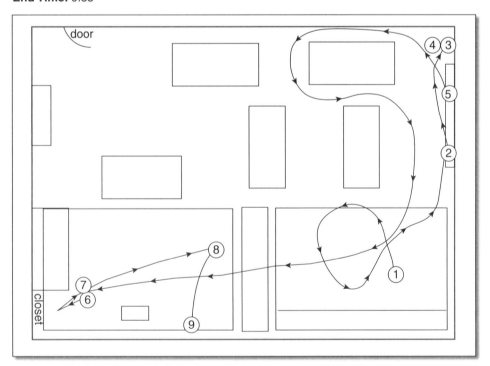

Source: Hillary Barranco-Casado, a NYC teacher and leadership candidate, adapted the form for student space utilization.

Tool 11: Feedback

Materials. A feedback chart outlining the seating arrangement of the particular class being observed (see, for example, Figure 3.6).

Explanation. A specified period of time to observe the lesson is agreed upon. At a planning conference, the teacher informs you that he or she is interested in whether or not he or she prompts, probes, and encourages student responses. He or she is also interested in how often positive reinforcement is used and how often pupils' responses are discouraged. A key then is developed collaboratively by the observer and the observee during the planning conference. Once categories and the key are approved, the observation may be scheduled.

A reproducibile version of Figure 3.6 is provided in Resource D as a training tool for interpreting the recorded feedback.

Figure 3.6   Feedback

Class: 5.2

Date: 9/27

Time: 2:20–3:00

D,D,Pr	Pr,D,D	E,Pb,Pb,O	Pb,Pb,E,O
Jaime	**Renee**	**Peter**	**Michael**
D	Pb,E	D,D,Pr	D
Juan	**Natasha**	**Frances**	**William**

Key: Pr = prompted; Pb = probed; E = encouraged; O = positively reinforced; D = discouraged pupil

Reflect and Practice

Refer back to the lesson transcript at the beginning of this chapter. Create a tailor-made technique to ascertain some aspect of the quality of Clara's teaching style. Discuss your findings with a colleague. Did your recordings match your colleague's observations?

Postnote. Can you develop another chart that might be keyed to another concern a teacher might have?

Tool 12: Teacher-Pupil Interaction

Materials. A Teacher-Pupil Interaction chart (see, for example, Table 3.10).

Explanation. In this case, the teacher wants the observer to focus on an individual student. The teacher informs you that he or she is having difficulty with Steve. The teacher complains that Steve's behavior gets progressively worse during a lesson and that the teacher is at his (or her) wits' end. A specified period of time to observe the lesson is agreed upon. The observer observes and records the student's behavior as well as noting the teacher's reaction.

A reproducible version of Table 3.10 is provided in Resource D as a training tool for interpreting the teacher-student interaction during this particular lesson.

Table 3.10   Teacher-Pupil Interaction

Student: Steve

Teacher: Clara Weingarten

Date: 9/13

Time: 9:05–9:30

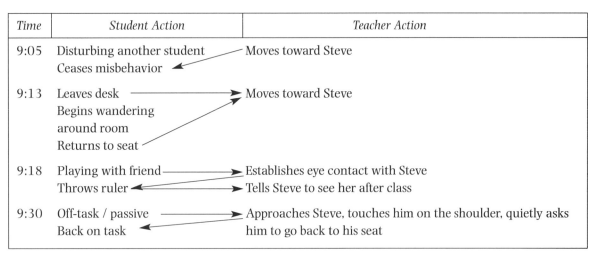

Time	Student Action	Teacher Action
9:05	Disturbing another student Ceases misbehavior	Moves toward Steve
9:13	Leaves desk Begins wandering around room Returns to seat	Moves toward Steve
9:18	Playing with friend Throws ruler	Establishes eye contact with Steve Tells Steve to see her after class
9:30	Off-task / passive Back on task	Approaches Steve, touches him on the shoulder, quietly asks him to go back to his seat

Source: C. D. Glickman, S. P. Gordon, and J. Ross-Gordon, *SuperVision and Instructional Leadership: A Developmental Approach* (6th ed.). Copyright © 2004 by Allyn & Bacon. Reprinted/adapted by permission.

Reflect and Practice

Postnote. How does this tool differ from the student space utilization tool? Compare the teacher's concerns in these two tools.

Tool 13: Indicators of Culturally Diverse Learners

As much of the predominantly English-speaking world becomes culturally and linguistically diverse, supervisors need to attend to teachers' awareness of this diversity and their efforts to address it in the classroom. The performance indicator instrument shown in Table 3.11 can form the basis for that discussion and even lead to appropriate professional development.

Table 3.11   Indicators of Culturally Diverse Learners

Class: 8-4

Date: 10/19

Time: 10:00–11:00

Teacher Indicator	Response			Comments
	Yes	No	N/A	
Displays understanding of diverse cultures	☑	☐	☐	Spoke to student before class about parents
Displays personal regard for students of diverse cultures	☑	☐	☐	
Uses instructional materials free of cultural bias	☐	☐	☑	
Uses examples and materials that represent different cultures	☑	☐	☐	Asked for analogous examples from different cultures
Promotes examination of concepts and issues from different cultural perspectives	☑	☐	☐	
Intervenes to address acts of student intolerance	☑	☐	☐	Addressed student teasing
Uses "teachable moments" to address cultural issues	☑	☐	☐	
Reinforces student acts of respect for diverse cultures	☑	☐	☐	Asks related questions about students' cultures

Source: C. D. Glickman, S. P. Gordon, and J. Ross-Gordon, *SuperVision and Instructional Leadership: A Developmental Approach* (6th ed.). Copyright © 2004 by Allyn & Bacon. Reprinted/adapted by permission.

Tool 14: Strategies for Diverse Learners

This tool has as a focus the teacher's strategies to reach all children in the classroom. It is applicable to all classrooms because diverse learners exist in any environment where people come together. Nonetheless, it is particularly pertinent to teachers who have students with disabilities integrated into the general population.

Table 3.12   Strategies for Diverse Learners

Class: 2-1

Date: 4/10

Time: 9:40–10:45

Teacher Indicator	Response			Examples
	Yes	No	N/A	
Proximity to students	☑	☐	☐	Constantly walks around room to check on individual students

Teacher Indicator	Response			Examples
	Yes	No	N/A	
Different ways of encouraging students	☑	☐	☐	Uses different vocabulary to praise
Positive reinforcement techniques	☑	☐	☐	See above
Modifications for individual children or types of learners	☑	☐	☐	Use of paraprofessional to adapt for individual children
Use of children's strengths	☑	☐	☐	Multiple intelligences integrated
Multiple ways in which lesson is unfolding	☑	☐	☐	See above
Integration of grouping according to needs and skills	☑	☐	☐	Changes grouping for different subject areas
Scaffolding of instruction	☐	☑	☐	Not apparent

Tool 15: Accommodations and Modifications for English Language Learners

Table 3.13   Accommodations and Modifications for English Language Learners

Class: ESL

Date: 3/10

Time: 11:05–11:30

Accommodation Modification	Was This Element Present?			What Is the Evidence?
	Yes	No	N/A	
Teacher talk is modified: slower speech, careful choice of words, idioms, expressions	☐	☑	☐	
Teacher allows wait time and monitors teacher input vs. student output	☐	☑	☐	Sometimes moves too quickly to next volunteer
Definitions and language are embedded in content/context	☐	☑	☐	
Real-world artifacts present that support comprehension	☑	☐	☐	Constant use of visuals—either real world or virtual
Elicits and draws on students' backgrounds to build prior knowledge	☑	☐	☐	Refers to home life and everyday USA experiences
Teacher uses nonverbal cues to support comprehension	☑	☐	☐	Uses hands a lot

Tool 16: The Differentiated Classroom

Materials: A performance indicator chart keyed to classroom characteristics of differentiated instruction. The observer and the observee have chosen to focus on which classroom activities differentiate instruction. It is preferable to observe the entire class. The observer describes the elements present during the lesson and comments on their absence or presence.

Explanation: Differentiated instruction takes place when teachers are aware and able to consider and deal with different learning needs and abilities of their students. The following chart contains many of the classroom activities that promote differentiated learning. No classroom can or should exhibit all of these characteristics at once, and others not included in the chart may be displayed.

Postnote: This tool is appropriate for most classrooms. Can you think of specialized classrooms where these activities might be particularly important?

Table 3.14   The Differentiated Classroom

Class: 3-11 Language Arts

Date: 5/14

Time: 1:30–2:15

Classroom Characteristics	*Presence of Element*			*Comments/Description*
	Yes	*No*	*N/A*	
1. Range of activities				
• whole-class instruction	☑	☐	☐	• Mini-lesson
• small-group activities (pairs, triads, quads)	☑	☐	☐	• Turn & talk at end of mini-lesson
• individualized activities (e.g., learning centers, independent study)	☑	☐	☐	• Independent reading while teacher conference with individual students
• student-teacher conferences	☑	☐	☐	
2. Students express themselves in diverse ways				
• artistically	☐	☑	☐	
• musically	☑	☐	☐	• Class sang a song related to read-aloud
• technologically	☑	☐	☐	• Some at computers during independent reading
• scientifically	☐	☑	☐	
• athletically	☑	☐	☐	• Stretching to song before independent work
• through drama/speeches	☐	☑	☐	
• traditional compositions	☐	☑	☐	
• building models	☐	☑	☐	
• other	☐	☑	☐	
3. Students construct meaning on their own; take responsibility for their own learning; plan activities on their own	☑	☐	☐	Children chose their independent activity

Classroom Characteristics	Presence of Element			Comments/Description
	Yes	No	N/A	
4. Learning activities are provided for students who complete work before others	☑	☐	☐	Children could choose multiple independent activities
5. Peer tutoring to reinforce more advanced learners and support less advanced	☐	☑	☐	Might be a suggestion for future independent work time
6. Different types of assessment are ongoing and integrated	☑	☐	☐	Teacher assesses during conferences; independent activities contain self-assessments

Tool 17: Guided Reading

Table 3.15 Guided Reading

Class: 2-3

Date: 5/5

Time: Literacy Block

Guided Reading Teacher Indicator	Yes	No	N/A	Comments/Examples
Management				
Was the transition from the mini-lesson to group work implemented in an orderly fashion?	☑	☐	☐	• Children for guided reading were told in advance that they would meet • Independent work and book exchange were addressed before splitting up into groups
Were the other children on task while the teacher was in small-group instruction?	☑	☐	☐	• Teacher did not have to interrupt group to attend to other students until the very end of session, after about a 45-minute period • Teacher left guided reading group while they were reading independently to walk around and monitor/ conference with others
Was the time allotted for the guided reading group appropriate?	☐	☑	☐	• Guided reading session lasted for 47 minutes • Recommended time is 15–20 minutes
Instruction (article for instruction: "Beverly Cleary")				
Was the text for guided reading introduced in a manner that provided knowledge? Was there support so that students could read independently and successfully?	☑	☐	☐	• Genre—a biographical article, columns, and how to read them • Activated prior to reading Beverly Cleary books • Nontext information—pictures, captions, lists

(Continued)

Table 3.15 (Continued)

Guided Reading Teacher Indicator	Yes	No	N/A	Comments/Examples
Instruction (article for instruction: "Beverly Cleary")				
Were the children interested in and did they grasp the concepts being taught?	☑	☑	☐	• Girls seemed more interested than boys • 3 out of 4 students were able to touch on the main idea
Was the text appropriate for the group with respect to the level, content, and interest?	☐	☑	☐	• Level seemed too difficult • Interest—boys were not as interested as girls
Were support, challenges, and opportunities for problem solving provided?	☑ ☐	☐ ☐	☐ ☑	• Support—text was introduced with a variety of strategies, main idea was finalized as a group, teacher led students through each paragraph to find details • Challenge—didn't seem appropriate. The text was challenging in itself as well as the activity
Did the students read independently?	☑	☐	☐	
Did assessment take place? What types?	☑	☐	☐	• Students wrote main idea in sentence form independently • Students highlighted details and were asked to justify their selections
Did the teacher allow students to be responsible for what they already know?	☐	☐	☑	
Did questions include the full range of Bloom's Taxonomy?	☑	☐	☐	• Knowledge • Comprehension • Evaluation—students had to support and justify answers
Did the teacher help students strengthen their strategies?	☑	☐	☐	• Students were asked to justify which details supported main idea. This developed the process behind the strategy. • Students were directed through each paragraph to break material into manageable chunks. This modeled how to approach the text. • Teacher told students how they can transfer what they did to other reading and writing

Source: This instrument was adapted from one that Suzanne Dimitri, a Brooklyn, N.Y., literacy coach, created. It is used with her permission.

Tool 18: Read-Aloud/Story Time

The following balanced literacy read-aloud tool is adapted from a tool that Lorraine Call, a preschool teacher on Staten Island, created. With slight adaptations, it can be used for any read-aloud lesson.

Table 3.16   Read Aloud/Story Time

Class: Pre-K   **Date:** 10/19   **Time:** 8:45

Title of book: *The Busy Little Squirrel*   **Author:** Nancy Tafuri

Type of book:

New words:

Other comments: Appropriate book choice and activities

Teacher Behaviors	Yes	No	N/A	Comments/Examples
Introduces book by showing cover and reading title. Encourages students to share thoughts about book based on these features.	☑	☐	☐	Teacher showed cover, asked who remembers what book about. Encourages with "What else?"
Reads name(s) of author and illustrator. Asks students to point to title, author, illustrator, and encourages discussion about these features.	☑	☐	☐	Teacher asks, "Who can tell me what the author does? What the illustrator does?"
Introduces at least three words that will be in story by showing cards with words and pictures representing them.	☑	☐	☐	Teacher covers picture part of word cards and asks who remembers the word. Then shows picture.
Attempts to capture/maintain students' interest. Uses facial expression and changes in tone, pitch, and so on to represent different characters and emphasize words or facts.	☑	☐	☐	Teacher uses loud and soft voice throughout. Hesitates when vocabulary word appears, allowing children to fill in word.
Involves children throughout the story by encouraging comments and questions.	☑	☐	☐	Asks other children if they know response to classmate's question "What's the squirrel doing?"
Asks open-ended questions, such as What if? What would you do if? and so on, and provides wait time. When voluntary responses are limited, initiates discussion of facts, plot and/or characters.	☑	☐	☐	Teacher asks, "What would you do if you were a squirrel?" "What do you think it feels like to roll around in those leaves?"
Involves children in extension activities by creating charts or other visuals, for example, T charts, story maps, word/character webs.	☑	☐	☐	Evidence of extension: leaf rubbings, fall collages, KWL chart about fall
Invites children to retell story in their own words (through pretending to read the book to the class, using puppets, etc.).	☐	☑	☐	

Tool 19: National Council of Teachers of Mathematics (NCTM) Standard 3

The mathematics tools included here are based on National Council of Teachers of Mathematics (NCTM) standards for school mathematics.

The NCTM Standards for School Mathematics are divided into two types. Standards 1 through 5 are known as content standards. These standards describe student outcomes along content lines (i.e., number and operations, algebra, geometry, measurement, and data analysis and probability). Since different content standards are emphasized in particular lessons and at certain grade levels, we provide an example of the application of outcomes for one content area: geometry. The supervisor and teachers can create similar performance indicator tools for each area.

Table 3.17   National Council of Teachers of Mathematics (NCTM) Standard 3—Geometry

Class: Sophomore Geometry Class

Date: 6/9

Time: 1:35

Students Can	Response Yes	No	N/A	Observations
Analyze characteristics and properties of two- and three-dimensional geometric shapes and develop mathematical arguments about geometrical relationships	☑	☐	☐	Students identified congruent triangles. They used sine function to determine the length of a side of the triangle.
Specify locations and describe spatial relationships using coordinate geometry and other representational systems	☑	☐	☐	Students determined the midpoint of a line segment, given the coordinates of its endpoints.
Apply transformations and use symmetry to analyze mathematical situations	☑	☐	☐	Students were able to reflect a triangle over the line $x = 0$.
Use visualization, spatial reasoning, and geometric modeling to solve problems	☐	☑	☐	Students had difficulty drawing a scale model of the floor plan of the classroom.

Note: We thank Judy Walsh, an instructor of math methods at the College of Staten Island, CUNY, and a former supervisor and teacher of mathematics, for her lead role in developing the math tools.

Tool 20: National Council of Teachers of Mathematics (NCTM) Process Standards (Standards 6–10)

Standards 6 through 10 are known as process standards. These standards describe student outcomes along process lines (i.e., problem solving, reasoning and proof, communication, connections, and representation). The categorical frequency tool can be used to record evidence of activities in the mathematics classroom that require students to engage in the process named. Each distinct activity should be counted only once in any given standard. However, an activity may meet several of the standards at the same time. For example, students working in cooperative groups may be meeting the problem-solving and communication standard.

Table 3.18   National Council of Teachers of Mathematics (NCTM) Process (Standards 6–10)

Class: Algebra 1

Date: 5/30

Time: 1:55

Activity Category	Tally	Total	Percentage
Problem solving	√√√√	5	25%
Reasoning and proof	√√√	4	20%
Communication	√√√	4	20%
Connections	√√	2	10%
Representation	√√√√	5	25%

Note: We thank Judy Walsh, an instructor of math methods at the College of Staten Island, CUNY, and a former supervisor and teacher of mathematics, for her lead role in developing the math tools.

Tool 21: Teacher Behaviors Keyed to Accountable Talk

A learning concept that has recently emerged from the accountability movement and cooperative learning is accountable talk. It is based on the principle that classroom talk that is accountable to the learning community and to the academic disciplines is essential to learning. The following observation tools are based on the four ways that student talk should be accountable: accountable to the community (polite listeners), accountable to knowledge (use evidence), accountable to standards of reasoning, and accountable to standards of reasoning appropriate to a subject area. For further information on accountable talk, contact the Institute for Learning at the Learning Research and Development Center at the University of Pittsburgh or click on the following link: http://www.teachersnetwork.org/tnli/research/achieve/Watson% 20%20072601.pdf.

Table 3.19   Teacher Behaviors Keyed to Accountable Talk

Class: 9-2

Date: 4/17/04

Time: Humanities Block

Teacher Indicators	*Response*			*Observations*
	Yes	*No*	*N/A*	
Engages students in talk by: • Providing opportunities for students to speak about content knowledge, concepts, and issues	☑	☐	☐	Teacher consistently waited for students to answer. You could see her thinking about the response. At the end of the class, group reflectors reported on the process in their groups.
• Using wait time/allowing silence to occur	☑	☐	☐	
• Listening carefully	☑	☐	☐	
• Providing opportunities for reflection on classroom talk	☑	☐	☐	
Assists students to listen carefully to each other by: • Creating seating arrangements that promote discussion	☑	☐	☐	The class reviewed the guidelines for discussion before going into circles of small groups where a reflector and facilitator were chosen. No time remained at the end of class to review group work.
• Providing clear expectations for how talk should occur	☑	☐	☐	
• Requiring courtesy and respect	☑	☐	☐	
• Reviewing major ideas and understandings from talk	☐	☑	☐	
Assists students to elaborate and build on others' ideas by: • Modeling reading processes of predicting, looking for key words, engaging prior knowledge, and so on	☑	☐	☐	The introductory whole-class discussion of the topic allowed the teacher to model the skills the students needed in their small-group discussions. She asked the class what reading process she had just used at least three times. No time to debrief about the discussions at the end of class.
• Facilitating rather than dominating the talk	☑	☐	☐	
• Listening carefully	☑	☐	☐	
• Asking questions about discussion ideas and issues	☐	☑	☐	

Teacher Indicators	Response Yes	No	N/A	Observations
Assists in clarifying or expanding a proposition by:				The teacher modeled all these methods in the introductory discussion and encouraged them as she walked from group to group.
• Modeling methods of restating arguments and ideas and asking if they are expressed correctly	☑	☐	☐	
• Modeling and providing practice at responding appropriately to criticism	☑	☐	☐	
• Modeling expressing own puzzlement or confusion	☑	☐	☐	

Tool 22: Student Behaviors Keyed to Accountable Talk

Table 3.20   Student Behaviors Keyed to Accountable Talk

Class: Social Studies

Date: 2/2

Time: 2:15

Student Indicators	Response Yes	No	N/A	Observations
Students are engaged in talk when they:				The whole-class and small-group discussions were very lively. Many students spoke, primarily to each other. Sometimes they interrupted each other.
• Speak appropriately in a variety of classroom situations	☑	☐	☐	
• Allow others to speak without interruption	☐	☑	☐	
• Speak directly to other students	☑	☐	☐	
Students are listening attentively to one another when they:				It was often difficult to determine if eye contact was being made. Students usually referred to the person whose ideas they were addressing.
• Make eye contact with speaker	☐	☐	☑	
• Refer to a previous speaker	☑	☐	☐	
• Connect comments to previous ideas	☑	☐	☐	

(Continued)

Table 3.20 (Continued)

Student Indicators	Response			Observations
	Yes	*No*	*N/A*	
Students elaborate and build on others' ideas when they:				Students stayed on topic, listened to each other. They were so engrossed in the issue that they did not bring up any related or new issue. One or two students referred to each other.
• Make comments related to the focus of the discussion	☑	☐	☐	
• Introduce new, related issues	☐	☑	☐	
• Listen carefully	☑	☐	☐	
• Talk about issues rather than participants	☐	☑	☐	
Students work toward clarifying or expanding a proposition when they:				Students actively reflected back what they heard and questioned what they didn't understand.
• Model methods of restating arguments and ideas and ask if they are expressed correctly	☑	☐	☐	
• Model and provide practice at responding appropriately to criticism	☑	☐	☐	
• Model expressing own puzzlement or confusion	☑	☐	☐	

QUALITATIVE OBSERVATION TOOLS

Tool 23: Detached Open-Ended Narrative

The observer records every person, event, or thing that attracts her or his attention, known as selective verbatim (Acheson & Gall, 1997) or script taping (Hunter, 1983). Whatever the observer considers significant is recorded. The observer simply records exactly what is said during the lesson; hence, a verbatim transcript is taken. Not all verbal communications are recorded but only those that the observer feels are significant or those communications agreed upon by both supervisor and teacher beforehand. Hence, only selected portions are recorded. Of course, no prearranged categories or questions are developed.

Selective Verbatim

Materials. A notepad or laptop to record observations.

Explanation. Supervisor and teacher collaboratively agree that anecdotal evidence will be collected during a specified period of time. The goal is to *describe,* as objectively as possible, the key events and actions that occur. It will be impossible to record everything. The observer must try to choose what he or she believes is indicative of the teaching and learning observed.

Open-Ended Narrative

Fifth-grade class; 13 boys and 12 girls; self-contained classroom; Amy Clayman, teacher; 9:45 a.m. I enter as Ms. Clayman tells class to take out their math books. As Ms. Clayman gives instructions for the math assignment, four students (two male and two female) are out of their seats, hanging their clothing in the rear classroom closet. The girl is talking. Ms. Clayman tells her to be quiet and sit down. Teacher takes attendance by reading class roster, name by name. After about 3 minutes, a monitor enters classroom, and teacher is recording daily attendance; noise level in class rises. Monitor leaves room. Teacher walks back and forth as students get quiet. At 9:53 a.m., Ms. Clayman asks a girl to tell the class what the answer to the first math problem is. Student responds; class attentive. Ms. Clayman asks a boy, "Can you answer question No. 2?" Student responds. Teacher calls on a boy who also responds, with a different answer. Ms. Clayman probes and asks boy to explain. Ms. Clayman asks another student to answer the question. Girl responds. Teacher asks another question to a boy and probes. Teacher proceeds this way for the next 15 minutes. Ms. Clayman then asks the class, "How may we figure out how much carpet to buy if the room is 10 feet by 15 feet?" No one raises a hand to answer. Ms. Clayman repeats the question. Still no response. Teacher draws a diagram on the board and then James calls out, "Oh, I know." Students giggle. Ms. Clayman tells class, "Now, stop that. Pay attention. Go ahead, James, tell us." James mumbles something. Ms. Clayman requests that he speak more clearly. James is silent. Teacher then explains to the class how to compute the area of a rectangle. She writes several examples on the board and then calls on several students to answer them.

Reflect and Practice

Obtain a video of a lesson and practice taking selected verbatim information. After recording is completed, share notes with a colleague.

Then view the video again, taking note of inaccuracies and missed information. Keep practicing until you're satisfied that you've recorded all that you wanted to.

Postnote. The ability of the observer to accurately and quickly record information is essential. Recording such information may appear simple, but much practice is required. Be certain to practice Activity 1.

Tool 24: Participant Open-Ended Observation

Participant open-ended observation refers to a situation in which the observer partakes in the classroom activities. The observer may assist in the instruction by working with a group or helping individual students.

The observer may take notes or just jot down some ideas for later recall. The advantage of having the observer participate in the class is that many insights may be culled from direct participation that might otherwise be missed from detached observations.

The types of observation possible are similar to detached open-ended narratives. Using this procedure, the observer either makes notes during the activities or simply summarizes events after the observation period. The essential element here is that the observer is in a unique position to better understand classroom interactions because he or she actively is involved.

Observers should feel free to vary their approaches (detached or participant), depending on a given situation. For example, sometimes a teacher may feel uncomfortable having the supervisor participate, explaining that it may be distracting. We highly suggest arranging the format of observation with the teacher in advance.

Practice participant open-ended observation as you did previously with the detached open-ended narrative.

Tool 25: Child-Centered Learning Observation

Based on constructivist learning theory, *child-centered learning observation* focuses primarily on the learner, the student, rather than on the instructor. By incorporating a qualitative approach, the observer may record observations in response to these and other learner-centered questions:

1. Were the children learning/thinking? What indications were there that the children were learning/thinking?

2. What kinds of questions were being asked (e.g., open-ended)?

3. How were the children treated?

4. What opportunities were provided for the children to learn in different ways?

5. Who is the source of knowledge?

6. Were the children talking to other children?

7. Were the children designing their own learning?

8. Who assesses learning? How was learning assessed? What was the role of the student?

9. What did we learn about the children?

Child-centered learning observations provide invaluable insights into student learning that would otherwise be overlooked by focusing on only the teacher. They also allow the teacher to reflect on the causes of the student's behavior or response, which may have originated in the teacher's interaction with the student. We suggest you practice this technique as you did the others.

Tool 26: Nonverbal Techniques

Materials. Nonverbal observation chart (see, for example, Table 3.21).

Proxemics is the teacher's use of perception and space. The closer a teacher is to a student, the less likely the student is to behave inappropriately. For example, the teacher may stand near or move toward a potentially disruptive student as a behavior control strategy. This technique works best with teachers who customarily stand and move about. Another use of proxemics is to arrange classroom furniture in such a way as to convey warmth and closeness.

Kinesics is the teacher's use of facial and body cues, such as smiling, frowning, staring, pointing, or hands on hips. These cues communicate strong messages, work well from a distance, and help signal individuals and groups when they are disrupting others. Kinesic cues should be considered as an aid to conventional classroom management methods. The best way to learn these cues is to practice them with others and in front of a mirror.

Prosody is concerned with tone, pitch, and rhythm of the teacher's voice, and communicates the importance of what is being said. Teachers who use this tool know that yelling and high-pitched voices tend to excite rather than calm students. Effective use of prosody can convey caring, empathy, and warmth as well as a love of teaching and students.

Immediacy is the degree of perceived or psychological closeness between people. Teachers who use this technique are physically close to students, use socially appropriate touching, exhibit warmth, and use open body postures while communicating. For example, lightly touching a student's shoulder or upper arm while explaining an assignment tells that student the teacher cares and wants him or her to be successful.

Explanation. Observations are collaboratively arranged and made in a series of short visits at various times during one day or over several days. Although a checklist can be used noting each time the teacher uses a particular nonverbal technique, we prefer the observer to keep a running record of the types of non-verbal interactions used, along with annotations describing the nature and impact of those interventions.

Table 3.10 in Resource D is provided as a training tool to interpret the teacher-student interaction during this particular lesson.

Table 3.21   Nonverbal Techniques

Class: 9th grade English

Date: 11/4

Time: 8:35

Nonverbal Technique	Frequency	Anecdotal Observations/ Student Responses
Proxemics • Standing near student(s) • Moving toward student(s) • Touching student(s) • Moving about room	√ √ √ √ √ √ √ √ √ √ √ √ √ √	Teacher frequently moving around room, especially during independent work

Kinesics
a. Affirmation
  • Eye contact
  • Touching
  • Smiling
  • Nodding
  • Open arm movements
	√ √ √ √ √ √ √
	
	√ √ √ √ √
		Eye contact during mini-lesson and discussion
		
		Frequent smiling
		
		Tendency to keep arms crossed

(Continued)

Table 3.21 (Continued)

Nonverbal Technique	Frequency	Anecdotal Observations/ Student Responses
b. Disapproval • Frowning • Stern look • Finger to lips • Pointing • Arms crossed • Hands on hips	√ √ √	Finger to lips to quiet students during independent work See above
Prosody • Varies voice tone • Varies pitch • Varies rhythm	√ √ √	Clearly aware of need to vary tone, pitch, and rhythm during mini-lesson
Immediacy • Responds with warmth	√	Generally responds with warmth without touching

Source: C. D. Glickman, S. P. Gordon, and J. Ross-Gordon, *Supervision of Instruction: A Developmental Approach* (4th ed.). Copyright ©1998 by Allyn & Bacon. Reprinted/adapted by permission.

Tool 27: Questioning Techniques

Explanation: Questions play an important role in the development of a lesson. Effective questioning starts students thinking and guides the class from one important concept to another. In the Quantitative Tool section, two tools are provided to assess the level of questioning according to Bloom's Taxonomy and Webb's Depth of Knowledge. In this qualitative questionnaire, we look at how questions are asked and how the teacher responds to the answer, two equally important but different skills from the level of the questions themselves.

1. What classroom rules exist for students asking and answering questions?

2. How does the teacher direct questions?

3. How does the teacher address wait time for students to think about answers?

4. How does the teacher address a lack of response to a question?

5. Are questions directed to both volunteers and nonvolunteers?

6. How does the teacher handle other students' comments to student responses?

7. How does the teacher handle praise and other reactions to questions?

8. How were students encouraged to ask questions? Or discouraged?

9. How did the teacher's position in the room affect class participation?

10. How many questions beginning with "how," "why," "explain," or "compare" were asked?

These questions were adapted with permission from the New York City Teacher Academy Fieldwork Guide.

Tool 28: Strategies for Diverse Learners

This focused questionnaire can be used as a basis for ascertaining how the teacher is meeting the needs of all the children. The following brief questionnaire is an adaptation of the Indicators of Culturally Diverse Learners chart (Tool 13) in the quantitative section.

1. How does the teacher encourage students?

2. What positive reinforcement techniques does he or she use?

3. What kinds of modifications for individual children or types of learners are evident?

4. How does the teacher use the children's strengths?

5. Where are the students situated in the room and why?

6. What are the opportunities for small-group work?

7. How does the teacher address grouping according to needs and skills?

8. What evidence is there of scaffolding of instruction?

9. How does the teacher adapt materials and instruction to different student learning styles?

10. What is the teacher's proximity to the students?

11. How are the children interacting?

12. What else is special about the treatment of the children?

We hope that these examples of two tools—one quantitative and one qualitative—for the same focus will facilitate your ability to create your own tools.

Tool 29: Differentiated Instruction

Differentiated instruction can occur when teachers are aware and able to consider and deal with different learning needs and abilities of their students. The following questionnaire addresses many of the classroom activities that promote differentiated learning. No classroom can or should exhibit all of these characteristics at once, and others not included in the questions may be displayed. This questionnaire can be adapted to include activities mentioned in the quantitative Differentiated Classroom tool and vice versa.

1. What preassessments of student knowledge are included prior to instruction?

2. How does the teacher incorporate multiple intelligences into the lesson?

3. How are different learning styles addressed?

4. What assessment strategies are used and when?

5. What homework options are offered?

6. Are all students prompted and probed equitably during questioning?

7. How is wait time for different students addressed?

8. What kind of grouping procedures are used (whole class, diads, triads, quads)?

9. Is peer tutoring used? If so, how?

Tool 30: Guided Reading

A Staten Island staff developer, Maria Casales, created a series of balanced literacy tools for her work with teachers.

Table 3.22   Guided Reading

Time: Literacy Block

Selects appropriate text for small-group instruction	*Helps children to think, talk, and question through the story*
Teacher uses book *The Birthday Cake,* written by Joy Cowley. Six students, 4 boys, 2 girls, receive a copy of the same book. They look at the cover of the book with curiosity and await teacher direction.	The teacher encourages her students to take a "picture walk" through the story. As they preview the text, Amanda questions an illustration, and Mark questions some of the words in print. Teacher briefly discusses their concerns.
Introduces story to the group as well as vocabulary concepts and text features	*Allows small groups to read independently with minimum teacher support*
The teacher brings the students' attention to new vocabulary words and to the ending punctuation. Children give the teacher sentences using the new vocabulary words. Teacher reviews telling sentences and question sentences.	The teacher allows the group to read the book independently. She lends support rarely and her students read the whole book (12 pages).
Provides or reinforces reading strategies and provides students with the opportunity to use the strategy	
Upon completion of reading the story, the teacher asks the students, "How many of you noticed the end of some sentences? Why are some sentences telling sentences and others question sentences?" Children are able to respond to teacher-posed questions. The teacher encourages the children to reread the story, focusing on ending punctuation and pauses.	
Records reflections on the students' reading behaviors during and after reading	*Engages students in a brief discussion after reading the story*
The teacher logs their reading behaviors as they relate to the skill and fluency. After they read, she adds some quick notes.	The teacher asks the students if they enjoyed reading the book. The students reply "yes." She then asks what they enjoyed the most and why.

Tool 31: Team Teaching in the Inclusion or General Education Classroom

The integrated or inclusion classroom usually includes a general and a special education teacher. In addition, team teaching has increased with the expansion of the integrated curriculum and longer and flexible time periods. Effective use of two teachers in one classroom is difficult to achieve. The following questionnaire can support collaborative team teaching. You can also create a performance indicator instrument to describe the teachers' roles.

1. Describe the involvement of the general education teacher and the special education teacher with the whole class, with small groups, and with individual children.

2. What is the role of each teacher in the classroom? How is instruction organized between the two teachers?

3. Who guides the curriculum?

4. What is the curricular role of each teacher?

5. Who attends to the individual needs of the children?

6. What accommodations are available for special needs students?

7. How are the accommodations for children with special needs handled?

8. How is responsibility for children with special needs divided between the teachers?

Note: Thanks to Claire Wurtzel, Director of Professional Development for the Churchill School and Center, for her suggestions for the inclusion tools.

Tool 32: Classroom Assessment in the Differentiated Classroom

Assessment has taken center stage in the efforts to raise achievement for all children. Ongoing and multiple forms of assessment provide crucial knowledge for differentiating instruction. The following questions will assist the teacher in determining whether multiple forms of assessment are facilitating learning.

1. How does the teacher preassess students?

2. What different forms of assessments are used?

3. What is the role of the student in classroom assessment?

4. Is peer assessment used? If so, how?

5. How is it determined that the students are ready to proceed to the next step or level?

6. How does the teacher adjust and/or modify the lesson in response to student needs and varying master levels?

7. How do assessments address multiple intelligences and learning styles?

8. How do students demonstrate to the teacher and to one another that they have achieved the goals of the lesson (quiz, test, written assignment, project, discussion, a variety of media, etc.)?

Adapted with permission from the NYC Teacher Academy Fieldwork Guide.

Reflect and Practice

We have presented 32 practical tools and techniques to assist your observations of classrooms. Some tools are certainly more appropriate than others in various situations. You know best what may be needed in a given situation. For instance, a teacher may request that you examine her verbal interactions with students since she tends to lecture too much at times and answer her own questions. You might suggest, therefore, the tool dealing with Teacher Verbal Behaviors. For this activity, use the following list of the 32 tools and create a scenario or situation in which each tool might be most appropriate. Share your list with a colleague. You will notice that different colleagues may have varied uses for even the same tool. Discuss the advantages and disadvantages of each tool selection.

1. Teacher Verbal Behaviors

2. Teacher Questions Using Bloom's Taxonomy

3. Teacher Questions Using Webb's Depth of Knowledge

4. Student On-Task and Off-Task Behaviors

5. Gardner's Multiple Intelligences

6. Hunter's Steps in Lesson Planning

7. Johnson and Johnson's Cooperative Learning Criteria

8. Group Performance: Assessment of Individual Participation

9. Diagram of Verbal Interactions

10a. Diagram of Teacher Space Utilization

10b. Diagram of Student Space Utilization

11. Feedback

12. Teacher-Pupil Interaction

13. Indicators of Culturally Diverse Learners

14. Strategies for Diverse Learners

15. Accommodations and Modifications for English Language Learners

16. The Differentiated Classroom

17. Guided Reading

18. Read-Aloud/Story Time

19. National Council of Teachers of Mathematics Standard 3—Geometry

20. National Council of Teachers of Mathematics Process Standards (Standards 6–10)

21. Teacher Behaviors Keyed to Accountable Talk

22. Student Behaviors Keyed to Accountable Talk

23. Detached Open-Ended Narrative

24. Participant Open-Ended Observation

25. Child-Centered Learning Observation

26. Nonverbal Techniques

27. Questioning Techniques

28. Strategies for Diverse Learners (Qualitative)

29. Differentiated Instruction (Qualitative)

30. Guided Reading (Qualitative)

31. Team Teaching in the Inclusion or General Education Classroom

32. Classroom Assessment in the Differentiated Classroom

SUMMARY

We have described two approaches to observation: quantitative and qualitative. A total of 32 tools and techniques were reviewed and practiced. We have not included videotaping and audiotaping as separate tools; rather, they are valuable instruments that can be used with any of the tools and techniques described in this chapter. According to Acheson and Gall (1997),

> Videos and audiotapes are among the most objective observation techniques. . . . They allow teachers to see themselves as students see them. . . . [T]hey can pick up a great deal of what teachers and students are doing and saying. A good recording captures the "feel" of classroom interaction. (p. 111)

Videos and audiotapes, according to Acheson and Gall (1997), are examples of "wide lenses" that are particularly useful "in supervising teachers who are defensive or who are not yet ready to select particular teaching behaviors for improvement" (p. 107). Acheson and Gall conclude, "After reviewing wide-lens data, these teachers may be more ready to reflect on their teaching, identify specific teaching behaviors for focused observations, and set self-improvement goals" (pp. 107–108). We agree.

At this juncture, we would also like to offer our perspective on the use of the tools and techniques presented in this chapter within a standards-based environment. In the 2000 edition of his book on different approaches to clinical supervision, Ed Pajak asks "whether clinical supervision is compatible with the principles of systemic reform and exactly how clinical supervision is being implemented in standards-based contexts" (p. 295). In our own work in the field and through feedback teachers and administrators have given us, our impressions are that the revised observation forms that districts often require are variations on the same old theme. Instead of an arbitrary list of categories of behaviors to be observed, the "new" standards-based formats address a range of standards. The supervisor fills out either a checkoff list or short narratives or a combination of both. The result for the teacher is the same: He or she scans the list in relief and files it, or reacts in disbelief to the areas requiring attention. The postobservation conference may provide valuable feedback, but the form itself is of limited value. Too many areas are observed simultaneously. The teacher becomes frustrated because he or she cannot focus on multiple areas effectively at the same time.

We propose that supervisors and coaches use the principles of the reflective clinical supervision cycle in a standards-based environment. Rather than create checkoff lists to verify if learning outcomes are being met, we suggest that each observation focus on one learning outcome, standard, or teaching skill.

In this chapter, we have provided some sample tools that are already in use or that we have created to meet some of the current learning outcomes and standards. The overarching standard, currently expressed as "leave no child behind," is the underlying theme of most of these tools. We have found that performance indicator instruments, categorical frequency instruments, and focused questionnaires can be easily adapted to meet most outcomes and standards. The samples that we have provided are primarily based on these three types of instruments, so that you can see the facility with which you and the teacher can discuss a focus, choose and adapt these tools, or create your own. We address diversity of backgrounds, learning styles, math standards, balanced literacy, differentiated instruction and assessment, and other strategies to enable all children to reach their potential. Since most of these tools are variations of performance indicator instruments, categorical frequency instruments, and focused questionnaire tools, we have not included postnotes for all of these tools.

Another practice in the standards-based environment that we will address is the "walk-through," traditionally termed the *informal observation*. The walk-through, which was developed as a means to improve instruction through teacher collaboration, will be presented in Chapter 5 as an alternative to traditional supervision. We believe that supervisors often use the walk-through or informal "pop-in" primarily as a monitoring method. In the best-case scenario, the supervisor has met with the teacher at the beginning of the year to talk about goals. Subsequently, the supervisor makes brief visits to a set of classes at regular intervals to ascertain if the agreed-upon goals are being implemented. More often, supervisors pop into classrooms unannounced and follow up the visit with a commendation or recommendation. We believe these informal or formal short visits are evaluation or monitoring practices that do not promote teacher-centered improvement of instruction. Supervisors should be present daily in classrooms and even take on teaching assignments. The goal, however, should be to get to know the children and how they are learning and to build a community of learners.

CONCLUSION

Research demonstrates that teachers are likely to change their instructional behaviors on their own after their classroom has been described to them by an observer. Observation is a mirror and thus a stimulus for change. Effective supervision is about engaging teachers in reflective thinking and discussion based on insightful and useful observation tools and techniques. In the next chapter, we place these observation tools within the context of a reflective clinical supervision program.

NOTES

1. We would like to acknowledge Glickman et al. (2004) for their excellent discussion of observation instruments. Our framework is drawn, in large measure, from their work. Their division of instruments into quantitative and qualitative approaches makes the most sense.

2. These categories were developed by Glickman et al. (2004).

An Introduction to Reflective Clinical Supervision

4

The way in which supervisors try to bring about change largely determines how teachers respond to the challenge. Supervisors can mandate change externally; or they can, together with teachers, build collaborative cultures that encourage the seeds of change to take root and grow.

—Grimmet, Rostad, & Ford, 1992, p. 185

CHAPTER OVERVIEW

1. Definition of Clinical Supervision

2. The Reflective Clinical Supervision Cycle

   a. The Planning Conference

      • Scenario A
      • Scenario B

   b. The Observation

   c. The Feedback Conference

      • Scenario A (directive informational approach)
      • Scenario B (collaborative approach)
      • Scenario C (self-directed approach)

   d. Collaborative Reflection

3. Conclusion

The first chapter traced the emergence of clinical supervision in the 1960s. In this chapter, we first present and explain our definition of clinical supervision and then offer an adaptation of clinical supervision we call *reflective clinical supervision*. An outline of the steps for each part of the cycle (except the actual observation) is accompanied by brief case studies. Opportunities to practice each phase are included. Finally, we detail how the whole process can be simulated in the course before trying it out on-site. By the end of this chapter, you will be prepared to complete the final assignment of conducting a whole cycle in your schools.

A DEFINITION OF CLINICAL SUPERVISION

Although the sequence of a preconference, classroom observation, and feedback conference already existed in the 1920s, during the era of democratic supervision, Morris Cogan is credited with developing the elaborated concept and techniques of the clinical supervision cycle, which has emerged as a major force in educational supervision since the 1960s.

Edward Pajak (2000) said that Cogan "viewed clinical supervision as a vehicle for developing professional responsible teachers who were capable of analyzing their own performance, who were open to change and assistance from others, and who were above all, self-directing" (p. 76). This definition encompasses some of the assumptions that we believe underlie effective supervision: It does not explicitly restrict supervision to the supervisor, opening up the possibility that change and assistance can come from many sources; and it emphasizes self-analysis and self-direction, important components of reflective practice. We expand the definition to include classroom teaching and learning as the focuses of improvement and collaborative as well as individual analysis and reflection.

Before we define supervision, and learn and practice an adaptation of the clinical supervision cycle, it is important to understand that clinical supervision is not only a structure but a concept, and as such, it contains a series of assumptions. Goldhammer, Anderson, and Krajewski (1993) outlined nine major characteristics of clinical supervision that we believe are consistent with any of the approaches and structures in this book:

1. It is a technology for improving instruction.

2. It is a deliberate intervention into the instructional process.

3. It is goal oriented, combining the school's needs with the personal growth needs of those who work within the school.

4. It assumes a professional working relationship between teacher(s) and supervisor(s).

5. It requires a high degree of mutual trust, as reflected in understanding, support, and commitment to growth.

6. It is systematic, although it requires a flexible and continuously changing methodology.

7. It creates a productive (i.e., healthy) tension for bridging the gap between the real and the ideal.

8. It assumes that the supervisor knows a great deal about the analysis of instruction and learning and also about productive human interaction.

9. It requires both preservice training (for supervisors), especially in observation techniques, and continuous inservice reflection on effective approaches. (pp. 52–53)

> **REFLECTION (INDIVIDUAL AND SHARED)**
>
> *Formulate a definition of clinical supervision based on the preceding ideas and assumptions. Work in class in groups of three to five; share your definitions and come up with joint ones that designated group leaders will report to the whole class.*

THE REFLECTIVE CLINICAL SUPERVISION CYCLE

Richard Weller's (1971) formal definition of clinical supervision provides a basis on which we can develop our reflective cycle of supervision:

> Clinical supervision may be defined as supervision focused upon the improvement of instruction by means of systematic cycles of planning, observation, and intensive intellectual analysis of actual teaching performances in the interest of rational modification. (p. 11)

Weller referred to the three phases of the clinical supervision cycle as represented in Figure 4.1.

We add a fourth phase to the three activities of planning, observation, and analysis through a feedback conference that includes a collaborative reflection and analysis of the process and its findings. The fourth phase is professional development. If you juxtapose the four steps that we propose with the four steps of the reflective practice cycle (see Figure 4.2), you will observe that they are correlated: The planning phase of the clinical supervision cycle is similar to the

Figure 4.1   Three Phases of the Reflective Clinical Supervision Cycle

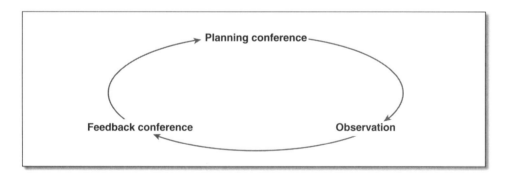

Figure 4.2   Comparison of Reflective Clinical Supervision With Reflective Practice

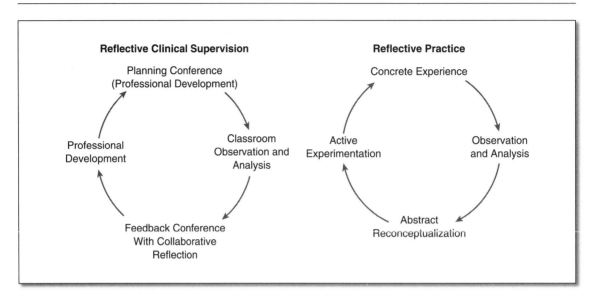

concrete experience or problematic or indeterminate situation of reflective practice (the goal is to pinpoint an experience for examination and analysis); we have also included professional development related to the observation focus as a possible part of the planning phase; the observation phase of clinical supervision, which is followed by individual analysis, is analogous to the observation and analysis stage of reflective practice; the feedback conference, which involves the joint analysis of the data and the reconceptualization and planning for the next cycle, is comparable to the abstract reconceptualization stage of reflective practice. The collaborative reflection concludes the third phase. It allows the supervisor and teacher to reflect on how the supervision process and its results worked before proceeding. In the fourth phase of the reflective practice model, the reconceptualized ideas are actually put into action, completing the cycle and simultaneously beginning another (Osterman & Kottkamp, 2004). In our fourth phase, professional development, the reconceptualized ideas are developed further. Thus, in the next cycle, the combination of the discussion of the observation and the further development through professional development prepare the teacher for a new planning cycle. If the observation does not result in a need for change in the practice, professional development can focus on a new instructional strategy.

It is apparent that in our model, the reflective process takes center stage in the clinical supervision cycle. The planning conference is the first step in the process and is crucial in determining the tone, content, and approach to the cycle. It can be the most important part of the cycle if, as in the Scenario B that follows, problem solving or professional development takes place before the observation.

The Planning Conference

Elena Santiago, the newly appointed principal of New Hope Middle School, whom we met in Chapter 2, began her first set of classroom observations as early as possible in the fall. She hoped to develop trusting relationships that would permit her and the teachers to focus on the improvement of teaching and learning, and not on the bureaucratic process of evaluation. Because her assistant principal could accomplish only some of the required observations and Elena wanted to be actively involved with what was going on in the classroom, she decided to meet with and observe herself the newest teachers first.

Elena set up a planning conference with a brand-new language arts teacher. She had heard that Sylvia, a recent graduate of a high-quality master's program, was having difficulty implementing her student-centered practices. Some of the students had not been exposed to cooperative learning groups before, and rumor had it that some of her classes were out of control. Nonetheless, Elena decided to query Sylvia about what she felt her concerns were. To make Sylvia comfortable, Elena set up a meeting in Sylvia's classroom, not in the principal's office.

We have found that the change process often begins during the planning conference. Therefore, we believe that two types of planning conferences can be effective. In the simpler form (see Scenario A), the teacher and supervisor identify the focus, choose an appropriate tool, and set the date and time of the observation and feedback conference. The supervisor can choose either the directive informational, collaborative, or self-directed approach to determine focus and tool. In the second type of planning conference (see Scenario B), the change process actually begins in the initial conversation. The discussion and choice of focus frequently lead to a decision to try new strategies. The teacher can practice the innovations(s) before the actual observation or implement them for the first time during the observation. Again, the supervisor chooses one of the three interpersonal approaches to determine focus and tool. In either case, some kind of professional development may also take place before the actual observation. That professional development could be as simple as a conversation and an intervisitation with a teacher expert in the chosen focus area.

Scenario A

Elena: Hi, Sylvia. How's it going?

Sylvia: OK, I guess.

Elena: Since I will be beginning nontenured teacher observations, I thought we could discuss a particular area, interest, or concern that could be the focus of the observation.

Sylvia: Gosh, I wouldn't know where to start. You pick it.

Elena: I know that you use a lot of exciting innovative teaching methods. Is there any one in particular that you'd like some feedback on?

Sylvia: Mmm . . . I've been trying to have the students work in cooperative groups to discuss their writing, and it doesn't seem to be working in some classes. I have a rambunctious seventh-grade class that doesn't work well in groups at all, and I can't seem to get control of the process. Could you sit in on that class?

Elena: Sure. Let me show you a couple of tools I could use to observe the groups and see which one you think might pinpoint your concerns.

They decide to use the cooperative learning performance indicator instrument created by Johnson and Johnson (1989).

Elena: What is a convenient time for me to visit when you will be using cooperative groups with the seventh graders?

Sylvia: How about third period next Tuesday? They're usually awake by then but not yet completely out of control.

Elena: Fine. Next Tuesday, October 1, third period. While we're at it, could we set a time to meet after the observation? How about during your professional period the following day?

<table>
<tr><td>

Reflection

What does Elena do to make Sylvia feel relaxed and at the same time focus on instruction? How does she get Sylvia to reflect on her own perceptions of her needs?

</td><td>

Sylvia: Sounds OK to me.

Elena: Agreed. Third period on Tuesday and second period on Wednesday. By the way, if you have any other input that would be helpful before I visit, don't hesitate to stop in and share it with me. I'm looking forward to seeing students using this wonderful method.

</td></tr>
</table>

Scenario B

Elena: Hi, Sylvia. How are you doing?

Sylvia: I'm at my wits' end.

Elena: You seem very frustrated. What's going on?

Sylvia: I've been trying to implement the cooperative learning theory I learned in college, and it just doesn't seem to be working.

Elena: How long have you been doing cooperative groups with the seventh-grade class?

Sylvia: I began last week. I explained the process to them, handed out guidelines, and asked them to study the steps and rules for their homework assignment. We tried groups the next day and they were *so noisy*. I made one more attempt the following day and had to abandon the process midway. It was so frustrating!

Elena: Did you model the process before you divided them in groups?

Sylvia: I thought that the sheets and my explanation would be sufficient. Maybe the change was too abrupt and extreme. Do you think one group could model without my losing control of the rest of the class?

Elena: Have you ever tried the fishbowl technique, where a volunteer group models the process in the middle of the classroom while the others watch and then comment at the end? If all the students keep their instructions in front of them, it will improve the fishbowl process and the ability of the rest of the class to comment.

Sylvia: Your suggestion could really help. It gives me another idea. I could have them make name plates for each role with a summary of the responsibilities on each card so the class would know who had each role in the fishbowl, and the list of steps on the other side would help everyone remember them. The list would also help them give feedback in the fishbowl and later in their small groups.

Elena: Your idea is very creative. Would you like me to visit when you do the fishbowl or when the whole class is in groups?

Sylvia: I think I could do both the fishbowl and cooperative groups in the double period we have the day after tomorrow. If I assign the name plates tomorrow, could you come the following day third and fourth periods?

Elena: I will make sure to be there. I'm very excited to see how it works.

They decide to use Johnson and Johnson's (1989) cooperative learning performance indicator instrument to observe the fishbowl and the subsequent groups. They confirm the time and location and set up a feedback conference time and place.

> **Reflection**
>
> *What are the major differences between Scenario A and Scenario B? What would help determine whether to use the approach depicted in Scenario A or Scenario B?*

Key Steps: Planning Conference

1. Decide the focus of the observation (choose a general approach: directive informational, collaborative, or self-directed).

2. Determine the method and form of observation. Problem solve or plan professional development where appropriate.

3. Set up the time of the observation and the feedback conference.

The goals of the planning conference are:

- To identify teacher interests and concerns in an appropriate manner (directive informational, collaborative, or self-directed) and offer professional development where appropriate.
- To clarify that the primary purpose of the observation is to improve teaching and learning.
- To reduce stress and make the teacher feel comfortable about the process.
- To choose an observation tool and schedule the visit and feedback conference.

The three steps of the planning conference are:

1. *Decide the focus of the observation.* Whereas the chief purpose of the observation is to improve instruction, it is essential to have the teacher's

perspective on his or her concerns and interests. Even a new teacher can help identify the primary or most urgent concerns. Change occurs most easily if the teacher has a role in providing the focus. The supervisor will use one of the three interpersonal approaches to guide the planning conference. Wherever possible, begin the problem-solving process related to the chosen focus of observation and include professional development.

2. *Determine the method and form of observation.* Once the focus is determined, the supervisor can discuss the appropriate tools. The supervisor will decide whether to include the teacher in making the choice of the observation tool. A newer or less secure teacher may have enough to cope with without taking part in that decision.

3. *Set up the time of the observation and feedback conference.* It is important, wherever possible, to provide the teacher with the opportunity to choose the day and time. The teacher knows in which class the focus that he or she has chosen can be observed best. Once he or she has had a role in deciding the focus, the choice is simplified. It becomes a learning experience with less likelihood of the visit being an occasion to put on a show.

Class Practice

During the week, think about two teachers in your school: an experienced, confident teacher and a novice. Imagine a planning conference with each one, and write a short dialogue based on the imaginary planning conference. In class, you will practice at least one of the scenarios in groups of three using the reflective practice guidelines. Keep your key steps cards and practice guidelines handy. Volunteers will model at least one scenario, which can be videotaped for their personal use and reflection.

Site Practice

Begin to think about a teacher who would be receptive to participating in a reflective clinical supervision cycle with you. Once you have found a volunteer, you can rehearse the planning conference in class and then actually schedule the site planning conference.

The Observation

Key Steps: The Observation

1. Finalize the choice of observation tool.

2. Conduct the observation.

3. Verify the feedback conference meeting time, and offer a copy of the observation tool to the teacher *before the feedback conference.*

4. Analyze facts of the observation and begin thinking of interpretations.

5. Choose a feedback conference interpersonal approach from Chapter 2.

---

1. *Finalize the choice of observation tool.* The supervisor finalizes the choice of an observation tool from those described in Chapter 3, preferably after consultation with the teacher during the planning conference.

2. *Conduct the observation.* The observation takes place at the agreed-upon time. The teacher should be less anxious about your presence and your writing because he or she has chosen the focus and is familiar with the instrument you are using to document it.

3. *Verify the feedback conference meeting time, and offer a copy of the observation tool to the teacher wherever appropriate.* At the end of the class, the supervisor reminds the teacher of their scheduled feedback conference. Where appropriate and feasible, the supervisor supplies the teacher with a copy of the completed observation tool so that they both can examine it individually before the conference.

4. *Analyze facts of the observation and begin thinking of interpretations.* It is preferable for the supervisor to analyze and interpret the observation tool as soon as possible after the class, while the observation is fresh in his or her mind. Study and analyze the facts and then begin to think about an interpretation of the findings. Don't jump to conclusions before meeting with the teacher. It is important to get the teacher's perspective before finalizing an interpretation.

5. *Choose a feedback conference interpersonal approach from Chapter 2.* Now that the supervisor has held the planning conference with the teacher and actually observed the teacher in the classroom, the supervisor should be able to determine which interpersonal approach is appropriate for the feedback conference.

The Feedback Conference

We now provide three scenarios based on the interpersonal approaches presented in Chapter 2. Before briefly reviewing the steps, try to identify which approach the supervisor chose.

Scenario A

In the first scenario, we return to Elena and Sylvia. You will remember that Elena is the recently appointed principal of New Hope Middle School, and Sylvia is a new, young language arts teacher who is trying to implement the cooperative learning methodology she learned in college and who is running into some difficulties. She asked Elena to observe her rambunctious seventh-grade class during a cooperative learning workshop on the writing process. Elena chose Johnson and Johnson's cooperative learning performance indicators as the observation tool (Table 3.8) and shared a copy of the results with Sylvia immediately, so she could review it before the feedback conference the following day. The scheduled meeting was in Sylvia's classroom during her professional period. This feedback conference is based on Scenario A of the planning conference.

Elena: Did you get a chance to look at the cooperative learning performance indicators?

Sylvia: I was devastated! Despite your attempts to write positive comments, it looks like I didn't get any of the responses right.

Elena: The students seemed to know what they were supposed to be doing because they kept on arguing about how they weren't following the rules! I didn't see them referring to written guidelines or following a clear sequence. How much preparation did they have before they began using the process?

Sylvia: I handed out a sheet one day for them to study at home, and then I had them try it out the next day.

Elena: Maybe it was too much too soon. Don't forget that some of these students haven't had much opportunity to work collaboratively. They are fortunate to have you as a teacher with all your current knowledge! This class in particular may need much more practice and role playing of the different roles before they can run their own groups. Have you ever tried the fishbowl technique, where a volunteer group models the process in the middle of the classroom while the others watch and then comment at the end? They also need to keep their instructions in front of them and make sure that the reflector has time to provide feedback at the end. Perhaps the reflectors can share who performed the roles most effectively in each group before the end of class. What do you think? Do you have any ideas?

Sylvia: I love your ideas, and they made me think of others. I can assign them as homework the job of making 3 × 5 cards for each job. They can then use the cards to direct their group work. And I could get a volunteer to videotape a group so they can see for themselves how they did.

Elena: Effective ideas! Let's review your plans and jot them down on the observation sheets so that we don't forget. First, you'll give them the 3 × 5 card assignment. The next day, a group will model the process using the fishbowl technique. Then you'll ask for a volunteer to videotape a group and ask the reflectors to identify who performed most effectively in each group. We can think of further incentives if these work. Do you want to go over them so we're sure we are on the same wavelength?

Sylvia: Sure. I can't wait to try these ideas. I'll give them the card assignment tomorrow. The next day, we'll do the fishbowl technique. Then I'll ask for videotaping volunteers. The following day, I'll explain the reflector's new role, and we'll try our first practice. How does that sound to you?

Elena: Terrific. How about meeting next week at the same time to touch base on how it's working? If it's going as planned, we can brainstorm some other refinements. Your feedback can help us decide if I need to revisit that class or if we can move on to another area.

Reflection

What does Elena do to take some of the heat off of Sylvia? What strategies does she use in giving suggestions? Why do you think Sylvia gets so excited? Which approach did Elena choose and why?

> **Key Steps: Directive Informational Approach**
>
> 1. Identify the problem or goal and solicit clarifying information.
>
> 2. Offer solutions. Ask for the teacher's input into the alternatives offered and request additional ideas.
>
> 3. Summarize chosen alternatives, ask for confirmation, and request that the teacher restate final choices.
>
> 4. Set up a follow-up plan and meeting.

Scenario B

Judy has been a French and Spanish teacher at New Hope for 5 years. As part of a state grant, all the foreign-language teachers have a bank of computers in their classrooms for the first time. Very little staff development accompanied the grant, so the teachers have been struggling to use the computers effectively. Elena is trying to get some funds to pay the foreign-language teachers to work on lessons for the wired foreign-language classroom.

In the meantime, Elena thought she might get the dialogue started by observing one of Judy's classes. At the planning conference, they decided that Elena would use the student on-task, off-task behavior tool (Table 3.5) to determine what is going on in the groups working on projects while Judy is helping the students on the computer. Elena gave a copy of the observation to Judy after class.

Elena: Did the on-task, off-task tool provide any helpful information?

Judy: It was actually pretty depressing. The students were off task much more than I had thought while I was helping at the computers. I guess that I was so immersed that I didn't realize how little work was getting done. On the other hand, when I left the computer group, they really stayed on task. I wonder what that means?

Elena: The students really can get involved in the computer work. It really has a lot of potential for foreign-language work. Your guiding them is so important. They are getting off on the right foot. What do you think you can do to get the rest of the class to stay on task while the computer group still needs assistance?

Judy: I guess I'm going to have to develop clear roles and processes for them to work together so I don't have to watch them all the time. I thought that writing and practicing scenes for a play they're going to perform would keep them on task. I have to remember that they're middle school students. Can you think of how I can organize them?

Elena: How about using some simple cooperative learning techniques—in French, of course—to keep the groups focused?

Judy: I guess they do need that structure. One could be the recorder for the scene and another could be the group leader. Do you think they need a reflector to report on how the group worked?

Elena: Maybe to start off with. Once you see that they are on task most or all of the time, you may or may not choose to do away with the reflector.

If this strategy works well, do you think one of the other foreign-language teachers could observe it?

Judy: I'd prefer not at this point. I'm not comfortable with either the technology or leaving the groups on their own. And I'm the least experienced of the foreign-language teachers.

Elena: OK. We can wait till the funding for your meetings comes through and start from there. So, you'll start training the students in cooperative learning techniques so they can work more effectively while you're working at the computers. Do you need any literature on cooperative learning?

Judy: No, thanks, I've got plenty.

Elena: Can we meet again next week at the same time to see how it's going? I'd also like your input on how the observation process worked for you. Would you like me to observe the groups again before we meet?

Judy: Let's meet first and see how it's working. I wouldn't want you to observe until I've gotten some of the kinks out.

Reflection

How does Elena respond to Judy's rejection of Elena's request? What do you think is Elena's ultimate goal? How can you tell which approach is being used?

Key Steps: Collaborative Approach

focus on instruction & learning

1. The teacher identifies ~~the problem~~; you solicit as much clarifying information as possible.

2. Reflect back on what you've heard for accuracy.

3. Begin collaborative brainstorming, asking the teacher for his or her ideas first. *Data collection strategies*

   Develop a plan to solve problem
4. Problem solve through a sharing and discussion of options.

5. Agree on a plan and follow-up meeting.

Scenario C

Several parents have already come in to complain to Elena about John O'Connell's class. A few have been trying to switch their children out of his class. As a result, Elena has decided she'd better see what's going on. It is going to be a difficult task because John has been teaching math at New Hope for more than 25 years, and from all accounts, he is teaching the exact same way he did 25 years ago.

Elena has an idea. At the planning conference, she asks John, as the senior math teacher, to try out some techniques that a math teacher in her previous school found exceedingly successful, especially in preparing students for the new state math test. Depending on how they work for him, they could discuss recommending them to the other math teachers, she says. Elena also offers John the opportunity to visit the math teacher from her previous school so he can see the techniques at work and talk about them with their originator. After much hesitation, John reluctantly takes her up on the suggestion. Elena then asks if she can observe him using the techniques and use the visit as her official observation. When Elena mentions observation tools, John immediately says that he prefers that she use the traditional narrative form. Elena convinces John to allow her to record verbatim as much as she sees, and he agrees that each of them will analyze the verbatim narrative separately.

Elena: Did you get a chance to look at the transcript of my observation?

John: No. I've been too busy. The visit to your old school really set my schedule off.

Elena: Can you take a few minutes now and give me your reactions?

John: (after a few minutes) Having the students work in twos to solve problems and then share their answers and processes with the closest set of twos just doesn't work for me. The desks got all messed up, the class was disorderly, and then it took me a long time to get them back to their regular work. It may work for your colleague, but not for me. Look at all the confusion and lost time.

Elena: I hear what you're saying. Besides the noise and confusion, how did the students work together?

John: They had a ball because they could talk away, but I had no way of knowing what was going on.

Elena: Do you have any ideas on how you could get rid of the glitches?

John: Your math teacher friend has the room set up differently, so she doesn't have to deal with students moving all over. I can't have them working at tables all the time. I can't teach that way.

Elena: How could you get around that?

John: Maybe I could have them rearrange the desks on Friday so the custodians could get them back in rows for Monday. But that would mean teaching the whole day with them in groups.

Elena: Could you arrange your schedule to do that?

John: I guess I could do problems on Friday and have them go over their tests for the rest of the period. They always have trouble concentrating on Friday anyway, so I won't have to deal with trying to make them listen all period.

Elena: Good suggestion. What do you think about getting feedback on their problem-solving processes and solutions?

John: I don't know. Your colleague has one student from each group write the solution and explain the process on the board. I'm afraid I'll lose control on a Friday if they're at tables. Maybe I'll have each table be responsible for writing one problem's solution and process on the board, and then ask for other suggestions. I don't know if it'll work. They may not stay as quiet as I like.

Elena: I think it's a terrific start. Let's go over what you're going to do. If it works, maybe some of the new math teachers can sit in on your class to see how it works.

John: I don't think so. They should concentrate on keeping order in their own classrooms. Some of the noise I hear coming out of those rooms. . . . So, I'm going to ask my homeroom to arrange the desks on Friday morning in tables of four. The students will first work in twos solving a problem, then they'll share their process and answer with the other two at the table. Then one person will put one process and solution on the board, and I'll ask for comments. Then they'll go to the next problem. If I have time at the end of the period, they can go over their weekly tests. The custodian will put the desks back in rows for Monday.

Elena: Fine. So Friday will be problem-solving day with the students at tables. If you make this an ongoing schedule, I could ask the custodian to rearrange the desks when he cleans on Thursdays. Can we meet a week from Monday to see how it's going?

> ### Reflection
>
> *What does Elena do to avoid feeding into John's negativism? How is she responding to the parents' complaints? How does she react to his resistance to do certain things? Which approach did Elena choose and why?*

John: Let's wait for two weeks. It'll give me a better idea if I want to continue with it. Since I get here early, you could come to my classroom on Monday before school starts.

Key Steps: Self-Directed Approach

1. Listen carefully to the teacher's initial statement.

2. Reflect back on your understanding of the problem.

3. Constantly clarify and reflect until the real problem is identified.

4. Have the teacher problem solve and explore consequences of various actions.

5. The teacher commits to a decision and firms up a plan.

6. The supervisor restates the teacher's plan and sets up a follow-up meeting.

Collaborative Reflection

The purpose of the collaborative reflection is to think about the value of the reflective supervision cycle just completed. This discussion can take place toward the end of the feedback conference, at a scheduled time after the feedback conference, informally soon after the feedback conference, or, if schedules are really tight, as written feedback. The questions asked are simple; in fact, they are a variation of the reflector's questions in the reflective practice guidelines presented in Chapter 2—What went well? What needs improvement? What would you do differently?—and are the prototype for most effective feedback processes. Remember that the focus of the collaborative reflection is the *process between the supervisor and the teacher, not the teaching that took place in the observation.*

Collaborative Reflection

1. What was valuable in the process we (just) completed?

2. What was of little value?

3. What changes would you suggest for the next cycle?

Class Practice

If you are able to schedule the planning conference or observation with your teacher volunteer before the next class meeting, be prepared to role-play the feedback conference in class. Decide on an interpersonal approach and create a description of the teacher with whom you met. Using the reflective practice guidelines, groups of three will practice as many of the scenarios as possible.

Site Practice

If the colleague on-site with whom you practiced the planning conference is not the participant for the whole clinical supervision cycle, find another teacher who will volunteer to do the complete cycle. Complete the cycle on-site and prepare the following written report:

A. Recount each phase of the cycle: planning conference, observation, feedback conference, and collaborative reflection. A video or audiotape can substitute for the written description.

B. Analyze the data from each approach choice you made and then interpret the data.

   1. How much teacher input was there in the planning conference? Would you recommend a change in the approach to this teacher in another planning session? Why?

   2. Did the observation tool reveal the behaviors on which you and your colleague agreed to focus? How or why not? Was the observation tool you chose appropriate and effective? Is it a tool you would use again? Why or why not? What other tool would you suggest?

   3. Which interpersonal approach did you use in the feedback conference? Why? What was the teacher's response? How well did it work?

   4. What were the teacher's reactions to the process? How effective was the collaborative reflection? What did you learn?

C. Provide a final reflection on the whole process, that is, your personal evaluation of what worked and was of value and what you will think about doing differently in the future.

CONCLUSION

This chapter has permitted us to expand our understanding of clinical supervision and become acquainted with the authors' version of reflective clinical supervision. The cycle presented consists of four stages:

1. The planning conference

2. The observation

3. The feedback conference

4. The collaborative reflection

Scenarios for some phases based on actual school contexts were presented, and exercises to practice the stages in class and on-site were created. Now that you are familiar with and have practiced various interpersonal approaches, tools and techniques of observation, and the reflective clinical supervision cycle, you can begin to think about the different ways that improvement of classroom instruction can be configured in a department, grade, team, or school. In Chapter 5, we present some of the significant alternatives to and variations on the traditional procedures for improving classroom instruction.

Alternative Approaches 5

Case Studies and Implementation Guidelines

CHAPTER OVERVIEW

1. Standards-Based Walk-Through

2. Mentoring

3. Peer Coaching

4. Critical Friends Groups (CFG)

5. Portfolio Assessment

6. Peer Assessment

7. Action Research

We have laid the foundation for a sound supervision program by discussing interpersonal approaches, reviewing observation instruments, and introducing a framework for a complete cycle of reflective clinical supervision. You also have had the opportunity to practice and reflect on each facet of this supervision program. In this chapter, we provide a unique compendium of alternative approaches to supervision. Each approach is presented through an actual case study[1] that highlights the successful implementation of seven alternative approaches to supervision of classroom instruction.

Stages for implementation accompany each approach. In addition, a few of the case studies focus primarily on the organizational processes that the individuals or group instituted to develop their procedures. Thus, these studies illustrate the way that instructional leaders introduce innovative supervisory strategies in the context of unique school settings. We are broadening the picture. Until now we have concentrated on the development of supervisory skills and practices; now we are beginning to look at supervision as one facet of instructional leadership.

STANDARDS-BASED WALK-THROUGH

The standards-based walk-through is unique because it does focus on enabling teachers to learn by exploring and relating to what other teachers are doing in their classrooms.

—Roberts & Pruitt, 2003, p. 121

Case Study 1

Dr. Christina Russo is an instructional supervisor in the Laurelton School District in El Dorado Hills, California.[2] She's been in that position in her district for the past three years and has a superb reputation as a constructivist educator who relates well to teachers and principals. As an innovative educator, Dr. Russo explored a range of alternatives to supervision and staff development. Having read about Sylvia Roberts's and Eunice Pratt's "walk-through" approach to promote a culture of collaborative inquiry among teachers, Christina volunteered to offer professional development workshops in the district. Mohammad Alauddin, principal of a K–5 elementary school, was particularly interested in nurturing a culture of collaborative instruction for his teachers. As a new principal whose predecessor was the classic administrator-bureaucrat, Mr. Alauddin wanted to implement alternatives to traditional supervision. First, however, he wanted to engage teachers in meaningful staff development. Having worked with Christina in the past, he invited her to conduct a walk-through in his school during a professional development day in November. Mohammad was particularly interested in the standards-based walk-through because principals in the district, as in many other locales, were required to pay close attention to the standards-based curriculum.

During her opening address to the faculty, Dr. Russo explained the walk-through as follows:

The walk-through is a structured process for opening up classrooms so that you can observe one another and learn from what occurs in other classrooms. How often are we isolated? We rarely have the opportunity to visit other classrooms in order to systematically observe what our colleagues are doing. Each of us can learn from one another. Great ideas are meant to be shared so that all students will learn. The walk-through is a great tool used by teachers for teachers. My role and that of Mr. Alauddin are meant uniquely to facilitate the process. The ultimate form and shape of the walk-through will be up to you.

Several models of the walk-through exist. I'd like to discuss the standards-based model since, as you very well know, our district has implemented an assessment system for the standards-based curriculum. Please note that after the approach is explained and tried at least once, you as a faculty will have the opportunity on your own to revise or even adopt another walk-through model.

Dr. Russo then explained the connection between the walk-through and standards.

Our model of the walk-through, based wholly on the work of Roberts and Pruitt (2003), is driven by the implementation of the content standards that have been adopted by school districts. This does not preclude a school from using the process to focus on other areas of interest. We initiated the process because building principals, with whom we were working, were struggling to identify ways of getting teachers to become comfortable with and respond to the standards that had been mandated as the focus of instruction in their districts.

We view schools as professional learning communities. Clearly, instructional practice and educational reform efforts have been profoundly influenced by the standards movement. Standards provide teachers with a blueprint for setting goals, planning curriculum, identifying effective instructional strategies, and assessing student performance. Once standards have been set, if teachers are to know what to do with them, they need ongoing direction and adequate support. We view the school walk-through as a strategy that serves this purpose by permitting teachers to observe their colleagues' work in relation to the standards, as they seek ways of improving learning opportunities for their students.

One of the teachers at the staff development introductory meeting interrupted Dr. Russo and asked, "What do we do on the walk?" Dr. Russo explained:

The tour is conducted on a professional development day when the students are not present in the school building. During the walk-through, the team members visit the classrooms to which they have been assigned and record their observations. They review student work for evidence of standards-related activities. They identify instructional activities, teacher-made instructional materials, and learning centers that might have implication for standards-based teaching in their own classrooms. They look for instructional activities that develop students' higher-level thinking skills. They make note of the layout of classrooms and content of bulletin boards and other displays in the classroom. If they are available, visitors may also review the teacher's lesson plans to see the scope and sequence used by the teacher for standards-related instructional planning.

As a team of teachers reviews the various artifacts in the classrooms, they share their perceptions with each other. It's important to remember that this process is not meant for evaluation.

Dr. Russo explained what happens after the walk-through:

After the walk-through, the teachers attend grade-level meetings to discuss their observations. Finally, they prepare a brief summary sheet listing (a) the things that they have learned about standards-based teaching and learning as found in their notes and (b) the ideas they would like to replicate in their own classrooms. All summary sheets are then submitted to the principal, and a brief report, indicating what the teachers have learned from the process, is prepared for dissemination to the faculty. This process will also cultivate classroom observation as a facet of your role as teacher leaders and enhance your overall leadership capacity.

The faculty committed to implementing the walk-through that year. The following comments were culled from the assessment Dr. Russo distributed to the participants at the end of the academic year:

- I ended up looking forward to the walk-through. We walked through twice, and most teachers enjoyed the process and learned a lot. It made me feel good about being a teacher.
- Finally, we spent valuable time on a professional development day. The walk-through is fun and a tremendous learning experience.

(Continued)

> (Continued)
>
> - The walk-through lets me see the teachers in my school in a different light. I am always surprised at the creative ways I see of teaching to and reinforcing the standards.
> - I am motivated to try new things with my class when I see how innovative some of the teachers can be.
> - I believe every good teacher is a thief. We all steal good ideas from one another. After the walk-through, I accumulate loads of new ideas.
> - After our last walk-through, a teacher from another grade level, whom I don't know too well, asked if she could come to my room to discuss how I used some of the instructional materials that I had made. I think the school walk-through is one of the better ideas that the principal has introduced to our school.

Source: S. M. Roberts and E. Z. Pruitt. (2003). *Schools as Professional Learning Communities: Collaborative Activities and Strategies for Professional Development.* Thousand Oaks, CA: Corwin.

A Definition

The *standards-based walk-through* provides for an organized tour of the building by teams of teachers who visit their peers' classrooms; observe the classroom environment and learning centers; review student work samples, special projects, and portfolios; and examine other classroom artifacts that the teacher has put on display for the walk-through (Roberts & Pruitt, 2003). Roland Barth (1990), noted educator, has pointed out that "teachers also need to be able to relate their classroom behavior to what other teachers are doing in their classrooms. Teachers *think* they do that. Many do, but many do not do it very systematically or regularly" (p. 49).

The standards-based walk-though is unique precisely because it focuses on enabling you to learn by exploring and relating to what other teachers are doing in their classrooms. Because it is designed and carried out by you, it helps to develop your leadership capacity. Please note that neither students nor supervisors are present during the walk-through.

The walk-through is a model or approach used to promote a culture of collaborative learning. Used as professional development or supervision, the walk-through engages teachers in meaningful activities to enhance the instructional process. Teaching can be a lonely experience. The walk-through gives colleagues an opportunity to see each other's work, reflect on the instructional process, and to collaborate on developing new and better ways to improve instruction and thus promote student learning (Roberts & Pruitt, 2003).

Stages for Implementation

Various formats of the walk-through are possible. Although the case study above focuses on using the walk-through to enhance professional development during professional development days, other models use it directly as an alternative to traditional observation (evaluation). For instance, a principal can forgo traditional observations of teachers who implement a walk-through, as described below. The walk-through can easily be done during the regular school day (not a professional development day), where a small group of teachers plan on walking through each other's classrooms when class is in session. What makes the walk-through successful is that it is a well-planned and systematic process.

Here are some general steps for implementing a walk-through as an alternative to supervision:

1. Meet with a supervisor and a teacher colleague to discuss using the walk-through as an alternative to traditional supervision.

2. Articulate a specific purpose for the walk-through.

3. Establish and maintain trust.

4. See the walk-through as an opportunity to collaborate in order to grow and learn as a professional.

5. Develop objectives for the walk-through.

6. Develop a form to guide the observation (based on the objectives).

7. Decide when and how the walk-through will take place. Will students be in the room during the walk-through?

8. Prepare your classroom for the visit by showcasing the aspects of the curriculum you want seen. For instance, if you decide that you want to show the science curriculum in action, make sure you put on display lessons and unit plans, student projects, science materials in use, student bulletin boards that focus on science, seating arrangements used, and so on.

9. Plan to meet during a common preparatory session or before or after school to share experiences.

10. Develop a plan of action. If the process is used as an alternative to supervision, the supervisor will likely want to see an action plan that summarizes the walk-through, what each teacher learned through the process, and the steps that will be taken to improve classroom instruction.

Reflective Practice

Activity 1

Groups of two or more research the walk-through. Can you find a school to visit that has implemented the walk-through? If so, interview the participants. What do you think are the advantages and disadvantages of the walk-through? How might you implement a walk-through with a colleague or an entire faculty at a given grade level?

Activity 2

Find a colleague who wants to develop a plan for the walk-through as an alternative to supervision. Assume that the supervisor has agreed to the walk-through in concept but wants to see a plan for implementation. Develop concrete objectives and, using the steps listed above in the Stages for Implementation section, establish a specific plan you would present to your supervisor. Be sure to demonstrate what you will do, what you might learn, and how the walk-through will contribute to your professional development and ultimately change teaching to improve student learning.

MENTORING

The mentor-mentee relationship is, indeed, a transformative one that can forever change the course of one's life.

—Cienkus, Grant Haworth, & Kavanagh, 1996, p. 2

Case Study 2

Mari Celi Sanchez is an experienced teacher in Northern Valley Regional High School District. After consulting with her assistant principal, James McDonnell, Mari Celi has decided to mentor Eric Jones, a non-tenured second-year teacher. Mari Celi is a dedicated teacher who has received two Outstanding Teacher of the Year awards over the course of her 18 years at the high school. As part of the professional development program, she opts for mentorship and receives release time to work with Eric.

Mari Celi meets with Eric to discuss their plans. She explains to Eric that she has no evaluative authority and will keep their conversations confidential. Although Eric will have to undergo at least three formal observations over the course of the semester, Mari Celi will not in any way participate in the evaluation process. "My job," she explains to Eric, "is to work with you as much as you'd like on areas that you feel may need improvement." Eric and Mari Celi develop a close professional relationship over the course of the next several months. He realizes that she in fact does not have any evaluative input, and his confidence in her grows daily. "You know," says Eric, "I feel I can really open up to you. More so than to a supervisor who I know will eventually evaluate me."

Eric's skills have improved dramatically. "You know," explains Mari Celi, "you are really a natural teacher. The kids love you, and your enthusiasm is infectious." Certainly Eric's evaluation reports in the year and a half he has been at the school have been exceptional. Eric attributes much of his success to the "expert and friendly assistance" he has received from Mari Celi.

While working on their second-semester instructional plans, Mari Celi shares some research she recently completed on gender bias in the classroom as part of her doctoral work. "Gender bias is quite common in many classrooms, you know," explains Mari Celi. Eric responds: "Oh, I believe that's overstated. I treat everyone equally in my class." "OK," says Mari Celi. "Let's see. I'll observe you." They discuss plans for an upcoming lesson during which Mari Celi will observe as both an independent observer and a participant observer using a qualitative research approach (Glanz, 2003). Mari Celi records the following notes during one segment of the lesson:

11th-grade class: 13 boys and 12 girls; self-contained classroom. Eric starts lesson at 9:45 a.m. I enter as Eric tells class to take out their readers. As Eric gives instructions for silent reading, three students (two male and one female) are out of their seats hanging their coats in the rear classroom closet. The girl is talking. Eric tells her to be quiet and sit down. During silent reading, students are reading quietly. After about 3 minutes, a monitor enters classroom and the teacher records the daily attendance. Noise level in class rises. Monitor leaves room. Teacher walks back and forth as students get quiet. At 9:49 a.m., Eric asks a boy to tell the class what the story was about. Student responds. Class attentive. Eric asks a girl, "Why do you think Billy in the story was so upset?" Student responds. Teacher calls on a boy who also responds, albeit differently. Eric probes and asks the boy to explain. Eric asks a girl another thought-provoking question. Girl responds. Teacher asks a boy another question—"Why was Jane so angry with Billy?"—and probes. (Ten minutes elapse and I note that it appears that Eric calls on boys and girls evenly, but that he consistently probes male responses but rarely probes a female response. Curious, ask Eric about this!) Time elapses. Teacher divides class into study groups; I join one of the groups with two boys and one girl. Teacher circulates. Students answer reading questions and discuss story. I ask them if they liked the story and to explain why or why not. Teacher requests attention from class. Eric continues by asking many thought-provoking questions and follows the same pattern of probing more for boys than for girls. Interestingly, when the boy sitting to my right in the group was asked a question, he was probed, but the girl to my left was not. I could not discern any concern among the students.

After the class, Mari Celi shares her observations with Eric. Eric, not defensive at all, was surprised. "Really? That's interesting. What do you think it means?" he asks. Mari Celi and Eric explore various possibilities in an atmosphere of trust, candor, and mutual respect.

A Definition

Mentoring is a process that facilitates instructional improvement wherein an experienced educator works with a novice or less experienced teacher collaboratively and nonjudgmentally to study and deliberate on ways instruction in the classroom may be improved. Mentors are not judges or critics but, rather, facilitators of instructional improvement. Like Northern Valley Regional High School, many schools have developed mentoring programs in which an experienced teacher is assigned or volunteers to work with a novice teacher for the purpose of "providing individualized, ongoing professional support" (Glickman et al., 1998, p. 353). In some parts of the country, such as Toledo, Ohio, mentoring is actually negotiated into the union contract as an alternative supervisory approach. Although some people in the field equate mentoring with supervision (Reiman & Thies-Sprinthall, 1998), we assert that mentoring is an alternative form of supervision.

Stages for Implementation

To implement mentoring effectively, the reader is advised to read *Teachers as Mentors: A Practical Guide* by Field and Field (1994) and to view the video that the Association for Supervision and Curriculum Development (1994) has produced on mentoring. We strongly recommend that mentors develop and use the supervisory skills presented in the preceding chapters. The stages for implementation that follow were developed at Northern Valley Regional High School District (1996) and are excerpted from a manual titled *Differentiated Supervision.*

Description

This model can incorporate a variety of possible applications. In all cases, an educator would agree to provide assistance, support, and recommendations to another staff member or staff members. A mentor could work with a non-tenured teacher or share expertise in a specific area with other educators. For example, a staff member with specific technical training may share this expertise with others. All interactions and recommendations between the mentor and staff members will be confidential.

Approach

The following guidelines are highly prescriptive; however, mentorship has proven successful as an alternative means of supervision at Northern Valley Regional High School.

1. Any educator may volunteer to be a support mentor. A supervisor or administrator, knowing of a certain staff member's expertise, may request that that individual serve in this capacity. If asked, a staff member must agree, not be directed, to serve.

2. A mentor plan is developed by the educator, approved by the supervisor, and shared with those individuals to be mentored.

3. The mentor implements the plan and reports on the plan activities to the supervisor.

Reflective Practice

A group of three students will develop a mentor plan. Then they will describe the plan and role-play a mentoring session in which the mentor shares his or her plan. What feedback approach would you use? Use the guidelines for reflective practice to provide feedback to the mentor and mentee.

PEER COACHING

When two teachers observe each other; the one teaching is the "coach" and the one observing is the "coached."

—Showers & Joyce, 1996, p. 15

Case Study 3

The International Institute is one of four mini-schools or institutes that are part of a large New York City middle school. It was previously one of the lowest-performing middle schools in the district. Nancy Brogan, an assertive, go-getter principal, was brought in to improve both achievement and image. Open to innovation and aggressive in pursuing funds, she broke up the 1,200-plus students into four theme institutes. The International Institute is composed primarily of Haitian, Russian, Spanish, Chinese, Bengali, and Urdu bilingual students. Because of the bilingual focus, the staff of the institute mirrors the diversity of the student body.

Through one of her outreach efforts, Nancy secured the assistance of one of the authors of this text. My (the author's) initial project was to help organize the governance committee of the institute. This task completed, our conversations veered more toward curriculum and teaching and learning issues. All of the teachers on the steering committee were committed, enthusiastic, effective, and creative teachers and, along with the institute director, Lynne Pagano, were open to anything that would promote student achievement. Because peer coaching was an approved choice in the new union contract's weekly period for professional development for each teacher, we decided to pursue the possibility of using this staff period to develop and implement the skills and practices of peer coaching. A second, recently approved union provision included the option of alternative assessment for tenured teachers. The director's reaction was,

These teachers are the best. They can all use the peer coaching as their official observations—even the one who is just shy of tenure. This way I can concentrate on the teachers who really need help. By the way, would you mind if I sat in on your meetings?

The prospective participants and I then made a site visit to a school that had developed a very sophisticated system of peer assessment. The teachers came back excited and ready to take on the challenge.

Next, we had to decide the focus of the peer coaching. Two of the teachers had been trained during the summer in the new standards required by the city and the state, and one teacher had been involved in developing the Spanish curriculum and city adaptation for the standards. Their enthusiasm about the work they had been doing and the need for implementation triggered conversation about two possible coaching models:

1. Peer observations based on the implementation of the curriculum for the new standards

2. Coaching where teachers would discuss classroom challenges or interests and conduct interclass visitations

Mannor Wong, the English as a Second Language (ESL) teacher, commented, "Since I'm not tenured yet, I'd prefer honing my general instructional techniques. I'd like someone to be able to give me feedback on the strategies I'm working on in the classroom and how the students are responding to them."

Farooqui Nasreen, the Urdu bilingual teacher, had the following conversation with Madeline Castaneda, the Spanish bilingual teacher:

Farooqui: Since you've already developed a curriculum in Spanish for the new standards, could I see how you're going to implement it in the classroom? Then maybe you could observe me as I try to use the adapted curriculum in my Urdu classes.

Madeline: That's a good idea. And the students will feel comfortable with you there because of the multicultural sharing we've been doing.

Lynn Lavner, an English Language Arts teacher with a strong performing arts background, began sitting in on our meetings unofficially. Her reactions were somewhat different: "I could use help as I try to develop our Facing History Through the Arts curriculum this spring, but I don't know about observing another teacher's class. I don't think that's for me."

The plan that emerged was for the participants to learn and practice interpersonal, observation, and feedback skills through observations of videotaped classroom instruction and role plays of interpersonal techniques and feedback approaches. They would then be prepared to help each other more effectively and become turnkey trainers for future coaching groups. A date for the first orientation and training meeting was set. In the interim, the volunteer group was to be finalized.

The Best-Laid Plans of Mice and Teachers

We began meeting in the director's office during the teachers' 40-minute lunch period. There were constant interruptions, time lost getting lunch, and teachers arriving late or not at all. Lynn Lavner hadn't been in on the original planning, which may have been the reason for her initial spotty attendance. Mannor Wong had not been involved in the early meetings either and may have had some initial apprehension. I decided that we needed to go back to the drawing board to look for a longer block of time at a different point in the day. Luckily, this particular group was involved in implementing a grant with some flexible funding. The coordinator of the grant, Elke Savoy (one of the participants), figured out that she could compensate the teachers to come after school for a series of two-hour workshops.

(Continued)

(Continued)

We had one more setback before launching the afterschool workshops. Through her ongoing outreach efforts, Nancy Brogan had procured additional professional development help to increase achievement scores. One strategy included daily brief observations by the directors in all classrooms and completion of checklists for each teacher. All staff were to follow certain procedures that the directors would verify in their visits. I met with the principal and Lynne Pagano to explain that this method was at odds with our peer-coaching goals. They agreed that the teachers involved in our project would be exempt from this requirement. In fact, Lynne was relieved because she was "going crazy" trying to keep up with the marathon visiting schedule.

Uninterrupted quality time, snacks, and compensation were a few of the elements that fostered time on task. The following weeks were spent perfecting the participants' interpersonal and feedback skills and using various techniques to observe videos of teachers and students. As the group simulated and role-played the skills in class, they began to practice observing colleagues' classes. Finally, they went through the clinical observation cycle with each other and other volunteers in the International Institute. Discussions and feedback took place at each session to fine-tune the process as we went along. Open communication about reactions to the process was encouraged.

Once the participants were comfortable with their observing and feedback skills, the next step was to set up individual or paired plans for their dialogues around curriculum implementation. The initial plans were set up at the last workshop because it was the last opportunity for quality time. We decided that each teacher or pair of teachers would write an action plan for his or her focus. Brief meetings would take place every two weeks to share experiences, provide feedback on what was and was not working, troubleshoot, and modify plans as needed.

I kept a running record of the process and provided both a qualitative and quantitative evaluation at the end of the semester. The participants were so enthusiastic that it was decided to involve more volunteers the following fall and share the experience with another institute.

> ### Reflection
>
> *What are the lessons to be learned from the initial meetings of the coaching group? What are a couple of underlying assumptions that the facilitators of this type of project must maintain for successful implementation?*

A Definition

Peer coaching is an umbrella term for the many different configurations of teachers helping teachers that have emerged primarily since the 1980s. Some of the other terms often used interchangeably with *peer coaching* are *peer assistance, collegial coaching, technical coaching, cognitive coaching, challenge coaching,* and *peer supervision.* Most of these models pertain to variations of peer-to-peer assistance of equals and do not involve evaluation. Mentoring programs that consist of master teachers helping less experienced or less well-trained colleagues are not included in our categorization. In this case study, peer coaching is defined as teachers helping teachers reflect on and improve teaching practices or implement particular instructional skills introduced through staff or curriculum development. Joyce and Showers (1980) specified the process as two or more teachers who meet regularly for problem solving using planning, observation, feedback, and creative thinking for the development of a specific skill.

Stages for Implementation

Goals for peer coaching include:

- Refine teaching practices
- Stimulate self-initiating, autonomous teacher thought
- Improve school culture
- Increase collegiality and professional dialogue
- Share in the implementation of new or common instructional skills

Key Steps

Teresa Benedetti (1997) outlined a simple set of procedures for teachers to initiate a peer-coaching system in their schools. The following procedures are an adaptation of her recommendations:

1. After obtaining permission from the appropriate administrators, suggest that your colleagues choose a peer whom they trust and with whom they feel they will work well.

2. Make sure that everyone is familiar with and able to engage in the cycle of clinical supervision. Ask assistance from supervisors or others familiar with clinical supervision.

3. Peers may have to help each other cover classes while their colleagues observe each other. Interested supervisors also can facilitate the freeing up of teachers. If scheduling conflicts occur, videotaping a class can provide the additional experience of viewing the class together. If both teachers teach the same content to similar classes, combining classes and observing each other's application of skills or team teaching can be very effective.

4. Organize weekly or biweekly seminars for peer coaching. The first sessions can be used to learn and review observation and feedback techniques. The opportunity to share experiences and brainstorm new ideas as well as modify the existing structure is essential.

Through the ongoing discussion of teaching and learning, curriculum development, and implementation, peer coaching can become the heart of professional development.

Reflective Practice

Site Practice

Each student will recruit a colleague who is interested in exploring peer coaching. Brainstorm with the teacher or teachers, if possible, about how peer coaching could be developed at your site. Record your ideas on chart paper and bring the actual sheets to class.

Class Practice

Divide the class into groups. Share the brainstormed ideas. Make a group list of the most promising ideas. The list can be developed by having each participant choose two or three favorites. The final choices will be the strategies that receive the most votes. Each group will report its results to the whole class. Students will then record their preferred strategies.

A JOURNEY: FROM PEER COACHING TO CRITICAL FRIENDS

In a Critical Friends Group context, critical means "important," "key," "essential," or "urgent" such as in "critical care."

—http://www.nsrfharmony.org/

Case Study 4

New Milford Middle School, a large intermediate school in a northeastern urban school district, has seen a recent and rapidly increasing number of English language learners (ELLs) enter the school over the past 5 years. Many of the new arrivals are Latino, but there is a sprinkling of Asians, Albanians, and several other nationalities. Unfortunately, the ESL teacher is not deemed an effective resource, adding to the teachers' frustration. Veteran staff members are not used to addressing the needs of non-English-speaking students, and the large number of new faculty are struggling just to survive in a large, somewhat anonymous environment. An ESL consultant, who had worked with one of the authors on a peer-coaching project, suggested that faculty work with the author on a peer-coaching model that would allow them to focus on their English language learners. Soon after, the end-of-the-year district report cited the school for poor results on standardized tests of its English language learners. Something had to be done! Thus was launched a new adventure in learning community building through alternatives to traditional supervision.

Professional development began with a series of meetings during which the participating group of teachers learned and practiced planning, observation, and feedback skills as a foundation for peer coaching. Practice scenarios were based as much as possible on real English language learner classroom dilemmas the teachers were facing. After each workshop, teachers practiced their new skills with each other and other colleagues. One teacher commented, "Practicing with each other using real classroom challenges is not only teaching us new skills, but we are actually solving problems in our workshop sessions." Another noted, "The lists of strategies that we have been building together are providing some of the support for ELLs that we have been lacking." The coaches then began to observe each other's classes using the Reflective Clinical Cycle.

As a result of their peer coaching, the participants realized that they still didn't have a grasp on the skills of certain ELL students. The author told them about Critical Friends Groups, professional learning communities consisting of approximately 8–12 educators who come together voluntarily at least once a month for about 2 hours. Critical Friends Group members are committed to improving their practice through collaborative learning (www.nsrfharmony.org/). She explained that problem-solving protocols or tools are often the basis of Critical Friends meetings and that they might try to use some student work protocols to examine the student work of the ELL students. She also thought that the protocols might serve as a springboard to creating a Critical Friends Group. The participants were willing and two teachers volunteered to bring in the student work of two struggling English language learners for the next meeting. Since the participants were quite familiar with each other's students, they decided that names would be left off to allow for a more objective description of the work.

At the next meeting, I introduced the protocol "Describing Students' Work." We began with a brief description exercise to prepare us for describing the student work. I gave the group the word "typhoon," to which each teacher responded with free association in a round-robin style. Next, the first teacher/presenter shared the student work describing the assignment. We then began descriptive rounds of the work, beginning with general impressions and physical description, continuing with "what the student is working on" rounds, which involves asking oneself what the student is trying to accomplish, what she or he values, knows how to do, and so on. Then we looked at the implications for teaching this child and what changes the teacher might make in working with this student. The culmination of the protocol was a round of "I wonder..." The teachers came up with perceptive thoughts and ideas. When we talked about what we learned about this student, we realized that the student had more knowledge and skills than the teacher had previously thought. The presenting teacher commented, "I really feel now that I can have higher expectations for Jorge and will try to challenge him more."

We described another piece of student work, and to our surprise, we came to a similar conclusion. Looking objectively and anonymously at the student letter that was shared, we were able to describe patterns of skills that no one had realized this student possessed. The teacher came away with a fresh, positive perspective of the accomplishments and potential of both of these students who the teacher had previously thought had few English skills.

The unexpectedly felicitous outcomes of the protocol led the group to decide to continue analyzing student work at the next meeting. I also decided to share the "Text Rendering Experience Protocol" with the group. Besides providing the opportunity to introduce another protocol, I felt that this protocol could be a bridge between using protocols for adults and children. The purpose of this protocol is "to collaboratively construct meaning, clarify and expand our thinking about a text or document" (National School Reform Faculty CFG Institutes 2004–2005). We used a text to which I had been introduced at a training session for Critical Friends facilitators, *Turning to One Another,* by Margaret Wheatley (Wheatley, 2002). I chose this text because it talks about perspectives and change—our willingness to be disturbed—in our complex world. I thought it appropriate for a school in transition and an empowering model for working with English language learners. Each participant chooses and shares first a sentence, then a phrase, and finally a word from the text. The facilitator then reads the group-created text. Upon completion of the process, the group discussed their reactions to the protocol and brainstormed ways to use this protocol in a class with ELLs.

At the conclusion of this session, our last for the year, the participants made three recommendations: (1) to request to use peer coaching as their alternative evaluation process (a choice in their union contract), (2) to create a Critical Friends Group where they would problem solve student, grade, and academy dilemmas, using additional protocols, and (3) eventually turnkey their new skills to other faculty. In addition, the end-of-the-year tests revealed that it is the special education English language learners who are having particular difficulty. The assistant principal in charge of our project recommended expanding the skill building to the faculty working with this targeted group of students.

However, the creation of a Critical Friends Group requires more than an outside facilitator on whom the group would be dependent and a small number of members familiar with only a few protocols. The author and the assistant principal, with the group's support, went to the principal with the two immediate requests: (1) a heads-up on the peer-coaching evaluation option and (2) professional development financial support to allow some of the group members to be trained as Critical Friends facilitators. The author, a trained Critical Friends facilitator, along with a recently relocated well-known facilitator, could incorporate the available members of the group into a seminar they would be running in the fall. The principal had recently been introduced to the concept of Critical Friends by a district leader who was encouraging the development of Critical Friends Groups in district schools. As a newly appointed principal in a large school with little sense of collaboration, she thought Critical Friends Groups could help begin the building of a learning community. Therefore, the principal arranged to release three teachers for three Friday sessions and three teachers agreed to attend two Saturday sessions to fulfill the required week of training. The school would then have a core of three trained teachers to promote the success of the first group and the expertise to turnkey to other faculty down the road. Finally, the principal also lent her support to the peer-coaching process as another means to build a professional learning community.

> ### Reflection
>
> *What attitudes do facilitators and leaders need when trying to develop new and/or alternative programs or projects? How does Michael Fullan's belief that "It is one thing to see an innovation 'up and running,' it is entirely another matter to figure out the pathways of how to get there in your own organization" (Fullan, 1999, p.14) apply to this case study?*

A Definition[3]

A *Critical Friends Group* is a professional learning community consisting of approximately 8–12 educators who have made the commitment to come together voluntarily at least once a month for about 2 hours to improve their practice through collaborative learning.

Stages for Implementation

The primary goals of a Critical Friends Group (CFG) are to:

- Create a professional learning community
- Make teaching practice explicit and public by "talking about teaching"
- Help people involved in schools to work collaboratively in democratic, reflective communities
- Establish a foundation for sustained professional development based on a spirit of inquiry
- Provide a consistent, ongoing context to understand work with students, relationships with peers, and thoughts, assumptions, and beliefs about teaching and learning
- Help educators help each other turn theories into practice and standards into actual student learning
- Improve learning and teaching

What does a CFG session look like?

Ideally, each session is approximately 2 hours. However, many protocols range from 1–2 hours providing flexibility in busy schedules. The session often begins with a "check-in"—an ice breaker, an exercise that previews the protocol, or a reflective question, such as, "So, what has transpired that's new or interesting as a result of the last meeting?" The coach may facilitate one of several protocols for examining a participant's student work (similar to the one in the case study). One of the members may bring in teacher work that the group can examine with teacher protocols. A text-based discussion of a topic of concern or interest to the group may take place, preferably with the use of a text-rendering protocol. Peer coaching may emerge among members in an ongoing or episodic manner.

Reflective Practice

Site Practice

Each student will recruit a colleague who is interested in exploring "Critical Friends." Go to the Web site of the National School Reform Faculty (NSRF), http://www.nsrfharmony.org/, and share the information with the teacher or teachers, if possible, about how a Critical Friends Group could be developed at your site. Record your ideas on chart paper and bring the actual sheets to class.

Class Practice

Divide the class into groups. Share the brainstormed ideas. Make a group list of the most promising ideas. The list can be developed by having each participant choose two or three favorites. The final choices will be the strategies that receive the most votes. Each group will report its results to the whole class. Students will then record their preferred strategies.

PORTFOLIOS FOR DIFFERENTIATED SUPERVISION

Case Study 5

When Carmen Farina became principal of the New York City elementary school PS 6, she faced many challenges, some more familiar to suburban principals than to urban ones.[4] She entered a school long renowned for academic excellence, located in one of the most elegant neighborhoods in the city. The previous principal presided over a building known as the private public school. Many of the parents had the means to send their children to private schools but preferred to send them to PS 6, generously funding the PTA to provide some of the extras that wealthy districts and independent schools often provide.

In her previous positions as a building principal and district staff developer, Carmen had transformed her school's language arts/social studies curriculum into an exciting interdisciplinary program called Making Connections and had overseen its implementation in the whole district. Carmen described the challenge at PS 6:

My dilemma upon assuming the principalship was that the students scored high on the standardized tests while little student-centered learning was going on. Veteran teachers, for the most part, ran traditional classrooms. How could I effect change in an environment where many parents and teachers were content with the status quo?

The approach I took was to begin visiting teachers on a daily basis and engaging them in conversations around their teaching practices. These visits allowed me to assess school strengths and weaknesses. Through constant class visits and discussion of successes and challenges, areas of concern and/or interest began to emerge. By the end of the year, we had been able to designate three priorities around curriculum needs and an area of interest for each teacher.

At that point, Carmen selected 10 teachers to participate in the first-year implementation of Portfolios for Differentiated Supervision. Although it was emphasized that participation was open to all faculty, a total of 16 teachers volunteered and subsequently took part in the process.

Laura Kotch, a staff developer, was key to the successful development and implementation of the model. The following remarks are some of the thoughts she shared in greeting a group of visitors to the school:

Each participating teacher is involved in creating a portfolio, a container for his or her area of inquiry. The decisions about which topics to study came from questions teachers had, their areas of interest, their curiosity, and experimentation with new classroom strategies and techniques. Some questions have lingered over time. A first-grade teacher's investigation originated with her question about practice that wasn't working. Her inquiry led to research on the most effective way to create competent and curious first-grade spellers. Other teachers began their portfolios by taking a risk and experimenting with new ways to integrate curriculum, such as Making Connections, author studies, and math/cooperative learning.

Laura concluded a workshop with these thoughts:

Teachers have been spending time talking together, reading articles and books written by the experts, and reflecting on their beliefs and practices. The task of writing ideas down in a portfolio requires us to clarify thoughts and ideas, refine our language, and find our writer's voice. The process of creating text has been both challenging and exciting. Writing together has allowed us the wonderful opportunity of forming a writing network, relating to each other not only as teachers but as authors as well. It will be worth all the hard work if the portfolio serves as a practical resource, while continuing to change and grow as our learning continues. As a facilitator, adviser, and friend working alongside the dedicated, hardworking, and talented professionals of PS 6, I am proud to be part of this exciting and innovative model of staff development.

A Definition

A *professional portfolio* can serve many different purposes. It can be, as it is at PS 6, a container for a particular area of inquiry. At PS 6, the portfolio not only documents the development of innovative and effective practices, it is a central vehicle for the growth of the teacher through self-reflection, analysis, and sharing with colleagues through discussion and writing. Although each PS 6 portfolio is different, each one includes teacher resources and references, professional articles, and practical suggestions.

Portfolios also can be used to support and enrich mentoring and coaching relationships. Although the portfolio does not replace the classroom observation, it extends and enhances the professional discussion by going beyond what is observed in the classroom on a given day. The advent of the electronic portfolio opens even more opportunities for sharing practices within a school, between schools, and beyond the teacher's district. When a teacher is applying for another position, an annotated collection of materials on a teacher's best classroom practices and work with colleagues supplements and strengthens the interview process (Danielson, 1996). One of us has repeatedly witnessed the influence that a well-crafted portfolio has on hiring committees.

Stages for Implementation (based on the PS 6 process)

Phase 1

A. Curriculum prioritizing

   1. Assess the school's strengths and weaknesses and develop a set of prioritized curriculum needs.

B. Portfolios for differentiated supervision

   1. Designate an area of expertise in each teacher's classroom, built through intensive class visitation and conversation around teaching practices.

   2. Solicit a group of volunteers or select staff to reflect on an area of expertise and share and provide materials for the school faculty and visiting colleagues.

   3. Criteria for inclusion of participants:

      a. Outstanding expertise in a certain area.
      b. A teacher who has not refined or reflected on a special talent.
      c. Teachers likely to respond to a collegial environment for self-improvement.

   4. Institute professional development to lay the groundwork for the creation of portfolios. Possible outcomes of the workshops are:

      a. Reflection on and analysis of the areas of expertise.
      b. Decision of some teachers to collaborate on their efforts and create a joint portfolio.
      c. Use of a letter format as a means of beginning faculty journals.

5. First drafts of the portfolios are submitted the following fall, and an administrator reviews the drafts and gives oral and written comments and suggestions.

6. When portfolios are completed, the principal writes a "dear author" letter to each participant.

Phase II

A. New portfolio cycle

1. Additional teachers choose to participate in the process.

2. Specialty faculty, such as ESL teachers, can complete their portfolios by adding to individual portfolios.

B. The reflective teacher

1. The process now involves semiannual "conversations" with the principal for a minimum of one uninterrupted hour to discuss portfolios and other areas of interest.

2. Teachers receive a summary of their conversation with the principal.

Advantages and Limitations of Process (according to PS 6)

A. Advantages

1. Affords the staff the opportunity to be reflective and analytical.

2. Encourages the teachers to work cooperatively together.

3. Allows the administration to get to know the teachers better and to encourage their growth in many areas.

4. Encourages the staff to read professional journals.

5. Gives a purpose for intervisitations.

6. Fosters professionalism in teachers.

7. Encourages teachers to apply for grants in areas of their expertise.

8. Enhances parents' view of the school.

9. Provides a focus for the two-way conversation with teachers.

10. Gives teachers more input.

11. Produces the "Hawthorne effect" when visitors come to the school.

12. Provides a vehicle for continuous inclusion of strategies (e.g., ESL, multiculturalism).

B. Challenges

1. Administration must develop a trusting relationship with the staff.

2. A lot of time is required.

3. Principal must be aware of what is going on in the classroom.

4. Teachers must be accepting of the process.

5. Inordinate amount of time is required for planning and writing.

6. Materials must be available.

7. Change is not immediate—it takes time.

> **Reflection**
>
> *How does this process differ from peer coaching? What are the similarities?*

Reflective Practice

Each student reflects on an area of classroom practice in which he or she has expertise or talent, about which he or she has questions, or with which he or she would like to experiment. Once everyone has come up with an idea, the class divides into small groups. After each person shares his or her area, the other members of the group offer suggestions of resources, professional articles and references, and strategies for creation of the portfolio.

PEER ASSESSMENT: SELECTION, SUPPORT, AND EVALUATION

Shared leadership can foster the professional growth and development of teachers, which in turn leads to the empowerment of students as successful learners.

—Personnel Committee, International High School, 1991

Case Study 6

The International High School, located on the basement floor of LaGuardia Community College, was a joint venture of the then New York City Board of Education and the Board of Higher Education of the City of New York. It is an alternative high school founded in 1985 to serve the needs of students with limited English proficiency. It describes itself as "alternative in its admissions policy, population served, school governance, teaching methodology, setting, and opportunities for both students and staff."

Some of the unique learning experiences for students developed over the past 13 years are the following:

- A focus on content-based English as a Second Language instruction
- Heterogeneous, collaborative groupings
- Career-oriented internships
- Organization of the entire curriculum around thematically based interdisciplinary cycles
- Team teaching
- Performance-based alternative assessment standards for course work and graduation
- The opportunity to take college courses with matriculated college students for both high school and college credit

The school is open to all students with limited English proficiency who reside in New York City, who have lived in the United States for fewer than 4 years, and who are entering ninth or tenth grade in the next school year. The diversity of languages, dress, and ethnicities that fills the halls dazzles the first-time visitor.

In a conversation, Eric Nadelstern, the founding principal of International High School, retraced the road that the staff traveled to reach their singular level of faculty and student empowerment:

The first years. In reflecting back, it was less about trying to figure out how to structure a school than trying to figure out how kids learn best—and through our discoveries, figuring out what a school would need to look like if it were built around our understanding about how kids learn best and in a way that allowed us to continue that level of inquiry, and then designing the school based on new learnings.

Given that, it's not surprising that the first year we opened, our school looked not too dissimilar from a traditional New York City public high school. We divided all knowledge into the same six arbitrary disciplines everyone else has been confined to for centuries. Periods were exactly 40 minutes long; we had eight of them a day. We made the mistake of thinking that if eight periods were good, nine must be better. So, going into the second year, we shaved 5 minutes off each instructional period and that gave an additional class.

The staff did meet together for 2 hours a week. Back then, it was as a paid-per-session afterschool activity. Since it was part and parcel of working here, it wasn't necessarily voluntary, although no one was forced to be here. We shared our insights on this common exploration about learning. And on the basis of those insights, we continued to rethink the way the school needed to be structured.

The first major step in that direction, or at least a milestone in it, was something we referred to as the Student for a Day Project. Everyone on staff was given the opportunity to be relieved of responsibilities, teaching and otherwise, for an entire school day, to spend a day with a kid. The staff member was to travel through the school as that kid did and attempt to see the school from the student's perspective. To avoid stacking the experiment, we selected 40 kids who were not as successful as we would have liked and asked the volunteers to spend the entire day with the student they chose. If that student had lunch during a particular period, they had to go to lunch with that student. If that student had gym, they had to bring their sneakers.

Over a 3-month period, everyone on staff volunteered for this exercise. We facilitated the shadowing opportunity by covering their classes. At the end of the experiment, we got together and shared our findings. In discussion, comments surfaced like, "The most interesting thing that happens in this school happens in the hallway in between classes." Or "Thirty-five-minute periods are insane. You can't do anything meaningful in 35 minutes, and to have to shift your focus every half hour is a crazy way of learning something."

So the curriculum committee decided to look at the structure and subsequently built a new one based on the 70-minute periods at LaGuardia Community College. I created a 2-hour block on Wednesday afternoon for the staff to meet. On Wednesdays, students can choose to stay at the school if they wish—the computer room is open, athletic and club activities are offered, or they can participate in college activities.

The key is that the staff meet together to identify their successes, failures, and kids' problems. As the staff learns what it isn't doing, the students learn from the staff's experience of trying to meet the kids' needs through inquiry. A principle emerged: Teachers best offer learning experiences for students that they experience first themselves. Therefore, peer assessment for children developed only after the teachers did it themselves.

Peer assessment. The peer assessment itself grew out of a small-school necessity. I realized that because of my small administrative staff, I needed to share responsibility. I was working a 70-hour week, seven days a week. So I started with personnel. I asked teachers if they wanted to participate in hiring. Prior to opening the school, I had interviewed 60 people for seven positions with each interview lasting 2 hours. In our first year, all seven staff members agreed to join the personnel committee and decided on a chair. They staffed the school for the second year. It did take time for them to become effective. By the end of that first school year, they weren't able to fill all the vacancies.

Having hired most of the staff, they had a vested interest in their hires becoming successful. The underlying assumption is that when staffing is a shared activity, the entire faculty accepts responsibility for orienting and supporting new members. Thus, the third year, the staff initiated peer support during the Wednesday afternoon meetings. Initially, peer support took place on Wednesdays without

(Continued)

(Continued)

involving evaluation. Once the faculty became accustomed to providing support, they began visiting each other's classes. As the observations increased, some written feedback began. Trust had to be built, and it took time. Providing written feedback to each other did not become widespread until the fourth year. And it wasn't until the fifth year that the personnel committee wrote and codified the schema for evaluation. Based on research showing that ideas from colleagues carry more weight than traditional evaluation procedures, the committee members concluded that a combination of self-evaluation and peer evaluation would be the most effective means to promote professional growth. By that time, my role was to meet weekly with the chair of the committee. The message to the faculty is that they are autonomous professionals who are trusted. The key to consensus in the school is that it is the faculty that shapes policy.

Ongoing development. Over the past few years, the staff has evolved into instructional teams that have become increasingly autonomous and have taken on more and more responsibilities. They schedule themselves for free periods, and they do their own hiring. These instructional groups have replaced the peer groups. The personnel committee has taken on more of a coordinating function. A coordinating committee oversees governance. I am a member of the coordinating committee and create my own portfolio, which my peer group evaluates.

At the time of the interview, Eric Nadelstern saw his own leadership role as threefold: First, he felt that his job was to model professional development, as in the portfolio that he created for his own assessment; second, he considers that training his staff to be leaders was one of his central roles; and third, a major piece of his responsibility was an external one—to protect and advocate for his school. In that role of advocate and liaison to the outside, he promoted the creation of an in-house, unpublished handbook titled *Personnel Procedures for Peer Selection, Support, and Evaluation* that International High School shares willingly with other professionals. We summarize some of the main assumptions and procedures for International's peer process as well as provide information on how you can request a copy of the complete handbook.[5]

Peer Support Groups

A Definition

The purpose of the *peer support group* is to provide a place for staff to exchange ideas, learn from each other, and support each other in reaching their professional goals. Groups composed of three to four members from at least two subject areas, one of whom is tenured, and including support staff, meet regularly and rotate every year.

Stages for Implementation

- Goals are established collectively at the beginning of the year.
- Meetings are scheduled to discuss progress and problems and provide timely feedback throughout the year.
- Staff visit each other's classes several times a year and write peer observations that reflect the goals of each staff member.
- Everyone in the group, including nontenured and provisional staff, writes at least one peer observation.
- The group provides support and feedback in the writing of self-evaluations, in the completion of the portfolio, and in the preparation of presentations before the peer evaluation teams.

Self-Evaluation

Self-evaluations can be as varied as the individuals on staff. The only requirements for the self-evaluations are that nontenured teachers must provide at least two every year and that tenured staff submit one at the end of the year. The self-evaluations can range from discussing growth to expressing disappointment, from looking at one course to comparing several, from focusing on content to examining skills. Because the portfolios are in a central location and open to all staff, faculty members can derive benefit from the insights of their colleagues.

Peer Evaluation

A Definition

The idea behind the *peer evaluation* team is that when a staff member needs feedback from the school at large, the staff member will make a presentation to a larger group of peers who represent the whole school. These presentations, as differentiated from the peer support group, often take place in passing through the gates that lead to tenure, that is, for appointment to a position, at the end of the first 2 years of teaching in the school, for continuation and completion of probation, and for granting of tenure. Tenured staff present every 3 years, a process that represents a form of renewable tenure.

Stages for Implementation

- The peer evaluation team is composed of staff members who have been in the school for a full school year, and the members are chosen from the following groups at random: a teacher or guidance counselor from the personnel committee to serve as team leader, a member of the subject area and other staff members, and the candidate's choice from his or her peer support group.
- The candidate prepares a portfolio that contains goals and objectives for the year; self-, peer, and administrative evaluations; two out of three student class evaluations for each semester; any professional work of the candidate's choice; and the annual end-of-term evaluation review.
- In the presentation, the team examines the portfolio materials, discusses the candidate's accomplishments and goals for the future, and makes a recommendation based on the portfolio, feedback from the peer support groups, and the discussion with the candidate.
- The following day, the candidate meets with the principal, the personnel committee chair, and the peer evaluation team leader to discuss the committee's recommendation and to develop a plan to meet the coming year's goals.

> **Reflection**
>
> *How does the portfolio in this process differ from the portfolio in PS 6? Where does the responsibility lie at the International High School for selection, support, and evaluation? To whom is each staff member accountable?*

ACTION RESEARCH

Although action research is not a quick fix for all school problems, it represents a process that . . . can focus the brain-power of the entire instructional staff on maximizing learning.

—McLean, 1995, p. 5

Case Study 7

Doris Harrington is a tenured math teacher at Northern Valley Regional High School, a school that comprises 1,100 students. Having taught in the school for 18 years, Doris is excited about the new program that Principal Bert Ammerman spearheaded to enhance professional development and instructional improvement: "I think it's neat that we now have a system in place in which we feel empowered. I mean, having an option, a choice in determining my professional development is certainly new and much appreciated."

Doris selects an action research plan as a part of the supervisory program that teachers, supervisors, and administrators collaboratively developed. "I've read so much about action research," she says, "and am so excited that others now appreciate how important it is to provide time for teachers to reflect about what we do every day in the classroom." Doris's observations confirm the views of many educators, who maintain that encouraging reflective teaching is one of the most important responsibilities of instructional supervisors (Schon, 1988).

Familiarizing herself with the literature on action research (Elliott, 1991; Glanz, 2003; Stringer, 1999), Doris reviews the four basic steps:

1. Selecting a focus for study

2. Collecting data

3. Analyzing and interpreting the data

4. Taking action

She wonders about her classroom. "What has been successful? How do I know these strategies are successful? What needs improvement? What mistakes have I made? In what ways can I improve my instructional program?" In collaborative conversations with her assistant principal, Jim McDonnell, Doris frames her project.

She wonders whether or not the time and energies expended on cooperative learning activities are worth the effort. Although she is familiar with the extensive research on the subject (Johnson & Johnson, 1989), Doris decides to compare her fourth-period math class with her sixth-period class in terms of how cooperative learning strategies affect student achievement and attitudes toward problem solving in mathematics. She chooses these two classes because they are somewhat equivalent in mathematical problem-solving ability. She selects a nonequivalent control group design commonly associated with ex post facto research because the study involves the use of intact classes (see Glanz, 2003, for an explanation of this research design).

She randomly assigns cooperative learning as the primary instructional strategy to be used with the fourth-period class, whereas the other class will work on mathematical problem solving through the traditional textbook method. After 6 weeks of implementing this plan, she administers a posttest math exam and discovers, after applying a *t*-test statistic, that the group exposed to cooperative learning attained significantly higher mathematical problem-solving scores than the group that was taught math traditionally.

Doris also keeps an anecdotal record throughout the research project on how students seemed to get along socially in both classes. Independent observers are utilized to ensure more reliable findings. She also administers an attitude questionnaire to ascertain how students felt about learning math using cooperative learning groups as compared to learning math in the more traditional format.

Based on her findings, Doris decides to incorporate cooperative learning procedures into all her classes. She still wonders whether or not, for example, cooperative learning will work for all math topics and whether cooperative learning is uniquely effective for problem-solving activities. In consultation with Jim McDonnell, she develops a plan to continue assessments throughout the year. Jim asks Doris to present her findings at both grade and faculty conferences.

Doris's enthusiasm for action research was emphatic:

Employing action research engenders greater feelings of competence in solving problems and making instructional decisions. In the past, I never really thought about the efficacy of my teaching methods to any great extent. The time spent in this project directly impacts on my classroom practice. I'm much more skeptical of what really works and am certainly more reflective about what I do. Action research should, I believe, be an integral part of any instructional improvement effort. No one has to convince you to change an instructional strategy. Once you gather and analyze your own data, you'll be in a position to make your own judgments about what should or should not be done. Action research empowers teachers!

A Definition

Action research is a type of applied research that has reemerged as a popular way to involve educators in reflective activities about their work. Action research is not a narrow, limited practice but, rather, can use a range of methodologies, simple and complex, to better understand one's work and even solve specific problems. Action research, properly used, can have immeasurable benefits such as:

- Creating a systemwide mind-set for school improvement—a professional problem-solving ethos
- Enhancing decision making
- Promoting reflection and self-improvement
- Instilling a commitment to continuous instructional improvement
- Creating a more positive school climate in which teaching and learning are foremost concerns
- Empowering those who participate
- Promoting professional development

Action research is an ongoing process of reflection that involves four basic cyclical steps:

A. Selecting a focus

    1. Know what you want to investigate.

    2. Develop some initial questions.

    3. Establish a plan to answer or better understand these questions.

B. Collecting data
  1. Primary
     a. Questionnaires
     b. Observations
     c. Interviews
     d. Tests
     e. Focus groups
  2. Secondary
     a. School profile sheets
     b. Multimedia
     c. Portfolios
     d. Records
     e. Others
C. Analyzing and interpreting data
D. Taking action

Stages for Implementation

To effectively implement action research, the reader is advised to read Glanz's (2003) *Action Research: An Educational Leader's Guide to School Improvement*, view videos produced by the Association for Supervision and Curriculum Development (1995) on action research, and even take a course at a local university or attend a workshop. Another resource is Hubbard and Power's (1993) *The Art of Classroom Inquiry: A Handbook for Teacher-Researchers.* The following stages for implementation were developed at Northern Valley Regional High School District (1996) and are paraphrased from a handout titled *Differentiated Supervision.*

Action Research

Description. The model allows the educator the chance to increase his or her scholarly background by encouraging him or her to examine and analyze pertinent documents. The educator might complete this independent study in one year. To complete the project, the educator will have periods designated for research and development during the year.

Before the beginning of the action research project, the educator will discuss the project with his or her supervisor reviewing goals and objectives and questions to be researched. Discussion of research methods should also be discussed to ensure that ethical guidelines for conducting research are maintained (see, e.g., Glanz, 2003).

At the end of the year, the researcher will submit a report to the supervisor. The report will highlight the project's significance, content, and conclusions, as well as pedagogically sound methods to teach the materials.

If the project's scope warrants an extension, the supervisor can recommend granting an additional academic year to complete the project. This model is applicable to all tenured staff and, in an exceptional case, could apply to an experienced but nontenured staff member.

Approach

1. Identify the importance of the research and suggest ways the project will enhance students' knowledge or improve services offered by the school district.

2. Identify the specific materials (primary and secondary sources) the educator will research.

3. Develop a schedule.

4. Limit the project's scope. Such delimitation will promote thorough rather than superficial research.

5. Study and analyze all materials for the project.

6. Develop and implement a unit or program based on the project.

The Northern Valley Regional High School District uses a prescribed set of guidelines that have resulted in a number of valuable research projects. In our experiences, without a formal structure to support such efforts, action research projects rarely, if ever, are successful. The implementation of this alternative means of instructional improvement in Northern Valley has furthered the efficacy of action research as an invaluable means to promote professional development. Action research as used at Northern Valley does not necessarily replace other traditional forms of supervision.

Reflective Practice

Groups of three to six students will consult Glanz's (2003) book, *Action Research: An Educational Leader's Guide to School Improvement,* and develop a workable research project whose aim is to improve classroom teaching. Describe the project and be as specific as possible. Incorporate both quantitative and qualitative approaches. Each group will present its project in a fishbowl. Sitting in a circle surrounded by the rest of the class, members of the group will describe different facets of the project. At the end of the presentation, the observers, or outer circle, will provide feedback, ask questions, and offer suggestions.

CONCLUSION

With these seven case studies of alternative approaches and the guidelines for creating a supervisory program that encompass alternatives to traditional supervision, you are now ready to consider what your next steps might be to improve the supervision of classroom instruction in your school and district.

NOTES

1. Most of the faculty in the schools involved in the case studies have encouraged us to use their real names.

2. This scenario is based on Sylvia Roberts's model and work with schools.

3. Most of the information in this section has been quoted or adapted from the Web site of the National School Reform Faculty (NSRF): http://www.nsrfharmony.org/.

4. The information for this case study was gathered from materials distributed at workshops held at PS 6 and through conversations with the then principal, Carmen Farina. Names have not been changed.

5. Copies of the complete set of procedures can be obtained from The Personnel Committee, The International High School, LaGuardia Community College, 31-10 Thomson Avenue, Long Island City, New York.

Supervision to Improve Classroom Instruction

6

Next Steps

Assume that any significant innovation, if it is to result in change, requires individual implementers to work out their own meaning.

—Fullan, 1991, p. 105

CHAPTER OVERVIEW

1. Supervisory Platform Guidelines

   a. Three Sample Platforms

2. A Case Study: Peer Assistance at Windham Southeast Supervisory Union

3. Next Steps

   a. Inner Circle
   b. School
   c. District

4. Conclusion—or Beginning?

In the preceding chapters of this book, we have tried to provide you with a foundation of knowledge, theory, and practice to permit you to formulate your own supervisory platform. With this goal in mind, we have provided you with (a) an overview of the history of classroom and instructional supervision, (b) guidance in developing an initial personal educational vision statement, (c) a description of the more recent approaches to supervision that aim to improve classroom instruction, (d) strategies and techniques for developing the skills needed to implement the different models and approaches, and (e) case studies that illustrate how individuals and schools have operationalized these models. We think that you now have the requisite knowledge, skills, and experience to draft your personal supervisory platform and begin to reach out to others. The goal of this final chapter is to facilitate the development of a personal plan to put improvement of instruction at the center of supervision in your professional environment. Our suggestions are designed to serve as a springboard for your own creativity, not as a recipe to follow.

Table 6.1 Supervisory Development Plan: Next Steps in Putting Improvement of Classroom Instruction at the Center of Supervision

For me, personally	
For my inner circle	
For the rest of the school	
For the district in the future	

Source: The late Nancy Mohr, former principal and leadership consultant, gave us permission to adapt her planning sheet.

NEXT STEPS

At this juncture, we encourage you to formulate your own beliefs related to supervision of classroom instruction and integrate them into your initial personal vision statements. Thus, next steps begin with "me," the clarification of your own supervisory beliefs. Once you have worked out your own meanings, you can begin to think about the next steps in your school environment. You can contemplate sharing them with your inner circle at school, be it the teachers on your grade level, in your department, in your cabinet, and so forth. After the inner circle has worked out a joint direction for itself, this small group can think about consequences and ideas for the whole school and eventually for sharing, dissemination, and development in the school district. The planning outline might look like Table 6.1.

GUIDELINES FOR CREATING A SUPERVISORY PLATFORM

Because we have focused primarily on supervision of classroom instruction in this book, we limit our guidelines for the development of a personal supervisory platform to classroom supervision. Although we recognize that it is impossible to isolate supervision of classroom instruction from the other facets of supervision of instruction, such as staff, curriculum, and group development, for the purposes of this book, we have placed supervision of classroom instruction at the center of professional development.

Your supervisory platforms probably will be as varied as your vision statements. We include some questions and sample supervisory platforms to facilitate the process of clarifying your beliefs and ideas. We suggest you use the same process that we outlined for your vision statement in Chapter 1:

- Prepare a first draft.
- Bring three copies to class.
- In groups of three, read each other's platforms one at a time.
- Provide descriptive feedback to the author after reading each platform.
- Revise your platform based on feedback and further reflection.

You can approach the following questions in at least two ways: (1) You can use some or all of your responses to these questions as a basis for your supervisory platform, or (2) you can write your platform first and verify that you have included some of the ideas contained in these questions.

1. How do you define supervision of classroom instruction?

2. What should be the ultimate goal of supervision of classroom instruction?

3. What assumptions, values, and beliefs underlie your goals and definition?

4. Who should make the decisions about supervision of classroom instruction for the school?

5. How do you envision the process developing?

6. What would the structure(s) of supervision of classroom instruction look like?

7. Who should be involved in the supervisory process? What should each party's role be? How would the roles differ?

8. What skills are needed for effective supervision?

9. What activities would be included in instructional supervision (e.g., staff development)?

10. How would you address the question of supervision versus evaluation?

11. What are your beliefs with respect to the role of the district in supervision of classroom instruction?

12. How would you assess the implementation of your ideas? What would be the indicators of success?

The following supervisory platform statements represent the thinking of students after one semester of developing their supervisory beliefs and practices.

Christine Drucker, a Staten Island, New York, high school teacher at the time, wrote the first platform; Linda Herman, a Brooklyn, New York, early childhood teacher at that juncture, submitted the second one; the third platform was written by Chris Ogno, then a Brooklyn, New York, elementary school teacher.

Supervisory Platform 1 (Christine Drucker)

Educating our children is not the job solely of the teacher. It is a result of a community of people working together to provide students with the skills they need to succeed in the world. This community includes parents, students, teachers, and supervisors.

Supervisors of curriculum and instruction hold a very important job—to ensure that students are receiving the best possible instruction they can from their teachers. Educators often discuss the role of the teacher as a mentor, inspirer, and facilitator for students. A supervisor holds that same role for the teacher—a mentor, inspirer, and a facilitator of learning.

The major role of a supervisor is to enhance the instruction of teachers. In order to perform this task, it is necessary for a supervisor to be a master teacher. This means that the supervisor must have a working knowledge of instructional techniques and curriculum. Teachers must have confidence and respect for their supervisor's knowledge in order to rely on that supervisor for assistance and advice. One way to accomplish this is for the supervisor to encourage teachers to visit the supervisor's own classroom. This is not only an opportunity to model teaching techniques, but it demonstrates the supervisor's confidence in teaching methods and classroom management.

Having knowledge of teaching and curriculum is helpful only if a supervisor has the ability to communicate. This is the key to successful supervision. The supervisor must develop relationships with the teachers where the teachers feel comfortable having discussions about their instruction. The relationship between the supervisor and teacher must be one of trust and mutual respect. Furthermore, teachers should be encouraged to communicate with each other. Creating the "open community" can lead to successful working relationships such as mentoring, team teaching, or coaching. It allows both teachers and the supervisor to be avenues of support, encouragement, and learning to their colleagues.

Most discussions between teachers and the supervisor are informal, and a comfort level should be developed between the teacher and supervisor through informal observations. The supervisor's presence should be commonplace—a consistent factor in the classrooms and hallways. This is very important in creating a comfortable atmosphere for the teacher and students during formal and informal observations.

Classroom observations are a key part of effective supervising. For observations to be effective, they must include communication. The communication process for classroom observations has three basic parts: the planning conference, the observation, and the feedback conference. During the planning conference, the supervisor and teacher confer about the purpose of the observation and they decide on a focus for the lesson. It should be the goal of the supervisor that the teacher be comfortable and knowledgeable enough about his or her teaching to decide what the observation should focus on.

It is important that observations be focused. When the supervisor and teacher decide to discuss, observe, and evaluate one piece of a lesson, that one piece can go into more depth. Furthermore, the teacher can feel more at ease when the focus is on a topic or issue that he or she has selected. The teacher can also feel secure in knowing that there is a valuable purpose to this observation.

In addition to deciding on a focus, the tool used for observation should be decided upon. The supervisor must have knowledge of a variety of observation tools that will assist both parties in focusing the observation and later evaluating it.

In order for the supervisor to be effective during the actual observation of a lesson, objectivity is essential. The tool selected by the teacher and the supervisor should act as a guide in focusing the supervisor and assist in maintaining the supervisor's objectivity. The supervisor's role in this step is to observe the behaviors, techniques, or issues discussed in the planning conference.

The supervisor should attempt to make the teacher as self-directed as possible during the feedback conference. At this point, the teacher, with the guidance of the supervisor, evaluates the lesson using the observation tool. If the teacher needs assistance in evaluating or understanding the observation tool, the supervisor assists while still trying to push the teacher toward independent reflection. This is the key to having successful observations. Once a teacher can look independently at observation tools and reflect on them, he or she can continue the process without the supervisor, either alone or with a colleague.

The teacher should feel comfortable at feedback conferences and be able to discuss any difficulties he or she may be having. The feelings of trust, support, and respect discussed earlier are imperative if any suggestions the supervisor makes to improve any difficulties are discussed. The focus of the feedback conference should be on the issues or topics that the teacher and supervisor agreed on earlier. This prevents the teacher from feeling overwhelmed and helps maintain the concept that the observation is to improve the instructional process, not pick on things that went wrong.

Part of enhancing the instruction of teachers is professional development. Not only should teachers be encouraged to attend workshops offered by outside organizations and through the school, but also the supervisor must create a variety of professional development activities. As the supervisor's classroom is open for teachers to visit, the teachers should be encouraged to do the same with each other. Teachers need to learn how to work with one another to share ideas, support, and advice. All teachers can learn from each other. Newer teachers can benefit from the seasoned teachers' experience in the classroom, and the seasoned teachers can learn from the new theories and practices that new teachers learned in college. Mentoring and coaching relationships can be created, and teams of teachers can work together on developing and expanding their instruction. Multiple possibilities of professional development should be available to the teachers. It demonstrates an appreciation of the diverse learning and communication styles of teachers—the same understanding of diversity that teachers are expected to have of their students.

Communication and community are the key elements of supervising instruction and curriculum. When a supervisor creates the sense of togetherness, the feeling that teachers and the supervisor are colleagues working to meet one mission—the successful education of students—there will be success.

Supervisory Platform 2 (Linda Herman)

I believe that the most important element of supervision is the tone that the supervisor sets in the school. When you walk into the building, you should feel the cooperation, support, care, common short-term goals, common long-term vision, lack of competition, safety, hard work, trust, and high expectations. It is in this kind of atmosphere, I believe, that teachers, supervisors, students, parents, and community leaders can do their best work to educate children.

I believe that supervision of classroom instruction is collaborating with teachers, helping them set their personal goals and classroom goals; helping teachers meet these goals; supporting and guiding teachers to be better teachers; helping teachers to see how their children are learning; and supporting teachers to help their children do even better. I also see supervision of classroom instruction as helping teachers enjoy teaching more, and realizing that they are not in this alone, that teaching is a "we" project. We can do together what we cannot do alone.

(Continued)

(Continued)

The ultimate goal of supervision of classroom instruction is that children learn and grow. We hope to help children not only do well on tests but also become lifelong learners who love books and discovery and see learning and school as an exciting adventure.

In order for my supervision to be effective, all or most teachers in the school need to be onboard. Like me, they also will want to improve as teachers and as coworkers. They will want to grow. They will want to see their students improve. They will want to see the parents and community become more a part of children's education. They will view education as a process. Hopefully, some will realize that we are on a wonderful path—working with children, helping them learn and grow, and that we are all on this path together.

When I begin supervising in a school, I will make an appointment with each teacher—to get to know them. I will ask them about their ideas for the school. What they think has worked. What they think can work. What hasn't worked. I will ask them how I can help them. I will ask them what their goals for themselves and their students are. I will ask them how I can help them realize their goals. I would set up a schedule with each teacher, where I could be in their classrooms once a week to assist them in their teaching. I feel that supervisors need to know kids and groups. Hopefully, it will begin to open up a dialogue and teachers will really feel comfortable coming to me for help. Teachers can realize that I am really there for them, for I truly am. If I support the teachers, they can do their jobs, which is my ultimate goal: to help the children.

For supervision of classroom instruction, I will meet with the teachers individually, talk about what they want to achieve, what they want to work on, what they want to know about their teaching. I will give them a copy of the supervision book, so they can decide what tool they want me to use when I observe them. We will set up a time for me to visit. I will use the tool they have chosen. I will then give the teacher a copy of my observation and make an appointment for discussion. We will meet and discuss what I have observed, how they felt, what they felt they would like to do differently, the same, what worked and what didn't. I will try to keep this experience positive, so that the teacher can feel safe and truly grow. I would tell the teacher that I would like to visit again in a month or so and maybe he or she could try another tool and look at a different area. Hopefully, I would be able to visit each teacher four times a year.

What I would really love to encourage in my school is peer observation, using the different supervision tools. I would like each teacher to have a partner to work with and help each other improve. They could observe each other's class often, learning and growing from each other.

I think that effective supervisors need to be good listeners. They need to be good observers. They need to be experienced teachers. They need to be compassionate. They need to be able to create a positive, open energy in the school. They need to be supportive. They need to be able to see teachers' successes and celebrate them, even the small ones. They need to be able to pat teachers on the back. They need to be able to pick teachers up when they are having a hard time, encourage them to see the light, and move forward. They need to have a lot of energy.

I also think that supervisors need to really know the curriculum in the school. They need to know what is being taught. They need to think about different ways to teach so that they can be a resource. Supervisors need to be able to go into a class and teach. A supervisor should be able to model lessons. If teachers are going for workshops for a new curriculum, the supervisor should go also. It should be clear that this is a learning community for all.

There should be much professional development to help teachers grow. Teachers should be encouraged to go to workshops at colleges, at the district office. A supervisor can invite a guest speaker in on a topic that the faculty is working on. Teachers in the building can develop their own workshops for each other, teaching what they feel passionate about to their peers. A schoolwide educational journal can be started— maybe twice a year—where teachers can write about their thoughts about teaching, ideas they have tried, or books or articles they have read. There should be a teachers' library where there are curriculum books, professional magazines, and articles. Teachers should be given the time to watch each other teach. Teachers should be encouraged to team teach. Supervisors should model a lesson. Teachers should be given time to visit other teachers in other schools. Teachers can watch an educational movie together and then have a discussion afterward. An instructional supervisor should make sure that there is a space for dialogue, where teachers can share ideas and grow.

Supervision for growth and evaluation should be separate. Supervision for growth should feel safe, so that the teacher can try new ideas and experiment and learn and grow.

I hope that I can work with other principals in the district to brainstorm ideas about how to supervise teachers better, to help children learn better, to include parents in the process. I hope that I can be instrumental in helping schools be less competitive and more cooperative, for we are truly all in this together.

I would feel successful if children liked coming to school. I want children to do well on tests. I want an active PTA where parents are involved in their children's education. I want teachers to feel happy working the best they can, but not stressed; to feel supported, to feel comfortable coming to me, to collaborate, to share ideas. I want a school that is always humming, always excited, always trying something new, alive. I think I would feel that I had really done a good job if in my second year, teachers walked in the first day and said how happy they were to be back in school!

Supervisory Platform 3 (Chris Ogno)

There is no more prodigious challenge than that of educating children. The role of the administrator must not be underestimated in this process. Educators are entrusted with the greatest gift the world can offer—the future. For educators are sculptors; they create and mold the minds of the future world. This is an awesome responsibility, especially in a world where drugs, technology, and the degeneration of the nuclear family have forced schools to take on new responsibilities. Teachers, as "the frontline soldiers," need support in undertaking such an enormous task. That support should come in the form of collaboration. The school, at all levels, must work together toward the common goal of educating children. Administrators must guarantee that these lines of communication both exist and stay open.

If the teachers are the "frontline soldiers" in the battle to educate our youth, then classroom instruction must be seen as the true "front line" of education. This is where the action and learning take place. It is here that the education process comes to its fruition, and it is the place where the administrator needs to be. The administrator can no longer be the field general on the hill (in an office) telling his or her troops what to do. The administrator needs to be in the "trenches" (classrooms) offering support, promoting communication between teachers, and encouraging professional development.

Communication must be the fundamental goal of any good administrator, for without communication, no growth can occur. As a leader, he or she must establish an environment that is free of fear and conducive to the sharing of ideas. The administrator's task is to ensure that teachers are afforded the opportunity to share ideas and work cooperatively toward the improvement of classroom instruction. Administrators cannot be critical and look for mistakes, or else they risk irreparable damage to this process by instilling fear and hindering dialogue. A good administrator cannot put him- or herself above the teacher. They must treat teachers with mutual professional respect. The administrator needs to foster an open, trusting relationship with his or her teachers. It is the administrator's function to serve the teacher as a resource in helping to improve instruction. He or she must be available to help and support the teachers of the school.

The administrator must "get dirty" by going into classrooms and working cooperatively with teachers on improving instruction. By being in the classroom, the administrator gets hands-on experience and can

(Continued)

(Continued)

better understand the needs of the teacher. The leader can then offer resources that will be effective in helping the teacher improve instruction. This in turn will keep the administrator's fingers on the pulse of the educational process.

Another way that having the administrator in the classroom can improve instruction is through observations. He or she can work collaboratively with teachers and set up observations to improve their teaching techniques. The key point in the observation process is to create an environment where positive feedback is promoted and fear and criticism are eliminated. During this process, administrators need to engage teachers in dialogue about their classroom instruction. It is through this personal reflection, which should be encouraged by the administrators, that teachers can do self-evaluation and real professional growth can occur. Classroom instruction then becomes a learning experience for the student, teacher, and administrator.

Finally, I believe that a good administrator should foster staff development. Teachers should be going into each other's classrooms and observing teaching. Ideas need to be shared and the classrooms are once again the "front line" of the educational process. The administrator should promote intervisitation by teachers for the enhancement of classroom instruction. I believe that by doing this, teachers will begin to see observations as a tool for improvement rather than a terrifying event that degrades and demeans the work that they do. Teachers and administrators can finally unite in a common effort to promote a system that strives to always improve classroom instruction in an effort to guarantee each child the finest possible education.

Peer Assistance at Windham Southeast Supervisory Union

Before suggesting some general guidelines for the development of next steps for your inner circle, school, and district, we provide an example of how peer supervision developed in a Vermont school district.[1] The Windham Southeast Supervisory Union (WSESU) spent several years attempting to improve its supervision and evaluation practices through research and discussion. This climate promoted the creation of two projects, one in the English department of the high school and a second one at the district level.

In June, the Brattleboro Union High School English department staff members decided that evaluation and supervision would be the department's theme for the following school year. The faculty felt that the department head, who was responsible for evaluation, budget, program development, curriculum, and scheduling and who taught two classes, could not provide substantive, clinical supervision for 16 department teachers. One of the teachers suggested that, given the expertise and professionalism of the department members, peer supervision could permit them to help each other with professional issues and provide mutual aid.

After considerable discussion, the English faculty decided that the department head should be an active support in the process without direct involvement. They felt that the inclusion of an evaluator would compromise a purely helpful, growth-oriented process. His help was, however, crucial in procuring the time, money, substitutes, and support services to make the experiment work.

Despite additional apprehension about the actual peer observation process, all members of the English faculty decided to serve at least once as an observer and once as an observee. After the first round, the full department discussed what had transpired and expressed nearly universal enthusiasm for the peer process. The members made two decisions based on their initial experiences:

- They decided to form small groups. Members of a group would have a clearer picture of who they were working with and could develop commitment and closeness. They could also cover classes for each other more easily.
- They also set up a clear clinical structure that included a preconference and feedback conference with specific goals.

Other challenges that were eventually resolved were:

- The establishment of voluntary participation
- The acquisition of district funds to permit training in observation and conference techniques and to relieve nonprofessional time
- The establishment of confidentiality and documentation for district approval through questionnaires, videos, and personal anecdotal records

The following year, a group of administrators, frustrated with the amount of time that evaluation consumes without improving instruction, initiated a district-level committee of volunteer teachers and administrators. The goal of their action plan was to establish a supervisory process for all staff members in the district that would both encourage professional growth and enhance learning. The supervisory process would be nonevaluatory and a separate administrative evaluation would determine job status. A district committee member discussed the pilot project with administrators, teachers, and paraprofessionals at each site and collected the names of volunteer pairs. Training was held at the district office; the number of participants was so large that each site had to provide financial support for the afterschool sessions. At the end of the pilot project, all the volunteers indicated that they wanted to continue their involvement. The district committee decided to design a plan for expansion in the next school year.

The lack of funds to support a district-level peer assistance coordinator was instrumental in the decision to move coordination of the project from the district level to each school and department. Each site's peer assistance leader would participate in a monthly meeting of a district Peer Assistance Steering Committee, which would facilitate communication between schools and departments and keep the process active. All the district and school administrators made a commitment to finding the time and money for three clinical supervision cycles for each participant and for training of new participants.

Despite setbacks due to unforeseen external circumstances, peer assistance survived and the steering committee introduced a cyclical evaluation model for the next year. Summative evaluation would occur every three years, with the two years between evaluations devoted to no evaluative supervision.

This model developed under the most propitious conditions: the steward-ship of two supportive superintendents and the buy-in of the individual school leaders.

"FOR ME, PERSONALLY": MY SUPERVISORY PLATFORM

We believe that the following ideas and suggestions for your inner circle, your school, and/or your district can be implemented in most school districts under many types of leadership and in diverse settings.

For My Inner Circle

Once you have completed your personal supervisory platform, you can reach out to colleagues in many ways. What we consider most important of all is to begin from the bottom up, that is, to find one or more colleagues who are amenable to beginning a conversation about transforming classroom supervi-sion from a required, primarily evaluatory process to one of shared growth in teaching and learning. It is also essential that project participation be voluntary.

The following suggestions are some of the innumerable strategies that can open up the conversation. Some of these ideas are teacher initiated; several can emanate from either teachers or supervisors.

- Share case studies from this book with one or more colleagues and then brainstorm possibilities for your inner circle. Invite a colleague to observe a challenge or success in one of your classes and provide you with feedback.
- Discuss with a colleague a curriculum area or approach you would like to try, and plan to team-teach a lesson or observe each other teaching the innovation and give mutual feedback.
- Offer to present an introductory workshop on alternative ways to look at supervision of classroom instruction.
- Discuss the possibility of building a peer-coaching component into an annual personal, department, or grade-level goal.
- Look into grant possibilities to support your project.

For My School

Although we advise that you begin the conversation about classroom supervision with a small group, it is sometimes possible to make inroads at the school level as you introduce the idea to your immediate colleagues. Some of the "inner circle" suggestions also are applicable to the school level. Therefore, a few of the following ideas are variations on the inner circle:

- Request that this book and other articles and books about innovative supervisory practices be purchased for your school's professional library.

- Spearhead a voluntary professional reading and sharing group in which alternative supervision is a topic.
- Suggest that innovative classroom supervision be a school goal for the year.
- Ask that a subcommittee on your school's site-based planning team be formed to discuss innovative classroom supervision.
- Offer to develop a series of workshops on observation techniques, feedback approaches, and alternative supervision for a group of volunteer teachers.
- Offer to set up a visit for interested colleagues to schools where successful alternative supervisory practices are being implemented.

For the District in the Future

Michael Fullan (1993) concluded that "effective schools are ones that are plugged into their environments. . . . A systematic, symbiotic relationship is required between schools and local agencies. . . . Leadership in successful systems *conceptualizes* the problem as continually negotiating school and district codevelopment" (p. 16). We endorse the idea that for reform to be successful, the district and school must support each other. If alternative supervisory methods are to succeed, the district will need to support them philosophically and financially.

Therefore, even as you begin to explore alternative supervisory methods with your inner group, it is important, wherever possible, to explore connecting with the district office. The district can facilitate the process at the site level from the outset. We recommend that you consider the following suggestions, but *only* after taking into consideration (1) that the individual, inner group, or school committee needs to consult with building supervisors before making contact with district-level employees and (2) that the careful application of problem-solving and decision-making skills is essential to determine if, when, and how to proceed.

- Offer to give an introductory workshop or a series of workshops on innovative supervisory practices.
- Request staff development funds so that teachers can be released for intervisitation or staff development.
- Apply for staff development funds or a grant to facilitate developing a pilot program.
- After completing a pilot program, request permission to ask other district faculty to visit the implementation of your project.
- Request permission to offer a presentation to other interested schools.
- Ask to set up a district schedule of intervisitation to other schools and districts involved in innovative supervisory practices.
- Procure funding to attend conferences on innovative practices.
- Apply to be a presenter at a conference as a representative of your school and district.
- Explore the feasibility of setting up a district-based committee on innovative supervisory practices.

- Discuss the possibility of including innovative supervisory practices as a district goal.
- Request district support in apprising you of grant possibilities and in writing proposals.

CONCLUSION—OR JUST A BEGINNING?

A major premise of this volume has been that supervisors can become a potent vehicle for the improvement of classroom instruction. We have attempted to highlight the tools, techniques, and strategies that we think are crucial in promoting instructional excellence. Yet, the challenge remains in your hands. We affirm what Harold Spears (1953) articulated more than a half century ago: "Supervision is and always will be the key to the high instructional standards of America's public schools" (p. 462). To ensure that supervision will continue as such, we have presented our modest proposal for effective supervision. We hope that you use our suggestions as a springboard for the improvement of teaching and learning in your professional environment. Please contact us (Susan Sullivan at Sullivan@mail.csi.cuny.edu or Jeffrey Glanz at glanz@yu.edu) to share your experiences, comments, and suggestions.

NOTE

1. This synopsis is based on a case study in *Supervision in Transition* (James, Heller, & Ellis, 1992).

Resource A

Microlab Guidelines

*M*icrolab is a term for a planned and timed small-group exercise that addresses a specific sequence of questions and promotes active listening skills in the process. Its structure is about equalizing communication and withholding judgment. It affirms people's ideas and helps build community.[1]

Aim

The aim is to help participants learn more about themselves and others and deepen the quality of collegial sharing using a timed small-group exercise.

Setup

All groups should consist of three to five people and be about the same size. It helps if people can pull chairs into a tight private group. The following techniques can be used to divide participants:

- Use cards with numbers on them such as three 1s, 2s, and so on. If the numbers come out uneven, avoid groups of five. Make two groups of four instead.
- Count off by three, four, or five.
- Group by level or category.

Time

It takes 15 to 40 minutes to complete a microlab; less time for groups of three addressing two to three questions; more time for groups of four to five addressing four questions. Allow time for the whole group to debrief at the end.

Directions for Leader

I'll be directing what we're going to be sharing. It's not an open discussion. It's about listening and sharing nonjudgmentally. I will pose one question at a time. Each person gets approximately one minute to answer it in turn. No one else is to talk or ask questions when it's someone else's turn. The goal is active listening. I will use a timer and tell the group when they should be halfway around. I also will tell you when the time is up for that question and what the next question is. If a person gets shortchanged on time for some reason, he or she can go first in the next round. It's about being open and honest and also about respecting confidentiality. What someone says in your group is not to be repeated by anybody else. Can you agree to that?

Guidelines

- Speak from your own experience. Say *I* when speaking about yourself.
- Stay on the suggested topic.
- Listen and discover rather than give advice.
- Avoid being judgmental.
- Respect shared confidences.
- It's OK to pass.

Debrief at the End

The whole group should discuss: What do we now know about each other's ideas or experiences? Commonalities? Differences? What was helpful or positive about the process? What was difficult? Is it something to revisit in our work? How could you use the process in your work?

Practice

Set up a practice microlab using the following questions from page 7:

Who or what in your personal or professional background influenced your present supervisory beliefs?

What are some positive supervisory experiences you have encountered?

What are some negative supervisory experiences you recall?

Why did you feel that way?

What does supervision look like in your school?

NOTE

1. We thank Emily White of Bank Street College of Education and Linda Lantieri of Educators for Social Responsibility for allowing us to adapt their guidelines.

Resource B

Fishbowl Guidelines

The fishbowl can be used either to discuss ideas generated in small groups in a large-group setting or to provide feedback to a small group that is modeling a role play, simulation, or another group process.

Aims

The aim of the fishbowl as follow-up to small-group discussions is to provide a forum for reporting on, sharing, and discussing the ideas generated in small groups. The fishbowl also allows a new process to be modeled with the goal of the volunteers learning the process, getting feedback, and helping the observers learn from the model's experience.

Setup

Discussion fishbowl. Place one chair per small group in a circle in the middle of the room. Provide an additional chair. Each small group chooses a representative for the circle to report on the group's discussion. The rest of the class observes without participating in the debriefing. If a class observer feels strongly about making a particular point, that person can sit temporarily in the additional chair in the circle to express that point. The observer then returns to his or her seat to free the empty chair.

Model fishbowl. Students volunteer to model a particular role play, simulation, or process. The players and an observer sit in the middle of the room surrounded by the rest of the class. Videotaping of the model is highly recommended. The volunteers model the process following the Guidelines for Reflective Practice. Once the observer in the small group provides feedback, class members can make additional observations. If a number of students want to comment, it is preferable to go around the outside circle in order, allowing the students to pass if they wish.

Time

The discussion fishbowl should be given a precise time limit; 10 or 15 minutes should be sufficient. The model fishbowl also should not take more than

10 or 15 minutes and should be abbreviated when necessary. Additional observations from the outer circle in the model fishbowl exercise should be limited by going in order and allowing only one comment per person.

Practice

Set up a practice fishbowl using the following scenario: An experienced teacher discusses a classroom challenge with a supervisor or teacher leader using the self-directed approach. A third person serves as reflector, and the rest of the class/group serve as observers and general reflectors.

Resource C

Technology in the Classroom

TIPS THAT SPAN THE TRADITIONAL TO THE VIRTUAL CLASSROOM

Feedback from instructors who have used the text in virtual or distance education environments confirms that careful planning can result in an almost oxymoronic success story: a hands-on virtual classroom. Most of these ideas can be adapted to enrich the traditional college classroom. School and teacher leaders can also use them for training in any of the alternatives to traditional observations. The suggestions are organized according to their versatility in different types of college classrooms or schools.

1. E-mail, discussion boards, blogs, wikis, asynchronized and synchronized programs. The materials in the book and the assignments are an effective source for myriad online activities. Discussion boards and blogs are a perfect means for students to obtain rapid assistance and feedback on site assignments. From the first school assignment on listening skills to the final reflective supervision cycle, students can query (through e-mail, discussion boards, blogs, and wikis) their colleagues and their instructors on how to approach a situation, how to handle the next steps, and how to discuss challenges and successes that took place. Microlabs can be organized online asynchronously on a discussion board or blog or through synchronized interactive programs.

2. Videos or DVDs, and to a lesser extent audiocassettes, can substitute for classroom feedback from instructors in the distance or virtual classroom. Viewing of the role plays on the video that accompanies the book can facilitate role playing and the practice of observation tools in the college classroom. Virtual classroom students can purchase the video, watch the role plays of the different approaches, and then re-create the role plays with willing colleagues, ideally videotaping them for subsequent reflection. Effective examples of role plays can be shared on the

Internet to allow students to observe as needed before class practices or recording their own site practices.

3. A highly developed technological environment can allow an actual classroom to be viewed in a smart college classroom or streamed online for a virtual course. The joint observation provides a common base for analysis and discussion.

4. If students are required to do paper or electronic portfolios, audiotaping or videotaping site practice conferences and assignments creates ideal portfolio artifacts. The DVD or video of the conference can be included in the paper portfolio or viewed live in the electronic portfolio.

5. Online professional development for peer coaching, mentoring, and other alternatives to traditional observations can be organized for a school district at individual school sites to avoid teacher travel during or after school.

Resource D

Observation Practice Sheets

Table 3.2   Teacher Verbal Behaviors

Class:

Date:

Time began:

Time ended:

Min.	Information Giving	Questioning	Teacher Answering Own Question	Praising	Direction Giving	Correcting	Reprimanding
1							
2							
3							
4							
5							
6							
7							
8							
9							
10							
11							
12							
13							
14							
15							
16							

Source: C. D. Glickman, S. P Gordon, and J. Ross-Gordon, *SuperVision and Instructional Leadership: A Developmental Approach* (6th ed.). Copyright © 2004 by Allyn & Bacon. Reprinted/adapted by permission.

Table 3.3   Teacher Questions Using Bloom's Taxonomy

Class:

Date:

Time began:

Time ended:

Number of questions asked:

Question Category	Tally 5 min.	Tally 10 min.	Tally 15 min.	Total	Percent	Comments
Creating						
Evaluating						
Analyzing						
Applying						
Understanding						
Remembering						

Source: C. D. Glickman, S. P. Gordon, and J. Ross-Gordon, *SuperVision and Instructional Leadership: A Developmental Approach* (6th ed.). Copyright © 2004 by Allyn & Bacon. Reprinted/adapted by permission.

Table 3.4   Teacher Questions Using Webb's Depth of Knowledge

Class:

Date:

Time began:

Time ended:

Question Category	Tally 5 min.	Tally 10 min.	Tally 15 min.	Total	Percent	Comments
Extended Thinking						
Strategic Thinking						
Basic Applications of Skill/Concept						
Recall						

Table 3.5   Student On-Task and Off-Task Behaviors

Class:

Date:

Time when sweep began:

Time ended:

Student	9:00	9:05	9:10	9:15	9:20	9:25	9:30	9:35	Observations

Key: A = at task; TK = talking (social); P = playing; O = out of seat; OT = off task

Source: C. D. Glickman, S. P. Gordon, and J. Ross-Gordon, *SuperVision and Instructional Leadership: A Developmental Approach* (6th ed.). Copyright © 2004 by Allyn & Bacon. Reprinted/adapted by permission.

Table 3.6 Gardner's Multiple Intelligences

Class:

Date:

Time:

Elements	Response Yes	No	N/A	Observations
Logical/mathematical	❏	❏	❏	
Bodily/kinesthetic	❏	❏	❏	
Visual	❏	❏	❏	
Musical	❏	❏	❏	
Interpersonal	❏	❏	❏	
Intrapersonal	❏	❏	❏	
Linguistic	❏	❏	❏	
Naturalistic	❏	❏	❏	
Emotional	❏	❏	❏	

Source: C. D. Glickman, S. P. Gordon, and J. Ross-Gordon, *SuperVision and Instructional Leadership: A Developmental Approach* (6th ed.), Copyright © 2004 by Allyn & Bacon. Reprinted/adapted by permission.

Table 3.7 Hunter's Steps in Lesson Planning

Class:

Date:

Time:

Elements	Response Yes	No	N/A	Comments
Anticipatory set	❏	❏	❏	
Objective and purpose	❏	❏	❏	
Input	❏	❏	❏	
Modeling	❏	❏	❏	
Checking for understanding	❏	❏	❏	
Guided practice	❏	❏	❏	
Independent practice	❏	❏	❏	

Source: C. D. Glickman, S. P. Gordon, and J. Ross-Gordon, *SuperVision and Instructional Leadership: A Developmental Approach* (6th ed.). Copyright © 2004 by Allyn & Bacon. Reprinted/adapted by permission.

Table 3.8   Johnson and Johnson's Cooperative Learning Criteria

Class:

Date:

Time:

	Response			
Elements	*Yes*	*No*	*N/A*	*Comments*
Explanation of academic and social objectives	❏	❏	❏	
Teaching of social skills	❏	❏	❏	
Face-to-face interaction	❏	❏	❏	
Position interdependence	❏	❏	❏	
Individual accountability	❏	❏	❏	
Group processing	❏	❏	❏	

Source: C. D. Glickman, S. P. Gordon, and J. Ross-Gordon, *SuperVision and Instructional Leadership: A Developmental Approach* (6th ed.). Copyright © 2004 by Allyn & Bacon. Reprinted/adapted by permission.

Table 3.9   Group Performance: Assessment of Individual Participation

Student:

Class:

Date:

Time:

	Regularly	Sometimes	Rarely	Comments
A. Contribution to group goals				
1. Participates in the group's activities				
2. Does his or her share of work				
B. Staying on the topic				
3. Pays attention; listens				
4. Makes comments to help group get back on topic				
5. Stays on topic				
C. Offering useful ideas or information				
6. Gives helpful ideas & suggestions				
7. Offers helpful feedback & comments				
8. Influences group decisions & plans				
D. Consideration of others				
9. Makes positive, encouraging remarks about group members & their ideas				
10. Shows & expresses sensitivity to the feelings of others				
E. Involving, working, & sharing with others				
11. Tries to get the group working together to reach group agreements				
12. Considers the ideas of others; exchanges, rethinks, defends ideas				
F. Communicating				
13. Speaks clearly; easy to hear & understand				
14. Expresses ideas clearly & effectively				

Source: Modified from the Connecticut State Department of Education; sponsored by the National Science Foundation.

Table 3.10   Teacher-Pupil Interaction

Student:

Teacher:

Date:

Time:

Time	Student Action	Teacher Action

Table 3.11 Indicators of Culturally Diverse Learners

Class:

Date:

Time:

Teacher Indicator	Yes	*Response* No	N/A	Comments
Displays understanding of diverse cultures	❑	❑	❑	
Displays personal regard for students of diverse cultures	❑	❑	❑	
Uses instructional materials free of cultural bias	❑	❑	❑	
Uses examples and materials that represent different cultures	❑	❑	❑	
Promotes examination of concepts and issues from different cultural perspectives	❑	❑	❑	
Intervenes to address acts of student intolerance	❑	❑	❑	
Uses "teachable moments" to address cultural issues	❑	❑	❑	
Reinforces student acts of respect for diverse cultures	❑	❑	❑	

Source: C. D. Glickman, S. P. Gordon, and J. Ross-Gordon, *SuperVision and Instructional Leadership: A Developmental Approach* (6th ed.). Copyright © 2004 by Allyn & Bacon. Reprinted/adapted by permission.

Table 3.12   Strategies for Diverse Learners

Class:

Date:

Time:

Teacher Indicator	Response			Examples
	Yes	No	N/A	
Proximity to students	❏	❏	❏	
Different ways of encouraging students	❏	❏	❏	
Positive reinforcement techniques	❏	❏	❏	
Modifications for individual children or types of learners	❏	❏	❏	
Use of children's strengths	❏	❏	❏	
Multiple ways in which lesson is unfolding	❏	❏	❏	
Integration of grouping according to needs and skills	❏	❏	❏	
Scaffolding of instruction	❏	❏	❏	

Table 3.13   Accommodations and Modifications for English Language Learners

Class:

Date:

Time:

Accommodation Modification	Was This Element Present?			What Is the Evidence?
	Yes	*No*	*N/A*	
Teacher talk is modified: slower speech, careful choice of words, idioms, expressions	❑	❑	❑	
Teacher allows wait time and monitors teacher input vs. student output	❑	❑	❑	
Definitions and language are embedded in content/context	❑	❑	❑	
Real-world artifacts present that support comprehension	❑	❑	❑	
Elicits and draws on students' backgrounds to build prior knowledge	❑	❑	❑	
Teacher uses nonverbal cues to support comprehension	❑	❑	❑	

Table 3.14 The Differentiated Classroom

Class:

Date:

Time:

Classroom Characteristics	Presence of Element			Comments/Description
	Yes	No	N/A	
1. Range of activities • whole-class instruction • small-group activities (pairs, triads, quads) • individualized activities (e.g., learning centers, independent study) • student-teacher conferences	❑ ❑ ❑ ❑ ❑	❑ ❑ ❑ ❑ ❑	❑ ❑ ❑ ❑ ❑	
2. Students express themselves in diverse ways • artistically • musically • technologically • scientifically • athletically • through drama/speeches • traditional compositions • building models • other	❑ ❑ ❑ ❑ ❑ ❑ ❑ ❑ ❑	❑ ❑ ❑ ❑ ❑ ❑ ❑ ❑ ❑	❑ ❑ ❑ ❑ ❑ ❑ ❑ ❑ ❑	
3. Students construct meaning on their own; take responsibility for their own learning; plan activities on their own	❑	❑	❑	
4. Learning activities are provided for students who complete work before others	❑	❑	❑	
5. Peer tutoring to reinforce more advanced learners and support less advanced	❑	❑	❑	
6. Different types of assessment are ongoing and integrated	❑	❑	❑	

Table 3.15   Guided Reading

Class:

Date:

Time:

Guided Reading Teacher Indicator	Yes	No	N/A	Comments/Examples
Management				
Was the transition from the mini-lesson to group work implemented in an orderly fashion?	❑	❑	❑	
Were the other children on task while the teacher was in small-group instruction?	❑	❑	❑	
Was the time allotted for the guided reading group appropriate?	❑	❑	❑	
Instruction				
Was the text for guided reading introduced in a manner that provided knowledge? Was there support so that students could read independently and successfully?	❑	❑	❑	
Were the children interested in and did they grasp the concepts being taught?	❑	❑	❑	
Was the text appropriate for the group with respect to the level, content, and interest?	❑	❑	❑	
Were support, challenges, and opportunities for problem solving provided?	❑ ❑	❑ ❑	❑ ❑	
Did the students read independently?	❑	❑	❑	
Did assessment take place? What types?	❑	❑	❑	
Did the teacher allow students to be responsible for what they already know?	❑	❑	❑	
Did questions include the full range of Bloom's Taxonomy?	❑	❑	❑	
Did the teacher help students strengthen their strategies?	❑	❑	❑	

Source: This instrument was adapted from one that Suzanne Dimitri, a Brooklyn, N.Y., literacy coach, created. It is used with her permission.

Table 3.16   Read Aloud/Story Time

Class: **Date:**   **Time:**

Title of book: **Author:**

Type of book:

New words:

Other comments:

Teacher Behaviors	Yes	No	N/A	Comments/Examples
Introduces book by showing cover and reading title. Encourages students to share thoughts about book based on these features.	❑	❑	❑	
Reads name(s) of author and illustrator. Asks students to point to title, author, illustrator, and encourages discussion about these features.	❑	❑	❑	
Introduces at least three words that will be in story by showing cards with words and pictures representing them.	❑	❑	❑	
Attempts to capture/maintain students' interest. Uses facial expression and changes in tone, pitch, and so on to represent different characters and emphasize words or facts.	❑	❑	❑	
Involves children throughout the story by encouraging comments and questions.	❑	❑	❑	
Asks open-ended questions, such as What if? What would you do if? and so on, and provides wait time. When voluntary responses are limited, initiates discussion of facts, plot and/or characters.	❑	❑	❑	
Involves children in extension activities by creating charts or other visuals, for example, T charts, story maps, word/character webs.	❑	❑	❑	
Invites children to retell story in their own words (through pretending to read the book to the class, using puppets, etc.).	❑	❑	❑	

Table 3.17   National Council of Teachers of Mathematics (NCTM) Standard 3—Geometry

Class:

Date:

Time:

Students Can	Response			Observations
	Yes	No	N/A	
Analyze characteristics and properties of two- and three-dimensional geometric shapes and develop mathematical arguments about geometrical relationships	❏	❏	❏	
Specify locations and describe spatial relationships using coordinate geometry and other representational systems	❏	❏	❏	
Apply transformations and use symmetry to analyze mathematical situations	❏	❏	❏	
Use visualization, spatial reasoning, and geometric modeling to solve problems	❏	❏	❏	

Table 3.18   National Council of Teachers of Mathematics (NCTM) Process
(Standards 6–10)

Class:

Date:

Time:

Activity Category	Tally	Total	Percentage
Problem solving			
Reasoning and proof			
Communication			
Connections			
Representation			

Table 3.19   Teacher Behaviors Keyed to Accountable Talk

Class:

Date:

Time:

Teacher Indicators	Response			Observations
	Yes	No	N/A	
Engages students in talk by:				
• Providing opportunities for students to speak about content knowledge, concepts, and issues	❑	❑	❑	
• Using wait time/allowing silence to occur	❑	❑	❑	
• Listening carefully	❑	❑	❑	
• Providing opportunities for reflection on classroom talk	❑	❑	❑	
Assists students to listen carefully to each other by:				
• Creating seating arrangements that promote discussion	❑	❑	❑	
• Providing clear expectations for how talk should occur	❑	❑	❑	
• Requiring courtesy and respect	❑	❑	❑	
• Reviewing major ideas and understandings from talk	❑	❑	❑	
Assists students to elaborate and build on others' ideas by:				
• Modeling reading processes of predicting, looking for key words, engaging prior knowledge, and so on	❑	❑	❑	
• Facilitating rather than dominating the talk	❑	❑	❑	
• Listening carefully	❑	❑	❑	
• Asking questions about discussion ideas and issues	❑	❑	❑	
Assists in clarifying or expanding a proposition by:				
• Modeling methods of restating arguments and ideas and asking if they are expressed correctly	❑	❑	❑	
• Modeling and providing practice at responding appropriately to criticism	❑	❑	❑	
• Modeling expressing own puzzlement or confusion	❑	❑	❑	

Table 3.20   Student Behaviors Keyed to Accountable Talk

Class:

Date:

Time:

Student Indicators	Response			Observations
	Yes	No	N/A	
Students are engaged in talk when they:				
• Speak appropriately in a variety of classroom situations	❑	❑	❑	
• Allow others to speak without interruption	❑	❑	❑	
• Speak directly to other students	❑	❑	❑	
Students are listening attentively to one another when they:				
• Make eye contact with speaker	❑	❑	❑	
• Refer to a previous speaker	❑	❑	❑	
• Connect comments to previous ideas	❑	❑	❑	
Students elaborate and build on others' ideas when they:				
• Make comments related to the focus of the discussion	❑	❑	❑	
• Introduce new, related issues	❑	❑	❑	
• Listen carefully	❑	❑	❑	
• Talk about issues rather than participants	❑	❑	❑	
Students work toward clarifying or expanding a proposition when they:				
• Model methods of restating arguments and ideas and ask if they are expressed correctly	❑	❑	❑	
• Model and provide practice at responding appropriately to criticism	❑	❑	❑	
• Model expressing own puzzlement or confusion	❑	❑	❑	

Table 3.21   Nonverbal Techniques

Class:

Date:

Time:

Nonverbal Technique	Frequency	Anecdotal Observations/ Student Responses
Proxemics • Standing near student(s) • Moving toward student(s) • Touching student(s) • Moving about room		

Kinesics
 	
a. Affirmation
  • Eye contact
  • Touching
  • Smiling
  • Nodding
  • Open arm movements
b. Disapproval
 	
  • Frowning
  • Stern look
  • Finger to lips
  • Pointing
  • Arms crossed
  • Hands on hips		

Prosody • Varies voice tone • Varies pitch • Varies rhythm		
Immediacy • Responds with warmth		

Source: C. D. Glickman, S. P. Gordon, and J. Ross-Gordon, *Supervision of Instruction: A Developmental Approach* (4th ed.). Copyright ©1998 by Allyn & Bacon. Reprinted/adapted by permission.

Table 3.22 Guided Reading

Class:

Date:

Time:

Selects appropriate text for small-group instruction	*Helps children to think, talk, and question through the story*
Introduces story to the group as well as vocabulary concepts and text features	*Allows small groups to read independently with minimum teacher support*
Provides or reinforces reading strategies and provides students with the opportunity to use the strategy	
Records reflections on the students' reading behaviors during and after reading	*Engages students in a brief discussion after reading the story*

Figure 3.3   Diagram of Verbal Interactions

Class:

Date:

TIme:

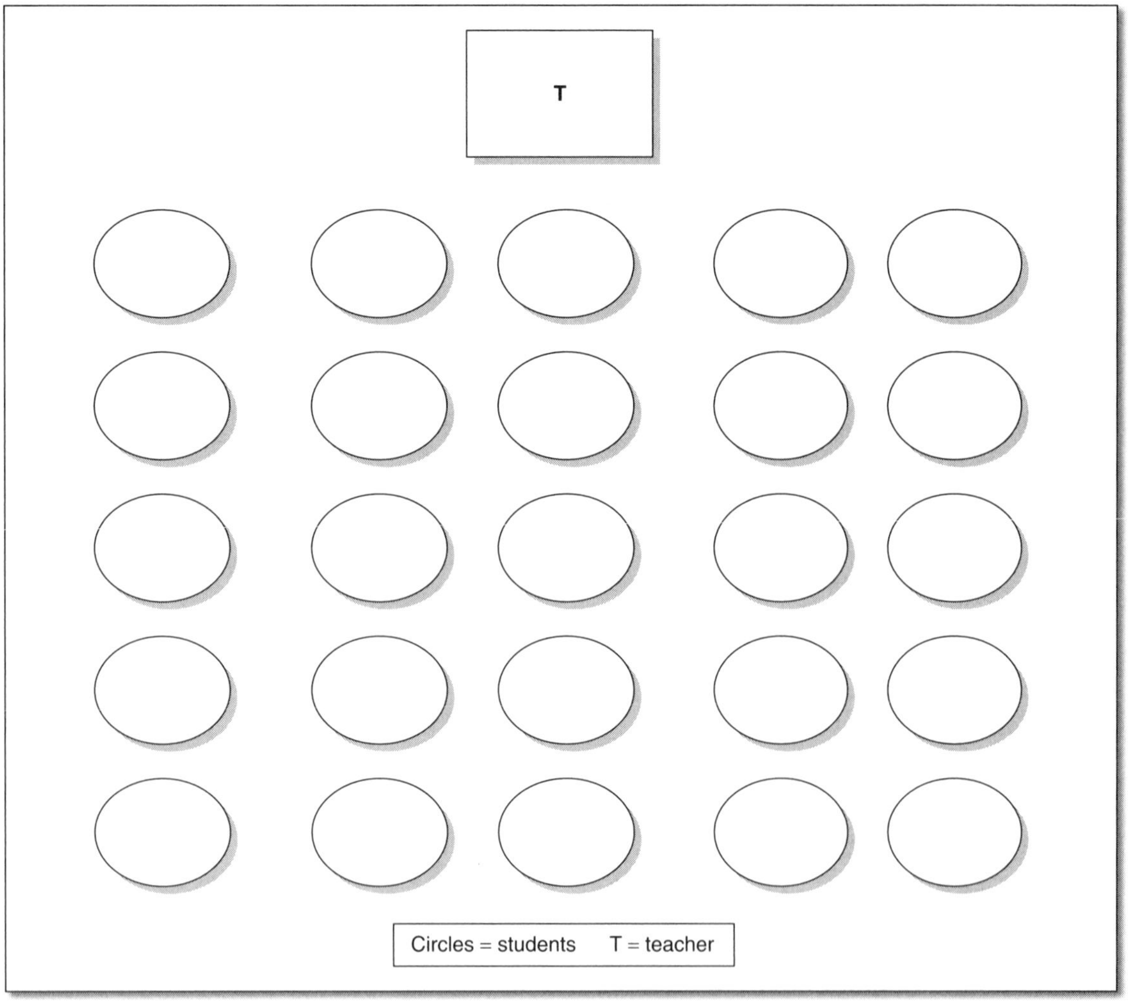

Circles = students   T = teacher

Figure 3.6   Feedback

Class:

Date:

Time:

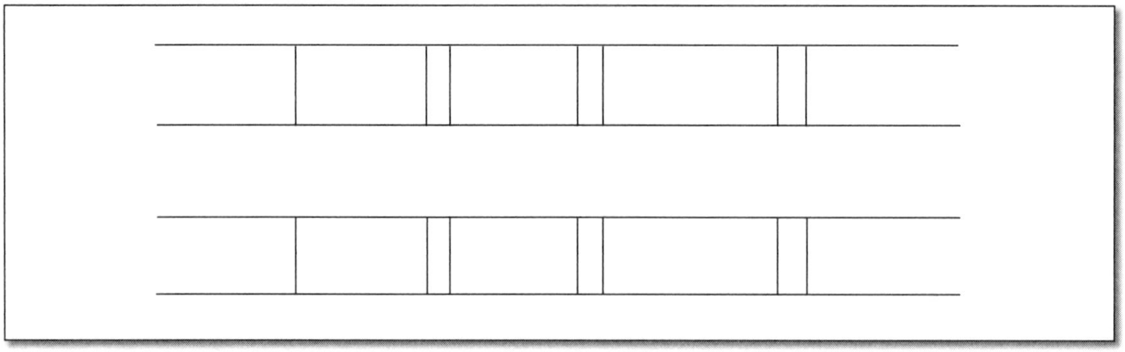

Key: Pr = prompted; Pb = probed; E = encouraged; O = positively reinforced; D = discouraged pupil

References

Acheson, K. A., & Gall, M. D. (1997). *Techniques in the clinical supervision teachers.* New York: Longman.

AchieveGlobal, Inc. (1995). *Frontline leadership series.* San Jose, CA: Zenger-Miller.

Alfonso, R. J., & Firth, G. R. (1990). Supervision: Needed research. *Journal of Curriculum and Supervision, 5,* 181–188.

Alfonso, R. J., Firth, G. R., & Neville, R. F. (1975). *Instructional supervision.* Boston: Allyn & Bacon.

Ambrose, D., & Cohen, L. M. (1997). The post-industrial era: Finding giftedness in all children. *Focus on Education, 41,* 20–24.

Anderson, R. H. (1993). Clinical supervision: Its history and current context. In R. H. Anderson & K. J. Snyder (Eds.), *Clinical supervision: Coaching for higher performance* (pp. 5–18). Lancaster, PA: Technomic.

Anonymous. (1929). The snoopervisor, the whoopervisor, and the supervisor. *Playground and Recreation, 23,* 558.

Association for Supervision and Curriculum Development. (1990). *Another set of eyes* [Video]. Alexandria, VA: Author.

Association for Supervision and Curriculum Development. (1994). *Mentoring the new teacher* [Video series]. Alexandria, VA: Author.

Association for Supervision and Curriculum Development. (1995). *Action research: Inquiry, reflection, and decision-making* [Video series]. Alexandria, VA: Author.

Balliet, T. M. (1894). What can be done to increase the efficiency of teachers in actual service? *National Educational Association Proceedings, 32,* 365–379.

Barr, A. S. (1925). Scientific analyses of teaching procedures. *The Journal of Educational Method, 4,* 361–366.

Barr, A. S. (1931). *An introduction to the scientific study of classroom supervision.* New York: Appleton.

Barth, R. S. (1990). *Improving schools from within.* San Francisco: Jossey-Bass.

Benedetti, T. (1997). Tips from the classroom. *TESOL Journal, 7*(1), 41–47.

Blase, R. R., & Blase, J. J. (1986). *Handbook of instructional leadership: How really good principals promote teaching and learning.* Thousand Oaks, CA: Corwin.

Bobbitt, F. (1913). Some general principles of management applied to the problems of city school systems. In *The twelfth yearbook of the National Society for the Study of Education, Part I, The supervision of city schools* (pp. 7–96). Chicago: University of Chicago Press.

Boehm, A. E., & Weinberg, R. A. (1997). *The classroom observer: Developing observation skills in early childhood settings.* New York: Teachers College Press.

Bolin, F. S. (1987). On defining supervision. *Journal of Curriculum and Supervision, 2,* 368–380,

Bolin, F. S., & Panaritis, P. (1992). Searching for a common purpose: A perspective on the history of supervision. In C. D. Glickman (Ed.), *Supervision in transition* (pp. 30–43). Alexandria, VA: Association for Supervision and Curriculum Development.

Bolton, R. (1979). *People skills.* New York: Simon & Schuster.

Borich, G. D. (2002). *Observation skills for effective teaching.* Columbus, OH: Merrill.

Bowers, C. A., & Flinders, D. J. (1991). *Culturally responsive teaching and supervision: A handbook for staff development.* New York: Teachers College Press.

Bridges, E. (1992). *Problem-based learning for administrators.* Eugene, OR: ERIC Clearinghouse on Educational Management, University of Oregon.

Bullough, W. A. (1974). *Cities and schools in the gilded age.* New York: Kennikat Press.

Burton, W. H. (1930). Probable next steps in the progress of supervision. *Educational Method, 9,* 401–405.

Burton, W. H., & Brueckner, L. J. (1955). *Supervision: A social process.* New York: Appleton-Century-Crofts.

Button, H. W. (1961). *A history of supervision in the public schools, 1870–1950.* Unpublished doctoral dissertation, Washington University, St. Louis, MO.

Calabrese, D., & Zepeda, S. (1997). *The reflective supervisor.* Larchmont, NY: Eye on Education.

Carnegie Forum on Education and the Economy. (1986). *A nation prepared: Teachers for the 21st century.* New York: Carnegie Corporation.

Champagne, D. W., & Hogan, R. C. (2006). *Interpersonal and consultant supervision skills: A clinical model* (4th ed.). Normal, IL: Business Writing Center.

Chancellor, W. E. (1904). *Our schools: Their administration and supervision.* Boston: D. C. Heath.

Cienkus, R., Grant Haworth, J., & Kavanagh, J. (1996). Editors' introduction. *Peabody Journal of Education, 71*(1), 1–2.

Cogan, M. L. (1973). *Clinical supervision.* Boston: Houghton Mifflin.

Costa, A., & Garmston, R. (1997). *Cognitive coaching: A foundation for renaissance schools.* Norwood, MA: Christopher Gordon.

Covey, S. R. (2005). *The eighth habit: From effectiveness to greatness.* New York: Simon & Schuster.

Cronin, J. M. (1973). *The control of urban schools.* New York: Free Press.

Danielson, C. (1996). *Enhancing professional practice: A framework for teaching.* Alexandria, VA: Association for Supervision and Curriculum Development.

Danielson, C. & McGreal, T. (2000). *Teacher evaluation to enhance professional practice.* Princeton, NJ: Educational Testing Service.

Daresh, J. C., & Playko, S. (1995). *Supervision as a proactive process.* New York: Longman.

Darling-Hammond, L., & Goodwin, A. L. (1993). Progress toward professionalism in teaching. In G. Cawelti (Ed.), *Challenges and achievements of American education* (pp. 19–52). Alexandria, VA: Association for Supervision and Curriculum Development.

Dewey, J. (1929). *The sources of a science of education.* New York: Liveright.

Dunlap, D. M., & Goldman, P. (1991). Rethinking power in schools. *Educational Administration Quarterly, 27,* 5–29.

Educational Testing Service. (1992). *The second international assessment of educational progress.* Princeton, NJ: Author.

Eisner, E. W. (1994). *The educational imagination* (3rd ed.). New York: Macmillan.

Elliott, J. (1991). *Action research for educational change.* Bristol, PA: Falmer.

Field, B., & Field, T. (1994). *Teachers as mentors: A practical guide.* London: Falmer.

Firth, G. R., & Eiken, K. P. (1982). Impact of the schools' bureaucratic structure on supervision. In T. J. Sergiovanni (Ed.), *Supervision of teaching* (pp. 153–169). Washington, DC: Association for Supervision and Curriculum Development.

Firth, G. R., & Pajak, E. F. (1998). *Handbook of research on school supervision.* New York: Macmillan.

Fitzpatrick, F. A. (1893). How to improve the work of inefficient teachers. *National Educational Association Proceedings, 31,* 71–78.

Fosnot, C. T. (1993). *In search of understanding the case for constructivist classrooms.* Alexandria, VA: Association for Supervision and Curriculum Development.

Fullan, M. (1991). *The new meaning of educational change.* New York: Teachers College Press.

Fullan, M. (1993). Coordinating school and district development in restructuring. In J. Murphy & P. Hallinger (Eds.), *Restructuring schooling: Learning from ongoing efforts* (pp. 143–164). Newbury Park, CA: Corwin.

Fullan, M. (1999). *Change forces: The sequel.* London: FalmerPress.

Fullan, M. (2006). *Turnaround leadership.* San Francisco: Jossey-Bass.

Garman, N. B. (1997). Is clinical supervision a viable model for use in the public schools? No. In J. Glanz & R. F. Neville (Eds.), *Educational supervision: Perspectives, issues, and controversies.* Norwood, MA: Christopher Gordon.

Glanz, J. (1991). *Bureaucracy and professionalism: The evolution of public school supervision.* Rutherford, NJ: Fairleigh Dickinson University Press.

Glanz, J. (1992). Curriculum development and supervision: Antecedents for collaboration and future possibilities. *Journal of Curriculum and Supervision, 7,* 226–244.

Glanz, J. (1998). Histories, antecedents, and legacies: Constructing a history of school supervision. In G. R. Firth & E. F. Pajak (Eds.), *Handbook of research on school supervision* (pp. 39–79). New York: Macmillan.

Glanz, J. (2002). *Finding your leadership style: A guide for educators.* Alexandria, VA: Association for Supervision and Curriculum Development.

Glanz, J. (2003). *Action research: An educational leader's guide to school improvement* (2nd ed.). Norwood, MA: Christopher Gordon.

Glickman, C. D. (1981). *Developmental supervision.* Washington, DC: Association for Supervision and Curriculum Development.

Glickman, C. D. (Ed.). (1992). *Supervision in transition.* Alexandria, VA: Association for Supervision and Curriculum Development.

Glickman, C. D., Gordon, S. P., & Ross-Gordon, J. M. (1998). *Supervision of instruction: A developmental approach* (4th ed.). Boston: Allyn & Bacon.

Glickman, C. D., Gordon, S. P., & Ross-Gordon, J. M. (2004). *SuperVision and instructional leadership: A developmental approach* (6th ed.). Boston: Allyn & Bacon.

Goldhammer, R. (1969). *Clinical supervision: Special methods for the supervision of teachers.* New York: Holt, Rinehart & Winston.

Goldhammer, R., Anderson, R. H., & Krajewski, R. J. (1993). *Clinical supervision: Special methods for the supervision of teachers* (3rd ed.). Fort Worth, TX: Harcourt Brace Jovanovich.

Goldstein, J. (2007, May). Easy to dance to: Solving the problems of teacher evaluation with peer assistance and review. *American Journal of Education, 113,* 479–508.

Good, T. L., & Brophy, J. E. (2002). *Looking in classrooms* (9th ed.). New York: Longman.

Greenwood, J. M. (1888). Efficient school supervision. *National Educational Association Proceedings, 26,* 519–521.

Greenwood, J. M. (1891). Discussion of Gove's paper. *National Educational Association Proceedings, 19,* 227.

Grimmet, P. P., Rostad, O. P., & Ford, B. (1992). Linking preservice and inservice supervision through professional inquiry. In C. D. Glickman (Ed.), *Supervision in transition* (pp. 169–182). Alexandria, VA: Association for Supervision and Curriculum Development.

Grumet, M. (1979). Supervision and situation: A methodology of self-report for teacher education. *Journal of Curriculum Theorizing, 1,* 191–257.

Hammock, D. C. (1969). *The centralization of New York City's public school system, 1896: A social analysis of a decision.* Unpublished master's thesis, Columbia University.

Harris, B. M. (1969). New leadership and new responsibilities for human involvement. *Educational Leadership, 26,* 739–742.

Hazi, H. M. (1994). The teacher evaluation-supervision dilemma: A case of entanglements and irreconcilable differences. *Journal of Curriculum and Supervision, 9,* 195–216.

Hill, S. (1918). Defects of supervision and constructive suggestions thereon. *National Educational Association Proceedings, 56,* 347–350.

Hill, W. M. (1968). I-B-F supervision: A technique for changing teacher behavior. *The Clearing House, 43,* 180–183.

Hoetker, W. J., & Ahlbrand, W. P. (1969). The persistence of the recitation. *American Educational Research Journal, 6,* 152–176.

Holmes Group. (1986). *Tomorrow's teachers: A report of the Holmes Group.* East Lansing, MI: Author.

Hosic, J. F. (1920). The democratization of supervision. *School and Society, 11,* 331–336.

Hosic, J. F. (1924). The concept of the principalship-II. *Journal of Educational Method, 3,* 282–284.

Howe, R. L. (1963). *The miracle of dialogue.* New York: Seabury.

Hubbard, R. S., & Power, B. M. (1993). *The art of classroom inquiry: A handbook for teacher-researchers.* Portsmouth, NH: Heinemann.

Hunter, M. (1983). Script-taping: An essential supervisory tool. *Educational Leadership, 41*(3), 43.

Jackson, P. (1990). *Life in classrooms.* New York: Teachers College Press.

James, S., Heller, D., & Ellis, W. (1992). Peer assistance in a small district: Windham Southeast, Vermont. In C. D. Glickman (Ed.), *Supervision in transition* (pp. 97–112). Alexandria, VA: Association for Supervision and Curriculum Development.

Johnson, D. W., & Johnson, R. T. (1989). *Cooperation and competition: Theory and practice.* Edina, MN: Interaction.

Johnson, S. M. (1990). *Teachers at work: Achieving success in our schools.* New York: Basic Books.

Johnston, C. A., & Dainton, G. (1997). *The learning combination inventory.* Pittsgrove, NJ: Let Me Learn, Inc.

Joyce, B., & Showers, B. (1980). Improving inservice training: The messages of research. *Educational Leadership, 37*(2), 379–385.

Kaestle, C. F. (1973). *The evolution of an urban school: New York City 1750–1850.* Cambridge, MA: Harvard University Press.

Kirby, P. C. (1991, April). *Shared decision making: Moving from concerns about restrooms to concerns about classrooms.* Paper presented at the meeting of the American Educational Research Association, Chicago.

Kolb, D. A. (1984). *Experiential learning: Experience as the source of learning and development.* Englewood Cliffs, NJ: Prentice Hall.

Lazerson, M. (1971). *Origins of the urban school: Public education in Massachusetts, 1870–1915.* Cambridge, MA: Harvard University Press.

Leeper, R. R. (Ed.). (1969). *Supervision: Emerging profession.* Washington, DC: Association for Supervision and Curriculum Development.

Leithwood, K., & Jantzi, D. (1990, April). *Transformational leadership: How principals can help reform school cultures.* Paper presented at the meeting of the American Educational Research Association, Boston.

Lieberman, A. (1995). Practices that support teacher development. *Phi Delta Kappan, 76,* 591–596.

Markowitz, S. (1976). The dilemma of authority in supervisory behavior. *Educational Leadership, 33,* 365–369.

Marshall, C. (1992). *The assistant principal: Leadership choices and challenges.* Newbury Park, CA: Corwin.

McAndrew, W. (1922). The schoolman's loins. *Educational Review, 22,* 90–99.

McBer & Company. (1994). *Inventories.* Boston: Author.

McLean, J. E. (1995). *Improving education through action research: A guide for administrators and teachers.* Thousand Oaks, CA: Corwin.

Murphy, J., & Hallinger, P. (1993). *Restructuring schooling: Learning from ongoing efforts.* Newbury Park, CA: Corwin.

Myers, I. B., & McCaulley, M. H. (1985). *Manual: A guide to the development and use of the Myers-Briggs Type Indicator.* Palo Alto, CA: Consulting Psychologists Press.

National Commission on Excellence in Education. (1983). *A nation at risk: The imperative for educational reform.* Washington, DC: U.S. Department of Education.

Newlon, J. H. (1923). Attitude of the teacher toward supervision. *National Educational Association Proceedings, 61,* 546–549.

Nolan, J., Jr., & Hoover, L. A. (2007). *Teacher supervision and evaluation: Theory into practice.* New York: Wiley.

Northern Valley Regional High School District. (1996). *Differentiated supervision.* Darnerest, NJ: Author.

Null, G. (1996). *Who are you, really? Understanding your life's energy.* New York: Carroll & Graf.

Osterman, K. E., & Kottkamp, R. B. (1993). *Reflective practice for educators: Improving schooling through professional development.* Newbury Park, CA: Corwin.

Osterman, K. E., & Kottkamp, R. B. (2004). *Reflective practice for educators: Improving schooling through professional development* (2nd ed.). Thousand Oaks, CA: Corwin.

Pajak, E. (1989). *The central office supervisor of curriculum and instruction: Setting the stage for success.* Needham, MA: Allyn & Bacon.

Pajak, E. (1993). *Approaches to clinical supervision: Alternatives for improving instruction.* Norwood, MA: Christopher Gordon.

Pajak, E. (2000). *Approaches to clinical supervision: Alternatives for improving instruction* (2nd ed.). Norwood, MA: Christopher Gordon.

Payne, W. H. (1875). *Chapters on school supervision: A practical treatise on superintendency grading; arranging courses of study; the preparation and use of blanks, records and reports; examination for promotion, etc.* New York: Van Antwerp Bragg.

Poole, W. (1994). Removing the "super" from supervision. *Journal of Curriculum and Supervision, 9,* 284–309.

Ravitch, D. (1995). *National standards in American education: A citizen's guide.* Washington, DC: The Brookings Institution.

Reiman, A. J., & Thies-Sprinthall, L. (1998). *Mentoring and supervision for teacher development.* New York: Longman.

Reitzug, U. C. (1997). Images of principal instructional leadership: From supervision to collaborative inquiry. *Journal of Curriculum and Supervision, 12,* 324–343.

Reports of the Record Commissions of the City of Boston. (1709). New York: Teachers College Archives.

Roberts, S. M., & Pruitt, E. Z. (2003). *Schools as professional learning communities: Collaborative activities and strategies for professional development.* Thousand Oaks, CA: Corwin.

Rousmaniere, K. (1992). *City teachers: Teaching in New York City schools in the 1920s.* Unpublished doctoral dissertation, Columbia University.

Schon, D. A. (1988). Coaching reflective teaching. In P. P. Grimmett & G. F. Erickson (Eds.), *Reflection in teacher education* (pp. 19–30). New York: Teachers College Press.

Seguel, M. L. (1966). *The curriculum field: Its formative years.* New York: Teachers College Press.

Senge, Peter M. (1990). *The fifth discipline: The art & practice of the learning organization.* New York: Currency Doubleday.

Sergiovanni, T. J. (1992). Moral authority and the regeneration of supervision. In C. D. Glickman (Ed.), *Supervision in transition* (pp. 30–43). Alexandria, VA: Association for Supervision and Curriculum Development.

Showers, B., & Joyce, B. (1996). The evolution of peer coaching. *Educational Leadership, 53*(6), 12–16.

Silberman, C. E. (1970). *Crisis in the classroom.* New York: Random House.

Smyth, J. (1991). Instructional supervision and the redefinition of who does it in schools. *Journal of Curriculum and Supervision, 7,* 90–99.

Spaulding, F. E. (1955). The application of the principles of scientific management. *National Educational Association Proceedings, 51,* 259–279.

Spears, H. (1953). *Improving the supervision of instruction.* Englewood Cliffs, NJ: Prentice Hall.

Stringer, E. T. (1999). *Action research: A handbook for practitioners* (2nd ed.). Thousand Oaks, CA: Sage.

Tanner, D., & Tanner, L. N. (1987). *Supervision in education: Problems and practices.* New York: Macmillan.

Taylor, F. W. (1911). *The principles of scientific management.* New York: Harper & Brothers.

Tomlinson, C. (1999). Mapping a route to differentiated instruction. *Educational Leadership, 57*(1), 1–8.

Tsui, A. B. M. (1995). Exploring collaborative supervision in inservice teacher education. *Journal of Curriculum and Supervision, 10,* 346–371.

Tyack, D. B. (1974). *The one best system: A history of American education.* Cambridge, MA: Harvard University Press.

Tyack, D. B., & Hansot, E. (1982). *Managers of virtue: Public school leadership in America, 1820–1980.* New York: Basic Books.

Weller, R. (1971). *Verbal communication in instructional supervision.* New York: Teachers College Press.

Wheatley, M. J. (2002). *Turning to one another.* San Francisco: Berrett-Koehler Publishers.

Wilhelms, F. T. (1969). Leadership: The continuing quest. In R. R. Leeper (Ed.), *Supervision: Emerging profession.* Washington, DC: Association for Supervision and Curriculum Development.

Willerman, M., McNeely, S. L., & Koffman Cooper, E. (1991). *Teachers helping teachers: Peer observation and assistance.* New York: Praeger.

Witcraft, F. E. (1950, October). *Scouting, 2.*

Zepeda, S. J. (2007). *Instructional supervision: Applying tools and concepts.* Larchmont, NY: Eye on Education.

Zepeda, S. J., & Ponticell, J. A. (1998). At cross purposes: What do teachers need, want, and get from supervision? *Journal of Curriculum and Supervision, 14*(1), 68–87.

Index

CORWIN

A SAGE Company

The Corwin logo—a raven striding across an open book—represents the union of courage and learning. Corwin is committed to improving education for all learners by publishing books and other professional development resources for those serving the field of PreK–12 education. By providing practical, hands-on materials, Corwin continues to carry out the promise of its motto: **"Helping Educators Do Their Work Better."**

Barriers to Communication

Barrier Type	Examples
1. Judging	1. Judging
• Criticizing	• "You are lazy; your lesson plan is poor."
• Name calling and labeling	• "You are inexperienced, an intellectual."
• Diagnosing—analyzing motives instead of listening	• "You're taking out your anger on her." • "I know what you need."
• Praising evaluatively	• "You're terrific!"
2. Solutions	2. Solutions
• Ordering	• "You must . . ." "You have to . . ." "You will . . ."
• Threatening	• "If you don't . . ." "You had better or else."
• Moralizing or preaching	• "It is your duty/responsibility; you should."
• Inappropriate questioning or prying	• "Why?" "What?" "How?" "When?"
• Advising	• "What I would do is . . ." "It would be best for you."
• Lecturing	• "Here is why you are wrong . . ." "Do you realize . . ."
3. Avoiding the other's concerns	3. Avoiding the other's concerns
• Diverting	• "Speaking of . . ." "Apropos . . ." "You know what happened to . . ."
• Reassuring	• "It's not so bad . . ." "You're lucky . . ." "You'll feel better."
• Withdrawing	• "I'm very busy . . ." "I can't talk right now . . ." "I'll get back to you . . ."
• Sarcasm	• "I really feel sorry for you."

Communication Techniques

Listening	Nonverbal Clues	Reflecting and Clarifying
"Uh-huh."	Affirmative nods and smiles	"You're angry because . . ."
"OK."	Open body language, e.g., arms open	
"I'm following you."	Appropriate distance from speaker—not too close or too far	"You feel . . . because . . ."
"For instance."		"You seem quite upset."
"And?"	Eye contact	"So, you would like . . ."
"Mmm."	Nondistracting environment	
"I understand."	Face speaker and lean forward	"I understand that you see the problem as . . ."
"This is great information for me."	Barrier-free space, e.g., desk not used as blocker	"I'm not sure, but I think you mean . . ."
"Really?"		"I think you're saying . . ."
"Then?"		
"So?"		
"Tell me more."		
"Go on."		
"I see."		
"Right."		

KEY STEPS—DIRECTIVE INFORMATIONAL APPROACH

1. Identify the problem or goal and solicit clarifying information.
2. Offer solutions. Ask for the teacher's input into the alternatives offered and request additional ideas.
3. Summarize chosen alternatives, ask for confirmation, and request that the teacher restate final choices.
4. Set a follow-up plan and meeting.

KEY STEPS—SELF-DIRECTED APPROACH

1. Listen carefully to the teacher's initial statement.
2. Reflect on your understanding of the problem.
3. Constantly clarify and reflect until the real problem is identified.
4. Have the teacher problem-solve and explore the consequences of various actions.
5. The teacher commits to a decision and firms up a plan.
6. The supervisor restates the teacher's plan and sets a follow-up meeting.

KEY STEPS—COLLABORATIVE APPROACH

1. Identify the problem from the teacher's perspective, soliciting as much clarifying information as possible.
2. Reflect on what you've heard for accuracy.
3. Begin collaborative brainstorming, asking the teacher for his or her ideas first.
4. Problem-solve through a sharing and discussion of options.
5. Agree on a plan and follow-up meeting.

KEY STEPS—PLANNING CONFERENCE

1. Decide the focus of the observation (choose a general approach: directive informational, collaborative, or self-directed).
2. Determine the method and form of observation. Problem solve or plan professional development where appropriate.
3. Set up the time of the observation and the feedback conference.

KEY STEPS—COLLABORATIVE REFLECTION

1. What was valuable in the process we just completed?
2. What was of little value?
3. What changes would you suggest for the next cycle?